Combat Chaplain

Combat Chaplain:
A Thirty-Year Vietnam Battle

By
JAMES D. JOHNSON

University of North Texas Press
Denton, Texas

6 5 4 3 2

The paper in this book meets the minimum requirements of the American National
Standard for Permanence of Paper for Printed Library Materials, Z39.48.1984

Permissions
University of North Texas Press
PO Box 311336
Denton, TX 76203-1336
940-565-2142

Library of Congress Cataloging-in-Publication Data
Johnson James D., 1940-
Combat chaplain : a thirty-year Vietnam battle / James D. Johnson.— 1st ed.
p.   cm.
Includes index.
ISBN 1-57441-133-0 (alk. Paper)
1. Vietnamese Conflict, 1961-1975—Personal narratives, American.   2. Vietnamese
Conflict, 1961-1975—Chaplains—United States.   3. Johnson, James D., 1940-   I. Title.

DS558.5 .J65 2001
959.704'37—dc21   [B]
00-069075

Dedication

Through history, it has been the males who go off to war and the females who are back home supposedly unaffected by battlefield trauma. I dedicate this book to four females who, directly and indirectly, were impacted by the trauma of the Vietnam war. All four have made a profound impact in my life, then and now.

Teresa Pina, Frank's daughter, and Kellie Johnson, my daughter were still in diapers in 1967–68. Both gave hope and reasons to live to two young men 10,000 miles away in a very bloody war. Nguyen Thi Hoang Yen (Yen-Nguyen), the same age, became a war refuge who survived continuous threats from the war to her family, home and herself. Even though from different places on the planet, these three could have easily been triplets.

Frank Pina, Pastor Ha and I could have easily changed places because of the love we had for our daughters which surely fueled a continuous desire to survive. Unfortunately, not all of us did.

Even though she was a toddler when she lost her father, Teresa's coming into my life in 1993 gave me emotional detergent for cleansing of my decades long wounds. Yen-Nguyen was placed by God on a small back street in Vietnam in 1996 so that the miracle of my finding her allowed healing and cleansing with international and intergenerational significance. Kellie, as my first born, gave me reasons to want to desperately come home whole. Now in their mid-thirties, Teresa in Texas, Yen-Nguyen in Vietnam, and Kellie in Louisiana, all have gone on with their lives as adults. But they may never know or appreciate the dynamic affect they have made on me, back then and in recent years.

Fourthly, there is Barbara, my wife of almost forty years, who has been a constant source of support, strength, encouragement, and love, not only during those terrible months in combat, but in the three plus decades since. If I never receive any more of God's grace, I can still count the gift of Barbara as a major element of who I am. Without her, my life would have been so drastically different.

Thank you, my "triplets", and my wife, for who and what you are to me.

Contents

Acknowledgments

From what began as personal therapeutic writings that migrated into a story and then into this book, I have many to thank. Through several drafts, I had wonderful administrative support from Evie Lichti, Sara Barefoot, Amy Parker and Stephanie Hoover. It was Stephanie, the daughter of a Vietnam veteran who encouraged and helped me see the importance that my story might have for the next generation, especially adult children of fathers who were in combat.

Structural and style assistance came from Clara Crocker, Gail Holland, Shannon Reichley, and Lynn Liles. Emotional support and encouragement came from my children, Kellie, Grey, Stuart and Eric and most especially from my wife Barbara.

My story would never had become a book without the knowledge, tenacity and belief in my journey by my literary agent, Jodie Rhodes. Finally, I thank the University of North Texas Press who had the willingness to invest in me and specifically to my editors, Ted Gittinger of the Lyndon Johnson Presidential Library, and Paula Oates, who have been professional, understanding, and sensitive to my odyssey.

Back to the Real World

TUESDAY, JUNE 25, 1968: The huge Boeing 707 rolls from the tarmac to the end of the runway. Movement seems to be at a snail's pace. *"Could one last mortar get us now?"* I wonder. The plane makes a wide turn onto the end of the runway. I try to will the pilot to gun the engines so we can leave this dirty, dangerous place called Vietnam. We sit on the end of the runway for what seems like an eternity. The thrust of the engines begins to move us forward. Not until the plane's nose lifts do I believe we're finally going home. One hundred and seventy-five GI's let out wild cheers. The tour in hell is finally finished. We're on the way back to a world of hot dogs, mom, and apple pie. It's a relief to know I'm leaving the nightmare behind.

By the time we reach 10,000 feet, I'm reflecting on my first eight and one-half months in this miserable land. I had hoped to serve with an infantry battalion, and, indeed I had. My mind races back. I once again feel the terror of being shot at for the first time, in an open pineapple field. I remember the all day and into the night ambush at Snoopy's nose with over 100 casualties; being the first person to jump on board another troop boat after it was hit by a B-40 rocket; leaving an entire twenty-nine man platoon wounded or dead except two. I recall landing by chopper, under fire, in a hot landing zone; being trapped behind a small rice paddy dike by a Viet Cong machine gunner as he blasts away, bullets showering me with mud as they explode into the dike. I remember pulling a lieutenant to safety after he's shot in an alley way; crawling through the mud under fire in the Jungle of Death; having an incoming artillery round explode five feet away, severely injuring my shoulder in the midst of that terrible fire fight that took the life of one of my best friends. And loading scores and scores of wounded soldiers on medevac choppers; sending many dead bodies from the field for the beginning of their last sad journey home.

I've experienced booby traps, snipers, ambushes, twenty-two different fire fights, ten major battles, numerous mortar attacks, fatigue, and emotional stress. Our small battalion usually had no more than 350 soldiers assigned at any one time, including non-fighting soldiers. Our four line companies often had no more than seventy-five riflemen per company who went into the field to actually fight. Of these, ninety-six were killed

1

outright, an unknown number died after being evacuated, and over 900 were wounded during my eight and one-half months with them. It didn't take any of us long to realize that if we're lucky, we'll only get wounded, not killed. Near death experiences were commonplace. It would be more accurate to say which day did I *not* have a near death experience?

As the huge airplane continues to gain altitude, much of this becomes a blur in my tired mind. It's all over now, or so I think. During the almost twenty-four hour flight back to the United States, I begin to experience the first of what will turn out to be a lifetime of dichotomy. My tour is finally over, and shortly I'll see my lovely wife and our two children. I haven't seen them in five and a half months since we were in Hawaii for Rest and Recreation—R&R. I think about my new assignment at Fort Bliss, Texas. A thousand other thoughts run through my mind. Even in my excitement, my heart aches over the loss of so many young heroes, a number of whom I'd been very close to. So many of them have gone home in body bags. My feelings are a mixture of gladness, sadness, and grief tinged with guilt. I'm making it out and they didn't.

By now, we're at 35,000 feet far out over the Pacific. With each passing minute, Vietnam is farther and farther away. But I sense it will never be completely gone.

After several stops for refueling, we land at Travis Air Force Base in California. When the wheels touch the asphalt surface of the runway, again we all let out a loud, wild cheer. Home again, thank God, we're finally home again.

As I disembark from the 707, the first thing I look for is a pay telephone. The terminal has a few, but I have to wait; it seems that every GI needs to make a call. When it's finally my turn, I break down as I tell my wife, Barbara, that I am finally, blessedly home. It will still be another day and more flights until I get to the East Coast to see her.

Someone once said, "You've never really lived until you've almost died." The trauma of combat never ends. Some of us who've experienced combat have almost died many times over. For anyone who's repeatedly experienced the terror of others trying to kill you, the feelings never go away. Combat is absolutely horrible. It placed my body and soul in the lost-and-found department for a while.

When I went to Vietnam as a twenty-six year old chaplain in 1967, I had a "parish" of 350 young soldiers. I had been to college at Wake Forest University for four years followed by three years of graduate work at a Baptist seminary and I was pastor of a small rural church for two years. But nothing could have prepared me for the eight and one-half months of combat that I experienced. I wasn't prepared, professionally or personally.

I had no apprenticeship, no blue print, and no mentor. There was only on-the-job training.

My ministry was always done in perpetual crisis. In Maslow's hierarchy of needs, survival is very basic. Nothing else matters unless one survives. As soon as one is in his first firefight, the quest for survival becomes the primary objective. Yet even in my quest for survival, I tried to never lose sight of my purpose, to be with my soldiers. I wanted to minister, encourage, and listen. I wanted to be a friend, advocate, and a figure of moral and spiritual authority. I wanted to love them always, but especially in combat, when they needed me most.

How did I survive? Physically, it was by the grace of God. Emotionally, I credit my survival to my strong faith in God, a loving wife, a wonderful upbringing by my parents, a strong sense of divine calling, a sturdy sense of humor, and perhaps even a bit of a hard head. I was lucky to have a "warm up" period of six weeks after I arrived in Vietnam before the real game called combat began. Then, the last three months of my tour, I had a transition time in a much safer and more secure assignment that served as my "basic untraining."

Upon reflection, I wasn't unique and certainly not a hero. Any deeds seen as heroic by others were merely my efforts to avoid being killed. I deeply respected and loved our soldiers, and I saw heroism in every encounter we had in combat. Patriotism usually did not enter into it. Soldiers fight for each other. When someone is trying to kill you, unique friendships are forged quickly. When lives are placed on the line, heroism becomes an almost every day event. I served with hundreds of heroes, most of who were never acknowledged or recognized. 1967–68 was like a ride on a roller coaster—wild, crazy, upside down, sideways, jerky, scary, fast, and nonstop.

All incidents in my story are true. Real names are used except where embarrassment or shame might be the result. In these cases, first names, no name, or a fictitious name is used. It certainly is not my intention to cause anyone residual pain or discomfort, especially three decades later. This war has caused enough of that.

My story is about more than just trauma. It's about me, and several hundred other young Americans, many of whom were objects of physical and emotional abortions. It's also about coping, feeling, growing up, bonding, being cynical, loving, being loved, being vulnerable, placing values in perspective, and even humor.

I write this almost verbatim from my diaries and extensive detailed journals that I kept. I also draw heavily from the letters and tapes my wife saved. All of these sources have helped me find and keep my perspective.

At times the language may offend some. Others might be surprised that a minister has feelings like I describe here. Maybe the typical minister doesn't, but few experience the continual onslaught I did during those eight and one-half months. The extreme feelings which accompany violence and trauma give birth to expressions that wouldn't be considered appropriate at Sunday lunch with one's parishioners. To mince words would dilute my story.

My story is personal. It reflects who I was at ages twenty-six and twenty-seven. It also reflects who I was in the ensuing thirty years. The correspondence and journal of thoughts and feelings are almost word for word, thus I make myself vulnerable.

No, my story doesn't end with my return flight home from Vietnam. It has continued for three decades. The latter part of my odyssey deals with events and circumstances, which are forever linked to my combat experiences.

The good news is that feelings, even bad ones, can be managed and controlled. I've learned that they don't have to rule me when they periodically resurface. For the better part of three decades, I've carried deep in my soul the hurt of those traumatic days spent with real heroes who were in their late teens and early twenties. Many would simply say, "Leave the war and move on." Do they understand what daily, life-threatening trauma does to a person? Ask the concentration camp survivor, or one who has been systematically raped as a child, or a combat infantryman. Yes, one can emotionally adjust and the trauma doesn't have to incapacitate. But making it go away is not easy.

Decades after my combat experiences, post traumatic feelings have periodically surfaced. These came about as a result of what others might view as seemingly benign events, but for me they were reflective of malignant emotions from deep in my soul. "Closure" never happened for me. "Cleansing" more accurately describes what happened to me years later.

I returned to Vietnam in 1996 where God allowed my "cleansing" to continue in truly miraculous ways. Returning with a few Americans and reconnecting to some Vietnamese, all who had impacted my life so profoundly, was a cause for my unbridled celebration. I feel several events in my return journey were absolute miracles.

Until now, no one has heard my complete story. Why? I'm not sure. Maybe no one asked—or knew what to ask. Maybe I just didn't know what to say.

Horrible as many of my experiences were, in a strange way, I'm a better person because of them. My "cleansing" has helped me as a pastoral counselor, and marriage and family therapist. I can more easily identify with and minister to persons who've been systematically abused—physically, emotionally and sexually—or those who have chronic illness, bad marriages, problem children, job difficulties, and mental illness. Victims are victims, and because I am also one, I have been able to help others over the years.

Some of my story is, of necessity, reflective of politics, theology and morality. But it's not about right or wrong. It is not a sermon, or even "religious" talk, or platitudes. This is about my odyssey; my combat experiences then and how they affected me in the intervening years. Thank you for listening.

CHAPTER ONE

June 28–August 18, 1967

WEDNESDAY, JUNE 28, 1967: What have I gotten myself into? Suddenly, I feel terribly, devastatingly alone. A part of me wants to turn around and return home. That's impossible. I'm over the Pacific with 175 other GIs heading to Vietnam. My mind is a blur as my thoughts hopscotch to so many events of the past few days.

I can still see my ten-month-old son, Grey, waving goodbye to me Sunday morning. I know he couldn't understand what was happening as I left to go to the airport. I was about to burst, not knowing if I'd ever see him again.

"Don't cry anymore, mommy," two and one-half year old Kellie had said to my wife, Barbara, in the Charlotte, North Carolina terminal. I can still see my daughter wiping her mother's tears as final goodbyes were spoken. The last thing I saw as I looked out the plane window was Barbara, Kellie and my parents all waving.

The whine of the engines seem to be telling me I must be crazy to leave my wonderful family and go to war. I feel sick to my stomach. After all, I did volunteer for this tour.

Five months ago at Fort Knox, Kentucky, I began to realize that I was getting closer and closer to receiving orders to go overseas. For a young chaplain on active duty, orders for reassignment after twelve months meant going to either Korea or Vietnam. I decided that if I was going to spend a year away from my family, I wanted to go to Vietnam.

A senior chaplain named Ed volunteered to make a call to Washington on my behalf. He said he could get me assigned to Vietnam. I remember stepping nervously into his office.

"Are you sure you want to go to Vietnam, Jim?" Ed grins, realizing he's about to show off some of his clout.

"Yes. I'm sure." But I don't sound too convincing, even to myself.

"Okay, here goes," he says, as he dials the number to the personnel department of the Chief of Chaplains Office in Washington, D.C.

"Nellie this is Ed at Ft. Knox. How is my favorite sweetie in Washington?" He winks at me, then goes on. "I have a sharp young chaplain here who wants to volunteer for Vietnam. Can you arrange it?" He paused and I realized hearing Ed say volunteer suddenly didn't sound so good.

During the following few weeks, I prepared baggage and attended special training. I learned how to shoot and dismantle an M-16 rifle and .45 caliber pistol, even though chaplains are prohibited by the Geneva Convention from carrying weapons of war. Nevertheless, I didn't want to find myself in a situation of needing to defend myself and not knowing how. This training was all "unofficial" and I was careful that none of it would be reflected on my records.

Now, as the pilot announces that we'll stop on Wake Island to refuel, I see Wake is nothing more than a pinhead in the middle of the Pacific Ocean. We disembark while the refueling takes place. It's here that I do my first Vietnam counseling. A young soldier, noticing the cross on my collar, approaches me, and asks if we can talk.

Outside, we find some privacy. It's late afternoon, only an hour before dark, and the sun's rays are glistening off the pacific waters.

"What's on your mind?" I say.

"Sir, I shouldn't be going to Vietnam. My mother's been sick." He proceeds to give me a litany of family problems, as if the longer the list, the greater the reason he shouldn't go.

"Have you put in for a compassionate reassignment or a hardship discharge?" This private doesn't seem to have a reason for either, but I don't tell him that. Now is not the time or place.

"They told me at Ft. Jackson that I'll have to do that in Vietnam."

"That's probably right." Right or not, he's now on the way and it can't be done here. "See your first sergeant when you get to your unit and also maybe your unit chaplain. Maybe they can help."

He is desperate and asks if I can't arrange for him to catch another plane back to the states. I guess he must think I am God, or at least a general.

"I'm sorry, there's no way you can stay here." He looks really disappointed, and I have the fleeting thought that if he were stateside, he might be a candidate for AWOL. But unless he's quite a swimmer, he won't get far. I think this poor nineteen year old kid is on his way to his first nervous breakdown.

FRIDAY, JUNE 30, 1967: It's 2:00 A.M. We've gained a day because of passing over the International Dateline. We're on our descent to land in Vietnam. I wonder what Barbara and the kids are doing now. The thought that it will be a year before I make the reverse trip again is sobering.

Only 365 more days to go! Already, that magic number is in my mind as it is with a prisoner. There's a sentence to be completed; a miserable thought, even though I have volunteered for the "sentence".

Everyone on the plane is quiet. The landing lights of the aircraft are on and, as I look out the window, I fully expect to see tracers from the Viet Cong (VC) weapons coming at us. There are none. My last phone call to Barbara just twenty-four hours ago at Travis Air Base now seems an eternity ago.

"Sug, how are you?" I had said when she answered the phone.

"Okay. Where are you?"

"Still at Travis, but we leave in a few minutes." She began to cry softly. "Are you okay?" I know that she isn't.

"I'm fine. I thought you'd already be gone. I miss you."

"I miss you too." Tears began to fill my eyes. "We'll just have to plan for R&R in Hawaii."

"Okay."

"How are the kids?" I ask.

"Fine, I guess. They don't know what to make of you not being here. Kellie cried for you last night."

I swallowed the pain I felt. "Well, just love them for me and know that I love you with all my heart. I'd better go. I'll write and make a tape soon."

"I love you, too."

I tried to think of something light or funny to say, but I was hurting too badly and my brain was a blank.

We touch down and taxi to a stop. A rather large Air Force sergeant comes aboard and tells us nonchalantly, and somewhat arrogantly, where to go when we leave the plane. Some of us want to tell him where to go. I make my way from the plane to a shelter a few hundred yards away. The only lights are four dingy bulbs and the glow of flares in the distance. I see several air police nearby who have clips of live ammunition.

After a half-hour, I finally find my baggage. Already, I am eager to leave Bien Hoa as the heat is beginning to have its effect on me even at 3:00 A.M.

Upon arrival at the 90th Replacement Battalion in Long Binh, we have paperwork and briefings. We draw linens for bunks, and perform several other small details. The first briefing is by a non-commissioned officer (NCO) who sounds like he has a mouth full of marbles. I finally catch a few winks of sleep about mid-morning. It's been a long time since I've been able to lie down and sleep. Being six feet six makes it impossible to sleep in the small seats of the airplane. Now, the heat of mid-morning makes it miserable to even lie still.

It had been my hope that I would be assigned to an infantry battalion during my tour. I get my assignment, the 9th Infantry Division. Great! Being away from home for a year anyway, I might as well live in the field with those who are doing the fighting. Besides, it'll be good for my career should I decide to stay in the army.

I write a letter to Barbara, because as tired as I am, sleep will not come. I wonder how she and the kids are. Artillery is being fired in the distance and mosquitoes bother me in spite of sleeping under a net. I wonder what incoming mortars sound like. I pray for my family, and for the scared kid I talked to on Wake Island. Only 362 days to go.

1:15 P.M.
Friday, June 30, 1967
Hello my three sweeties,
Well, I'm in Vietnam. I miss you three more than anything in the world.

SATURDAY, JULY 1, 1967: Shortly after lunch, my name is called on the compound loud speaker. Soon I'm on the way over the rough roads headed to Bear Cat, the division headquarters located about eight miles from Long Binh. The world is now left further behind.

On the ride to Bear Cat, I see my first rice paddies, water buffalo, Vietnamese hooches, and smell for the first time the unique odor of a Vietnamese village. Highway 15 leads to Vung Tau on the coast. Bear Cat lies just off this highway and is about thirty miles from Saigon. As we ride, Chaplain Charlie Meek, the division chaplain, briefs me on the current enemy situation around Bear Cat. The VC have been quiet for some time in this area. He does point out a hole in the road made by a mine that the VC had blown several days earlier. The roads are a mess, rough and dusty.

Arriving at Bear Cat, I'm surprised at its large size. Chaplain Meek has a good bed, stereo, refrigerator, and a homemade shower. I had assumed everyone in an infantry division would sleep either in tents or on the ground. Charlie is a kind, father type figure, which I badly need now.

"Jim, I'll be sending you down to Dong Tam in a few days." He tells me. "You'll join an infantry battalion; the 3/60th. They'll be going aboard ships for riverine operations at the end of the month."

I'm puzzled. I've never heard of riverine operations before. "Is it like the Marines?" Charlie is a former Marine, but I have forgotten that.

"No, nothing is as good as the Marines." He offers a slight grin.

I'm not sure what he means, but I'm certain I don't want to get into a Marines vs. Army thing.

"Riverine operations will be different from anything we're doing over here," Charlie says.

I don't even know enough to ask intelligent questions.

"I'll take you to Dong Tam tomorrow and you can see a little of what the Delta looks like."

SUNDAY, JULY 2, 1967: "Goooooooood morning, Vietnam" This trademark morning greeting from the Armed Forces Radio Station awakens me. Today Chaplain Meek has several services in different locations and tells me to just tail him wherever he goes so I can see how he operates.

We board a helicopter and head south into the Mekong Delta. From the air, I'm amazed at the number of rivers, canals and waterways. I learn that 2,400 kilometers of navigable natural waterways and 4,400 kilometers of man made canals make up the Delta. The waterways are sources of life for the Vietnamese. It's their source of food, means of transportation, washing machine, bath tub, and commode. The numerous rivers, canals, streams and ditches are heavily influenced by the tides and seasonal monsoon rains.

Our first stop is at Dong Tam, a base camp the size of four football fields. General Westmoreland, the U.S. Army, Vietnam commander, personally chose the name of Dong Tam. It means "united hearts and minds." He believed that the name would signify the bond between the American and Vietnamese people in the combined objective in the Delta. Also, he thought it would be an easy name to pronounce and remember.

We fly to a maintenance unit at Ben Luc. The place is a sea of mud as we are in the midst of the monsoons. They last six months, and you feel as if you are caught under a shower. You can't get away from the rain. The saying is, "It only rained two times last week, once for three days and the second time for four days."

Back at Dong Tam, I meet another "Jim", whose place I'm taking in the 3/60th. He is to be moved to the 3rd Surgical Hospital, also located here at Dong Tam. This is the first that he has heard of this reassignment and he seems surprised.

Returning to Bear Cat, we fly over what the French used to call the "Paris of the Orient," Saigon. It is a sight to behold for this country boy. The houses and buildings are close together and the streets are a mass of humanity. We fly low which allows me the opportunity to see the city from almost tree top level.

MONDAY, JULY 3, 1967: After breakfast I take my first malaria pill. Monday is the day we all must take this, to forget is to risk malaria. There is also a personal dilemma involved here; many tell me the pills cause diarrhea. But Malaria can kill, diarrhea can't!

Today I go to Saigon and meet with the USARV Chaplain, the senior chaplain in all of Vietnam. Just north of Saigon, I'm impressed by a roadside memorial, a huge statue of a tired looking Vietnamese soldier sitting down, staring out into space. He's dressed in full battle gear. I realize this must be the way many Vietnamese GI's think. They've been fighting for many years; their tour isn't over at twelve months.

In Saigon I'm utterly amazed. Lambrettas, small three wheeled vehicles resembling a motorbike with a cab, are everywhere, along with bicycles, scooters, taxis. Some of the vehicles look like mopeds with side cars. The streets have no markings and everyone just noses through the intersections. There are few stop lights and most don't work.

The USARV Chaplain had been my post chaplain at Fort Knox, Kentucky for a short period of time, so I know him fairly well. He asks how things are and welcomes me to Vietnam. He remains seated at his desk, shakes my hand, and gives me a short briefing on what to expect and what to do in different situations. I listen attentively in spite of his arrogance and patronizing attitude. He keeps talking about our obligation to the American public, but I really don't know what he's talking about. Vietnam probably seems like a 100,000-piece jigsaw puzzle to most Americans. If a parent has a son here, that's the only piece of the puzzle that matters.

When the briefing is finished, I salute and leave. Here at the HQ, brass are everywhere. I feel out of place and I'm glad to get out of brass hat boulevard.

As we drive back through Saigon after getting my baggage, my driver gets lost. I have been lost from the time we left Bear Cat this morning. We finally find our way out and head home. I've been here two days and I'm now calling it "home."

My driver drops me off at the finance office for processing. Here, I'm given "military pay certificates" (MPC) for my green backs. MPC is supposed to be used only internally by the military. Vietnamese accept it, but if and when MPC is changed, the MPC held by the Vietnamese will be about as valuable as Mardi Gras beads. I don't imagine I'll see greenbacks again until I go on R&R in January.

The first major battle of my war begins for me today and it's not a battle fought with guns, artillery, air strikes and gun ships. This battle is with loneliness, homesickness, frustration, fear, and despair.

The first "ambush" occurs on my return from Saigon back to Bear Cat. I'm soaked from a monsoon downpour while riding in the open Jeep. It's been one week since I left my family but it seems like a year. I'm beginning to feel like I'm in a bottomless pit.

TUESDAY, JULY 4, 1967: The fourth of July! A year ago I spent this holiday quietly with my family. This morning I draw my equipment. I now have some jungle fatigues and jungle boots. Even though they aren't faded like some of the "veterans" at least I don't have the tale-tell sign of stateside fatigues that shout to everyone how new I am. I mope around most of the day, feeling sorry for myself. I smile outwardly but inside I'm dying.

Late in the afternoon, I call home via a Military Affiliated Radio System (MARS) station, which enables me to call the United States through ham operators. The connection is so bad that Barbara's voice is garbled, but at least I hear her and know that she is okay.

In the evening, the division band has a concert. I'm still feeling down, however, I do find their last piece quite amusing. It is the 1812 Overture and ends with 105 millimeter howitzers firing live rounds out at the enemy.

Back at the hooch, I take out the pictures of my family. This depression is about to kill me. My prayers seem so empty. My personal enemy continues his frontal assault as I sleep; I dream of missing my family.

WEDNESDAY, JULY 5, 1967: I awake and my "battle" continues to rage. The only good news is that Chaplain Meek tells me that I'll be reporting to my new unit tomorrow instead of waiting until next Sunday.

Walls of self pity wash over me. I get a second plague shot. With my luck, the antidote will give me the disease.

THURSDAY, JULY 6, 1967: I'm able to laugh in the early morning light as I go out to catch the aircraft that will take me to Dong Tam. The sign over the shelter at the little dirt airstrip reads, "Bearcat International. Elevation 32 ft. Please don't pee on the Runway." I chuckle and this humor is good for me.

The sun is just beginning to cast its rays over the eastern horizon. With the fog lifting from the water-soaked rice paddies and with wisps of smoke rising from the Vietnamese hooches below us, you'd never guess from high above in our helicopter that a war was going on. Can God actually be in this forgotten place? The gunners on the helicopter suddenly open their doors, and cool morning air rushes in. As we descend for our approach to Dong Tam, I'm still amazed at the waterways.

Paul, my chaplain's assistant, is waiting for me at the Dong Tam air strip. It takes only four or five minutes to get to my new home which is on the other side of our base camp.

The hooch has tropical wood siding, slanted for vision and cross ventilation, but it keeps the rain out. The floor is wood and the top is a general purpose small tent. A built-in desk is ample for writing and typing. Two wall lockers are sufficient for extra fatigues. Footlockers fit snugly under the folding cots. At least I know the hooch floor will not be littered with dirty underwear. I am advised that due to the wet conditions in the Delta, no one wears any!

By now, the midday heat is rising. Inside the hooch, it feels hot enough to bake biscuits. I'm also told that Dong Tam is very secure. It has been mortared only once and that was in February, five months ago. Still, I'm shown where the protective bunker is, "Just in case."

Dong Tam is located eight kilometers southwest of the city of My Tho, pronounced Me Toe, and sits at the intersection of the heavily traveled, VC controlled Kinh Xang Canal and the My Tho branch of the Mekong River. The canal becomes known as "Route 66."

Six months ago, there was nothing but rice paddies in the area that has become Dong Tam Base. Then, two large dredges anchored in the river and began twenty four hour dredging of sand that was continuously piped on to Dong Tam. Slowly, the wet sand from the river bottom became firm enough on which to build Dong Tam Base. A fairly large turning basin has been dredged to accommodate the smaller river craft anticipated for use in riverine operations. This basin enables the boats to literally move to within a few feet of troop embarkation and disembarkation. This also allows for quick re-supply of ammunition, food, etc. So, Dong Tam is literally being built from the bottom of the My Tho River.

FRIDAY, JULY 7, 1967: The "enemy" that first attacked me on Monday returns with reinforcements today and he pounds me with his heaviest artillery yet. I'm tortured. How I miss my family.

SATURDAY, JULY 8, 1967: This morning the "battle" continues to rage. I know that something must change; this depression is killing me. I have prayed each day and night for peace in my personal war. God, where are you?

> *11:00 A.M.*
> *Saturday, July 8, 1967*
> *Hello Sweets,*
> *I'm having some second thoughts about staying in the army. I sure am anxious to know how Kellie is adjusting to my being gone. I know that all this is a strain on you, it's probably worse on you than on me. I have a new idea, maybe on R&R you could not only bring Kellie but Grey as well. He'd be eighteen months then. The food here is okay but not like yours.*

A miracle! That's what it is! I can't describe it any other way. A very heavy burden is suddenly and mysteriously lifted from my shoulders. I feel like the Apostle Paul must have felt after his blindness ceased following his Damascus road experience. My "battle" is over! I go to a staff meeting

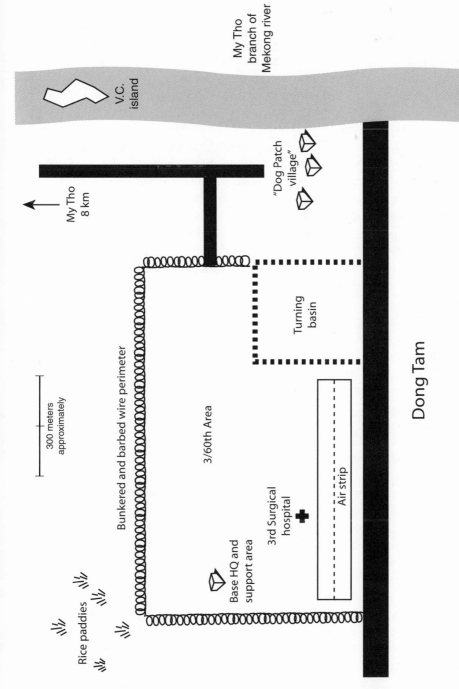

V.C. island

My Tho branch of Mekong river

"Dog Patch" village

My Tho 8 km

Turning basin

300 meters approximately

Bunkered and barbed wire perimeter

3/60th Area

3rd Surgical hospital

Base HQ and support area

Air strip

Rice paddies

Dong Tam

Dong Tam lay-out

at eleven o'clock a brand new man with a renewed spirit. I'm utterly amazed; the depression is gone. This happens so rapid that it's scary. I can truly say I've had a taste of hell, because of the intensity of my feelings. This must be God's way of allowing me to experience what many GI's feel.

SUNDAY, JULY 9, 1967: Today, I conduct my first services in Vietnam. The heat is terrible. I plan to establish a routine, meet people, plant seeds for future relationships, get adjusted to the climate, and explore ways to enhance my future ministry. We'll be moving from Dong Tam aboard the ships in three weeks, so I have this warm-up time to get adjusted. My goal is to see and be seen by every soldier in the 3/60th at least every other day. I want to know the soldiers on a first name basis, know their jobs, needs and particular situations. I want to be there, to encourage, to be connected to them, to heal by my presence with God's influence. Yes, ministry here will be indeed unique. But, this is a unique environment.

Grey was eleven months old yesterday. I'm missing so much as his father.

6:15 P.M.
Sunday, July 9, 1967
Hello Sweets,
If I thought I'd have to wait until next summer to see you, I'd go crazy. Are you afraid to stay by yourself?

MONDAY, JULY 10, 1967: Today I make a visit to a small orphanage in the city of My Tho, approximately five miles to the northeast of Dong Tam. This orphanage is operated by the only Protestant church in My Tho. Pastor Ha is a marvelous Christian. The orphanage has room for approximately thirty orphans. There are only two buildings in the orphanage proper. One is for living quarters and office space and the other is a school building consisting of three open air classrooms. The latter was completed just last week. It will school four hundred refugee children. What a marvelous attempt by these dedicated Christians to take care of the children who are innocent victims of this war. The kids are so lovable.

Now it's back home to Dong Tam. The mission now for the 3/60th is to provide defense for the construction of the base. This consists of limited small unit offensive operations just beyond the perimeter of the base, guarding the dredges and pipelines that funnel the wet sand, manning the perimeter and preparing to move aboard the ships in early August. I walk to the perimeter.

TUESDAY, JULY 11, 1967: The hospital calls almost daily for dustoffs bringing in soldiers with fragment wounds from booby traps. It is my understanding that a "dustoff" gets its name from the fact that when a soldier is wounded, a medivac chopper is called in as soon as safely possible. As the chopper comes in, the objective is to load the wounded on board quickly so the aircraft can leave immediately. In doing so, the rotor prop wash blows up a lot of trash and dust; hence the name "dustoff."

A booby trap is a favorite and inexpensive weapon the VC use regularly. It's a bomb using a grenade, mine or homemade explosive materials. Most have an almost invisible trip wire that causes the explosion when a soldier's boot contacts the wire or string. The VC use booby traps where GI's are likely to walk, such as trails and hooch entrances. Figuratively and literally, I am afraid we'll get a belly full of booby traps. I've never experienced people traumatically injured before.

WEDNESDAY, JULY 12, 1967: Secretary of Defense McNamara schedules a visit to Dong Tam. I already don't care! I'm beginning to feel that we'd be just as well off to build bonfires on the moon for what this war costs.

I now have a steady stream of GIs coming to me for counseling. I hear many of their problems each day, and I'm beginning to feel very much a part of the unit.

Chaplain Meek calls to inform me that I have a letter at Bear Cat. I am so happy, I can't wait to get back there to read it.

8:20 A.M.
Friday, July 14, 1967
My Darling Sweetie,
Boy, was I ever glad to get the mail from you. I know you'll have some bad days like I had last weekend. But, I am much better. It's beginning to be difficult to know the days and dates. Does Kellie still cry for me at night? That must be pretty hard on you. Only 175 days until I get to see you on R&R. Come hell or high water, I intend for you to get to Hawaii. We'll be together for 6 full days and nights!!!

I play numerous games of basketball with the soldiers. When we choose up sides, I am usually one of the first selected and am soon referred to as The Jolly Green Giant. Yes, I'm tall, and a good athlete, and I soon become known as a "force" on the court. These basketball games expose me to many soldiers in a short period of time. This will prove very beneficial in the months ahead, because whenever I see them in the field on combat operations, they'll already know who I am. Besides, playing basketball is fun. I'm one of only a few who can slam dunk the ball. That gets attention around the camp.

8:00 A.M.
Tuesday, July 18, 1967
Hello Sweetheart,
You wouldn't believe how little some of the girlfriends and wives write their men over here. I sure do appreciate your faithfulness in writing and everything else. I dream about you and the kids almost every night.

WEDNESDAY, JULY 19, 1967: I'm now receiving mail on a regular basis. This feels better than scratching an itch.

SATURDAY, JULY 22, 1967: I've never before heard an incoming mortar round, but, I immediately know exactly what it is. My adrenaline kicks into high gear!

"Incoming!" I yell to Paul.

"Hit the bunker!" It's 9:00 P.M.

We grab our flak vests and steel helmets and make a run out the front door to head for the bunker, about fifteen steps from my hooch. The first two rounds have hit just to our left front. As we run, the next round follows and explodes behind us. I hear the fragments hitting the tin roof of the new tropical barracks under construction just behind my hooch. As I slide into the bunker, my heart is pounding. Outside I hear the continual dull thuds of exploding mortars. It's pitch black.

I crouch in the bunker with about twenty enlisted men. A few soldiers light cigarettes which offer only a quick glow that reflects controlled fear on each face.

The mortar attack is over in about five minutes. The only sounds now are the hum of the generators, a far away helicopter, and a vehicle some distance away.

Safely out of the bunker, I quickly head in the darkness to the 3rd Surgical Hospital. Part of our mechanized company, C/5/60th, has been on the perimeter and has gotten into a fight with the VC. They knocked out the VC mortar that had been used to hit Dong Tam. The VC fired a recoilless rifle at an armored personnel carrier and even though the round missed the track, it exploded a few meters away. A fragment caught a soldier in his chest cavity. He's wet and terrified but very much conscious. I stay with him as they prep him for surgery. He's glad to be alive but anxious. I pray with him before he goes into surgery.

When I finally go to sleep in the wee hours of the morning, I have the feeling that I am fast becoming a veteran. I have now been under live fire.

SUNDAY, JULY 23, 1967: I'm already tired when I wake up, but I'm scheduled for five services since I'm the only chaplain on Dong Tam today.

Today is Barbara's birthday, and I miss her desperately. I hope she gets the string of pearls I bought at the PX and sent a few days ago. Poor Paul. He writes his wife daily, but receives only one letter a week from her. He says little about it but I can tell it bothers him. I'm more grateful than ever for my Barbara. I am just lying down tonight when I hear the first sickening explosion. It makes a direct hit on one of the new tropical barracks buildings under construction just to my rear. Fortunately, it is unoccupied. I immediately yell to Paul and we grab our flak jackets and steel pots and run for the bunker.

I run so fast that I "spin out" as I turn the corner near the bunker and come down hard on my knee. Inside the bunker, my leg burns badly from the abrasion. I feel some blood but it is too dark to assess my injury. After about ten minutes, we hear no more mortar rounds coming in, but there is a lot of small arms fire on the perimeter. I tell the soldiers in the bunker that I wish there was an infield fly rule for mortars like there is in baseball.

It's been four months since the first and only mortar attack on Dong Tam and now we've been hit two nights consecutively. I get out of the bunker and stand with several other soldiers for several minutes. The only illumination is the flares on the perimeter. I am shaking with fear. I know I must get to the hospital quickly because while we were in the bunker during the attack, I heard several cries of, "Medic, medic."

At the hospital, I help a wounded soldier into the pre-op ward only to find that the hospital is on secondary power. A nurse tells me that their main generator was knocked out during the mortar attack. All the hospital personnel had hit the floor. Two doctors are patching a soldier, and I see immediately that he is more seriously wounded than the one I helped in.

After about fifteen minutes, many other soldiers are brought in from throughout the base camp. I go from one to the other seeking to comfort them in their pain. Some are seriously injured, others have only minor wounds, but they all are very frightened. I forget my injured knee.

The hospital was the primary target. Each hospital unit is a small mobile, oblong, balloon-type ward that is held up by machine generated air pressure. Most units were deflated by fragments. As the first rounds exploded, several nurses quickly extracted their patients from their beds and laid them on the floor to get them out of harms way.

The only treatment that can be given to these wounded soldiers is first aid. No surgery can be performed because the hospital, for all practical purposes, is out of commission. An estimated twenty rounds have hit the immediate hospital area. Some of the wounded are in serious condition but none appear to be critical at the moment.

We begin evacuating all patients, old and new, to the hospitals in Saigon and Long Binh. We have about thirty-five newly wounded. The evacuation takes several hours to complete, even with several medevac choppers making flights back and forth. I stay with the wounded until the last one is evacuated.

Tonight, I've had my fill of torn flesh, fear, destruction and chaos.

MONDAY, JULY 24, 1967: Daylight reveals the extensive damage done. The nearby officer's hooches for the hospital have received a direct hit. One round actually landed in the bed of a physician who fortunately was in the operating room. If I thought I was exhausted last night, now I am dead. It was never like this when I was pastor of Gum Spring Baptist Church in Lilesville, North Carolina. I now realize there was nothing in my previous life that could have prepared me for this.

WEDNESDAY, JULY 26, 1967: We learn that one week from today we load aboard navy ships and become a part of the Mobile Riverine Force. Because of so much water in the Delta, a strategic decision was made to employ riverine operations using a floating base camp, water maneuverable assets, and combined army and navy forces. This concept will better utilize the wet terrain of the Delta. This is the first time in 100 years that the U.S. Government has attempted to combine infantry and small navy boats in combat operations. The last time was in the Civil War, and never on foreign soil. We're a part of history in the making.

I learn that my daughter Kellie has had the mumps and my concern is that Barbara may also get them. I know she didn't have them as a child. I worry some about this, but since I've only had seventeen hours of sleep since Saturday, I decide I can't spend energy worrying about what I cannot control. I can't do anything from 12,000 miles away.

SUNDAY, JULY 30, 1967: War highlights many personality types. Larry Garner is a lieutenant who commands our Charlie Company of the 3/60th. Actually, his company is only attached to us because they're a mechanized infantry unit and the rest of the 3/60th is called a "straight leg" infantry unit. This company is attached to us primarily to provide security on the roads within a short distance from the base camp, to patrol the roads in and around Dong Tam. Their vehicles are armored personnel carriers, simply referred to as "tracks."

Larry's presence is always known. He's loud but not obnoxious. He sports a moustache and close-cropped hair. He always carries two .45 caliber pistols hung on each hip, somewhat like Patton and his ivory-handled western-style six-shooters. He can carry on a knowledgeable conversation on any subject. Rumor has it that his IQ is 167.

Larry has become known as Bandito Charlie. When Larry took command of the company, he wanted to be unique so he had everyone in the company wear red bandannas. The battalion commander complained that they all looked like a bunch of Banditos, and the name stuck. In the company, Larry was called the Red Barron. To the rest of the battalion, he was known as Bandito Charlie. His reputation as a fearless and effective leader spread quickly throughout the division. As a lieutenant he's taken command of a company that was previously commanded by a captain. Larry has camouflaged his company's "tracks," painted skull and cross-bones on them and personally designed company flags. All other mechanized infantry companies have olive green paint and white markings.

Larry is also a master tactician. He has already won a Silver Star. He has guts, and everyone knows it. He stands in the gunners' position during operations wearing black pajamas, which are the VC uniforms, in an attempt to draw fire from the VC so his men can get into a good firefight. To say that his soldiers love him is an understatement. I hear many of them say that they would go to hell and back if they had Lieutenant Garner as their leader.

One of Larry's heroes is General Custer, and Larry knows Custer's tactics cold. Many of Charlie Company's Mechanized Infantry attacks are remakes of those cavalry charges. On Saturday, July 15th, Larry and I talked extensively in his hooch. We continued our talk over dinner and for an hour or so afterward. Even though I'm new to the battalion, Larry seems comfortable enough with me to vent some significant feelings. This is a part of him that others don't see, his feelings. I learn that he studied for the Catholic priesthood, but decided instead to get a degree in Military History. Earlier he pulled one enlistment in the Marine Corps.

On this afternoon and evening, he is disturbed because the division command is apparently having some difficulties with the unorthodox manner in which he commands his company. The commanding general of the division has learned about the dressing up of his armored personnel carriers and has ordered him to remove the flags and the skull and cross-bones. Larry feels that the commanding general simply doesn't understand tactics or even simple matters such as how these morale builders play important parts in winning battles.

Larry feels that this war is his ball game. Even though he's married and has two children the same ages as mine, he has decided to extend six months making his tour eighteen months instead of twelve. Larry seems to live to have contact with the VC. From our conversation, I come away thinking that he sees himself as immortal. This troubles me. No one is immortal. Infantrymen in battle seem to have some feeling that the person next to him may get hit but he won't. Maybe this feeling sometimes is the only thing that keeps a soldier going from day to day when he's fighting. I believe that Larry feels, even stronger than anyone else I know, that he'll never be killed.

I make a mental note that one of two things will happen to Larry if he stays in the army. Either he'll make general because of his intelligence, experience, common sense, and brashness or he'll get kicked out because of the unorthodox way in which he conducts his military business.

Tonight we talk again. Larry vents a considerable amount of his uncertainty about the future, primarily because of his perception of the lack of support from the powers at division headquarters. He's troubled and speaks from his gut.

A multiple battalion operation known as Coronado II has begun southwest of Dong Tam. Our base camp is a spring board for this particular operation. Because the 3/60th is preparing for riverine operations next week, our mission is only to provide security operations for Dong Tam. Numerous other battalions are to launch combat operations from Dong Tam, including a crack battalion of Vietnamese rangers. The C/5/60th is the only company from our battalion which will be actively involved and their job is simply to guard the extended perimeter of Dong Tam with their tracks. This consists of running short operations on the roads, meager as they are, in and around Dong Tam.

Just prior to the beginning of this operation, Larry turns over command to Dick Botello, a new infantry captain. Larry has fulfilled the normal time in command and is now due to a normal rotation to a staff position. For this operation Larry will be with Dick to help orient him to road runner operations. Tonight, they're on Highway 4 near Cai Lai. This is the only paved road that goes through the Delta, though "paved" is a bit of an overstatement; the road is pock marked, and some stretches are little more than rubble. It extends from Saigon down to Ca Mau in the Deep South. If the Viet Cong can control this highway, the many waterways, the people, and the rice flow to market, they can dictate their will to the rest of the country.

This morning at 4:30 A.M., I'm told that we have some dustoffs from C/5/60th coming in. I quickly go to the 3rd Surgical Hospital. The first man brought in is Lieutenant Billy Smith, the executive officer of C/5/60th.

This is the third time he has been wounded. He's not near death but is shot up pretty badly, and I imagine that this wound will end his war. Four other soldiers are also brought in, their wounds consisting mainly of fragment wounds. All told, Charlie Company has sixteen wounded.

And then, I'm startled nearly senseless when one of the wounded men tells me that three from C/5/60th have been killed and the bodies are still on the field. These are the first soldiers to die since my arrival. What shocks me into immobility is when he tells me that one of the three killed is Larry Garner. I don't believe it. I don't want to believe it. Then, another wounded soldier says, "Yes it's true," and goes on to add that he was with Lieutenant Garner when it happened. I still don't want to believe it. It can't be! The soldier then relates what happened.

He tells me that a medevac helicopter had been shot down nearby. Larry had said, "We must save these pilots if it costs us our lives." He and five others moved out on foot to secure the chopper and rescue the crew from the VC. The soldier says Larry had wanted to "charge those little VC bastards and put them out of commission." They fought their way to the chopper, beat back the VC and successfully evacuated the pilots and crew. Larry and his men formed a small security perimeter around the crippled chopper. Later in the night, the VC mounted a vicious counter attack, and Larry caught a VC bullet through the heart. He and two other soldiers were killed immediately.

Even though I knew Larry for only a brief period of time, I feel devastated at his death. He's the first soldier that I've known personally in my thus far short tour who is killed. When a good soldier like Larry dies, something inside me seems to die too. I feel his loss intensely, and am surprised by this intensity. Nothing seems to ease my pain in these early morning hours.

It's just beginning to get light when I leave the hospital and walk to the battalion area. I see the battalion executive officer as he is leaving his hooch, and I tell him about Larry. The operations center knew there had been three KIAs, but apparently no one had informed command that one was Larry, since he was no longer the company commander. Stunned, he suggests that I go tell Lieutenant Colonel Monk Doty, the battalion commander. I agree but I dread every step as I approach his hooch. I knock and LTC Doty opens the door.

"Good morning, Chaplain. Come in." He's his usual cheery self.

"Thank you sir."

"You caught me in the midst of my morning shave." His face is all lathered in white suds. I tell him to go ahead and finish, but he knows I wouldn't be here this early in the morning for small talk. He insists I tell him what is on my mind.

"I have some bad news, sir."

He pauses and looks at me in mid stroke. "Is it about my family?" Even through the lather, he looks startled.

"No sir." I hadn't thought he might consider that. "It's about C/5/60, Sir . . ."

"What about them?" He seems a little relieved.

"Larry Garner has been killed."

Even through the shaving cream, I see his features flinch and draw. "Killed? Are you sure?"

"Yes. He was shot early this morning."

Monk is completely silent. He turns his back to me and continues shaving. I can't see his face. I wonder if his eyes have tears, like mine do.

"Damn," he finally says intensely. After another pause, he asks for all the details and I tell him. He thanks me and I leave.

Everywhere I go today, people are asking me about Larry's death. Everyone finds it unbelievable. Many of these people didn't even know him but they talk as if he'd been member of their family. Most people felt that Larry was immortal because of his bravery and unorthodox way in which he fought battles. One bullet has destroyed such thoughts.

Two other men were also killed in the same fight that took Larry's life. But, no one speaks of these two soldiers, almost as if they never existed. People only want to talk about Bandito Charlie. A legend has been killed.

MONDAY, JULY 31, 1967: Late yesterday afternoon, a major battle developed and raged into the night. This morning I'm notified that many Vietnamese casualties will be coming into our hospital. After last week's mortar attack, the hospital was quickly brought back on line by replacing the damaged balloon-type units.

Shortly, the first helicopter arrives, the first of many flights in the next two hours. Over one hundred wounded Vietnamese ranger soldiers are brought in. Worse than that, forty-one additional Vietnamese rangers are dead.

This crack battalion of Vietnamese rangers had a battalion of Viet Cong bottled up. They attacked the VC by being airlifted practically on top of them. The VC counterattacked, resulting in absolute slaughter on both sides.

As the wounded arrive, oftentimes six or seven per helicopter, they're in various stages of emotional and physical trauma. As these Vietnamese soldiers are continually unloaded, my senses are bombarded. I'm almost emotionally washed away. None of the wounds that I've seen previously are anywhere near the gruesome types of injuries these Vietnamese rangers have. Some have limbs that are barely hanging on by shreds. Many have bones exposed through the skin. Some have their faces almost blown off but are still alive.

I help the medical personnel unload the wounded from the helicopters so more wounded can be picked up and brought in. I pass out cigarettes to those who want them.

I'm in shock. I've never experienced anything like this. The sights and the smell of blood and death hit me hard. I sweat profusely. Some of the medics helping have to take breaks and leave for awhile. My mind and heart are on overload.

One body in particular makes a memorable mark. A bullet has pierced a young soldier's head just above the bridge of his nose. The only thing left of his head is the bottom part of his eye sockets. Eyes, forehead, and the top of his skull, and all his brain are missing. I think of a volcano crater.

Very few of these Vietnamese soldiers whimper, cry out or make verbal expressions of their physical pain. Perhaps these young Vietnamese soldiers have grown up in poverty and have already experienced a great deal of suffering. Maybe they just accept pain as a part of life. I have tremendous admiration for the way they are enduring.

As word quickly spreads around Dong Tam, reaction is similar to any mass casualty situation. Numerous soldiers come to the hospital area to see what's going on. Most are visibly shaken. They are various support personnel who have never experienced anything like this before. Some leave quickly. Others try to help. Still others just stand and stare, mesmerized.

We learn later that 180 VC were killed. However, death is death regardless of which side you're on. The downside of being an infantryman in combat is death. Who really cares about victory or defeat if you're dead?

I've yet to be shot at.

TUESDAY, AUGUST 1, 1967: Tomorrow we load the ships to begin riverine operations for the next three months. Instead of just protecting an area, we'll soon become aggressors. I know this will not be a child's game of cops and robbers.

My brigade chaplain, Lee Smith, has told me brigade intelligence is expecting at least sixty per cent of my men to be killed or wounded during our next three months. I'm astounded. I simply don't believe this.

WEDNESDAY, AUGUST 2, 1967: At midmorning I conduct my first memorial service. This is for Larry Garner. A tremendous number of people are present from other units. They come from the hospital, the engineers, and the various service units.

An M-16 rifle with bayonet stuck in the ground, and a steel helmet positioned on the rifle butt symbolizes the dead soldier. It is a striking reminder of the finality of war.

The wind blows hard during the fifteen minute, outdoor service. Monsoons threaten continually but fortunately the rains hold off. I offer a few remarks, some scripture passages, a prayer and the battalion commander says a few words. We have a roll call of the dead and it ends with a last salute to our fallen comrade. Fifteen minutes is enough.

Memorial services are always sad occasions. But they're expected because the very least we can do in remembrance of these who have died.

A little later, as Bravo Company is being extracted from just beyond our perimeter, a soldier steps on a mine and is blown to bits. One leg is located about fifty yards from the site of explosion. His other leg is never found.

Later it is moving time. The Mobile Riverine Force flotilla consists of two barracks ships, a barracks barge, a repair ship, and a supply ship. The USS *Benewah* is the headquarters ship. Aboard is the 9th Infantry Division's 2nd brigade headquarters, the navy command group, and has space to sleep eight hundred soldiers. It is a landing ship tank (LST) that has been redesigned. It has a small hospital component, dining facilities, a landing deck for helicopters and means to communicate to any place in the world. It carries a thirty day supply of frozen, chilled, and dry food. The second ship is the USS *Colleton*, which is almost an identical barracks ship to the *Benewah*. This is our battalion headquarters and houses most of our soldiers from the 3/60th. Each barracks ship has a pontoon type barge, known as an ammi barge, attached to the side to provide for loading and docking of the river assault boats. It also allows for space to clean and store ammunition and individual weapons.

I only take my chaplain's kit, which contains the necessary elements to have field services, some toiletry articles, writing papers, some pictures of Barbara and the kids, my jungle boots and fatigues, and my field gear, which I have yet to use. I'm assigned to a four man room with three other officers. The room is small but comfortable. It's quiet and air-conditioned.

Dinner is held in the officer's ward room. This is "high cotton." There's carpet, tablecloths, overstuffed chairs, and Filipino stewards. My bed is wonderful and cozy. There's no sound of outgoing artillery and mortars such as at Dong Tam. In fact, the only sound is the faint hum of the air conditioner.

THURSDAY, AUGUST 3, 1967: Turf quickly becomes an issue and it surfaces this morning. Navy regulations state that no alcoholic beverages are to be aboard a navy vessel. Last night, a sailor was caught drinking by his supervisor. When pressured, he reports that he received his booze from an arriving soldier. A big fuss develops. It is later learned that this navy chief petty officer keeps a private stock of booze stashed away for special occasions. Yet, when a rear end needs covering today, attempts are made to scapegoat the soldiers. Everything is quieted by apologies and promises that it won't happen again. The fuss was about booze and navy regulations, but I'm sure the real issue was about turf, control, and power.

I spend extra time with the C/5/60th this afternoon. Their morale is sagging significantly. They're still in shock that Bandito Charlie is dead. Plus, with our move, they now have been turned from a mechanized unit into a straight-leg infantry unit. Their pride is hurt and their 'remember the Alamo' spirit has vanished.

While I am in the troop's bunk area word comes that one of the track drivers was killed late last night. He stayed behind to turn in his vehicle, hit a mine, and the track flipped over on top of him.

At 10:00 P.M. an alarm sounds throughout the ship. Most of us in the army have no idea what the alarm is about. I soon discover that two sailors are overboard in the river. They were in a shuttle boat returning from an evening of drinking in Dong Tam. In the middle of the huge My Tho River, one either was pushed or jumped overboard and the other jumped overboard after him. They're both lucky to survive. At times, especially when the tide is falling, the current is rapid and treacherous. These two drunk sailors are fortunate that the tide is changing and the current isn't especially swift. Furthermore, in the darkness of the murky waters, they're lucky that the shuttle boat is able to quickly turn and locate them on the first pass.

This day has been so long.

FRIDAY, AUGUST 4, 1967: We are to move to Vung Tau for some specialized training before we begin large-scale riverine operations. This city is located oceanside, and is one of the in-country R&R areas for soldiers. Vung Tau is a relatively secure part of Vietnam.

This trip is my first ever on a real ship on the ocean. I'm excited. We pass some seagoing sampans with funny looking oriental sails, which are quite different from anything I've ever seen.

12: 15 P.M.
Sunday, August 6, 1967
Hello Sweets,
So you took Grey's bottle? You mentioned being concerned about something

happening to me. There is always the possibility, but I'm no fool, nor a hero. I'm being really careful.

TUESDAY, AUGUST 8, 1967: Today is Grey's first birthday. I vividly remember the first time I saw my son. It seems like more than a year ago that he was born at Ft. Knox, Kentucky. I'm a very lucky man. I sure love my two children.

During the next several days, we do training operations nearby. I stay aboard the aid boat, but this is not much fun.

MONDAY, AUGUST 14, 1967: I fly to Saigon to the 3rd Field Hospital. I'm still not accustomed to the tragedies of lost legs, or blinded eyes. These guys are always eager to learn what's happening back in the 3/60th. For most of them, I'm the only contact they have with what's going on. Those who are to be evacuated to Japan or the US for further treatment will, in most cases, never see their buddies again.

WEDNESDAY, AUGUST 16, 1967: Today is party time. Our training operation is over which means our pre game warm up training is about to end. Since we are to relocate shortly, this is a good break. The party is on the nearby beautiful beach. The non-commissioned officer's club caters the party with fried chicken and charcoaled steaks. Cold beer and soda are plentiful.

All sorts of Vietnamese vendors have set up and are selling anything they think the GIs might buy including silk, bathrobes, and even empty jars and black market C-rations.

I take a swim in the warm ocean. What luxury! Later in the afternoon, there's entertainment from a rock-n-roll group from the Philippines who feature a very attractive, mini-skirted singer. She's an instant hit with the GIs. Her singing is not much but who cares?

Back at the ship, I have the unpleasant task of telling one of my soldiers about the death of his father. He sobs quietly for several minutes. Of course, he'll be given emergency leave to go home, but to be in such a faraway place and get news of your father's death is terrible. I know by the way he cries that he's close to his dad. I wonder how I might feel if I received the same news about my father, and I miss him suddenly and fiercely. I consider myself lucky to have my "Pop" as a father and pray I don't get news of his death while I'm in Vietnam.

FRIDAY, AUGUST 18, 1967: We leave Vung Tau heading to Long An Province, which lies west and southwest of Saigon. Our destination is the

Soi Rap River. Movement is slow because we tow the pontoon barges behind us. En route, the ships test fire their weapons.

I have a decision to make. In non-combat assignments, both stateside and Vietnam, the chaplain's "position" is normally at a chapel, or his office or hooch. Because of the Mobile Riverine Force, a totally new concept, I must decide where I will be located during combat operations to provide pastoral care to the troops.

Combat in World War I, World War II, and Korea proved that the chaplain's best location was at the battalion aid station, which would normally be positioned a mile or two to the rear of the front lines. This worked well in previous wars and it is on this basis that my division and brigade chaplains have directed that my post during combat operations should be on the aid boat.

Based on my experience in our recent training exercise, my role will be extremely limited if I restrict myself to the aid boat. I want to be with my soldiers. I want to act and interact with them wherever they are, whatever they are doing. I don't want to just react after they're wounded. I want to know them, to be known by them. Doing this only when they're in base camp or on board ship won't be sufficient. I need them to recognize that I care enough to be with them. I want to minister to them before, during, and after they fight. If I am to adapt the adage of a chaplain, "Bringing men to God, and God to men," then I *have* to be with them in combat.

I realize I have three choices: to be on the aid boat, which is strongly suggested by my chaplain superiors; to locate at the battalion rear, which is on board ship or at Dong Tam base; or to maneuver on the ground with the troops and be in their midst wherever they go. The first two simply don't seem feasible. However, to go with the troops means that I'll be exposed to daily dangers such as snipers, booby traps, and firefights. My supervisory chaplains have questioned me. What if I am wounded or killed, how might that impact the troops? I don't plan to be wounded, of course; however, it's a risk I feel I must take if I am to do the ministry God has called me to do. I'm the one who must now define how best to be pastor to these men. I decide not to leave this decision to my brigade and/or division chaplain supervisors; it is my decision.

And so, my decision is made. I will not be just a 'special teams' player. I will be offense, defense and special teams. I will, when possible, go on combat operations with the troops. I will be where they are, regardless. I may receive resistance from my chaplain superiors. They may even call my action one of defiance. But, they're not on the ground where I am. I will do what I must do to provide pastoral care to these heroes.

CHAPTER TWO

August 19–
September 26, 1967

SATURDAY, AUGUST 19, 1967: The Mobile Riverine Force base is anchored at the junction of the Soi Rap and Vam Co Dong Rivers south of Saigon. Our area of operation will be about twenty miles away northwest of Ben Luc.

At our pre operation briefing, we're told that over two hundred Viet Cong from the 506th Local Force Battalion have been spotted in a one by two mile area. That's exactly where Alpha Company is to operate. Since I'm going out with them, this gets my immediate attention.

Having decided that my position during combat operations will be in the field with the troops, the Alpha Company commander has asked if I'll go with his company. He's relatively new to the battalion having arrived two weeks after me. In fact, all the company commanders have arrived since I have.

This company commander is yet to lead his company in a real fight. He's a huge man and claims to have played football for a year with one of the professional NFL teams. I played football at Wake Forest and, had I not had a career-ending shoulder injury, would have been drafted by the Chicago Bears. Therefore, football is a natural link between us.

After supper I try to sleep for an hour. I know we have an all night boat ride and tomorrow will be a challenging day for me. But, I'm too keyed up to sleep. My mind races wildly. I think of home. I'm afraid of booby traps. At six foot, six inches I think I will be a perfect target for any tree-line VC sniper. I don't know what to expect tomorrow, so sleep won't come. I wonder what I have gotten myself into.

I finally get out of my bunk and write a letter to Barbara. The eerie quiet reminds me of a funeral home. I strap on my field gear and go to the wardroom for a 10:00 P.M. breakfast. Perhaps a dozen or so officers and soldiers I know comment that they can't believe that the chaplain is actually going out on combat operations. Several ask me why. This is obviously new to them, and they all seemed impressed. This makes me feel good.

31

I've been given a .45 caliber pistol and a few rounds "in case you need them." The Geneva Contention of many years ago precludes chaplains from carrying weapons since we are non-combatants. But, the VC don't operate under the guidelines of the Geneva Convention. They proved that recently when they mortared the hospital at Dong Tam. I wear a camouflaged cross insignia on my jungle fatigues. But bullets and booby traps don't distinguish between the cross and the crossed rifle insignia of the infantry, so I'm glad to have the .45 caliber.

I step from the pontoon onto our armored troop carrier (ATC). Each company is allocated three ATC's and twenty minutes to load. Each boat can transport about thirty soldiers, is diesel powered and heavily armed. However, night loading is treacherous, as we have only dim red lights by which to see. Normal lighting would make us an inviting target from the shore even though we're anchored in the middle of the huge Soi Rap River.

The ATC's pull up to the side of the pontoon, three at a time, and take their passengers on board. Only one man can climb over the rail and onto the ATC at a time. One slip means falling into the rapid, murky current. I'd just as soon forgo a night swim, thank you. Caution in loading takes considerable time. The navy has expert swimmers for rescue should a soldier accidentally fall overboard, but no one wants to put them to the test.

The boats form a single line formation and are off for one of the longest rides of any of our operations. We travel in the darkness for several hours up the Vam Co Dong River past the Ben Luc Bridge (Highway 4) and then for several more hours up the dwindling, winding waterway.

The boats are packed with soldiers. Because of heavy casualties in the future, this will be one of the last operations where all of our platoons are at full strength. It's hard to get comfortable lying in a pile of GIs. About every hour I stand up to try to get some circulation back into my legs and each time I do, I lose some of the precious space that I have on the floor of the boat. I'm soon in a fetal position. We are like a boat load of refugees. During the entire night, I don't even take off my gear. With it being so dark, I'm afraid that I won't be able to find all of it.

One day just melts into the other during the long ride. When first light finally begins to make its way over the horizon, I'm relieved; soon the cramped conditions will cease. Then, to my momentary terror, I realize that we'll also be on land, sweeping and looking for the VC. I'm not sure I like this trade-off.

SUNDAY, AUGUST 20, 1967: Just before sunrise, the order is given to saddle up and be prepared to beach. The hum of the ATC diesel engines, the sounds of gear being strapped on and weapons being checked overcome the low sounds of grumbling troops who are already tired. Convicts on death row the night before execution have it better than we did during the night.

As I look out over the top rail of the ATC, mist hangs over the placid waters of the small stream. A few water buffalo stand gazing at us. The vegetation along the shore is very thick but the rice paddies beyond are expansive and open. We pass some Vietnamese hooches but see no people. Perhaps they're in their bunkers or the VC have warned them away. Or maybe they're sleeping in this Sunday morning.

Artillery begins coming in on the banks of the stream up ahead. Our artillery, too, is waterborne and is located about three miles away. Each barge accommodates two tubes of 105mm howitzers. The floating barges of artillery are able to follow us wherever operations occur.

My anxiety rises. After a brief period of inactivity, all four machine guns on our boat and all the other boats begin firing toward the stream banks. The ATCs are doing reconnaissance by fire when we are seconds from beaching.

As quickly as it began, our firing stops. The ATC's simultaneously turn their bows sharply into the stream banks. My heart thumps wildly in my chest. The ATCs beach in groups of three, five to ten meters apart to maintain the integrity of the company. Each company is about two hundred meters apart. Our ATC slams into the bank, the front ramp is dropped and we run out of the beached boat and hit the banks of the stream as quickly as we can. I follow a rifleman for about twenty meters where we drop behind some foliage for cover.

"Well, Chaplain, we made it this far," he says to me. I'm too scared to respond except for a weak smile and head nod. Thank God, we received no fire yet. At least I can now stretch my legs.

Once the immediate area around the banks of the stream is secure, we begin moving inland. Within forty meters of beaching, we begin encountering numerous small canals and ditches two-to eight-foot wide. The first two I jump across. The third we have to wade across. It's time to go swimming. These jungle fatigues make odd bathing suits. I am immediately soaked up to my armpits. The water is cool. During the day we cross fifty to seventy-five small streams, most only two or three feet wide and knee deep. But, some are twenty-five to one-hundred-feet wide and are over my head. The going is treacherously slow due to the water and rough terrain. There is tall grass and undergrowth everywhere. My feet are never out of water.

Within twenty minutes of beaching, we run into a series of Viet Cong bunkers. They are unoccupied and the engineers with us blow them up with plastic explosives.

An hour and a half after we beach, I suddenly hear gunshots to our left rear about a quarter of a mile away. Moving on our left is our Bravo Company and to our right is our Charlie Company. Soon after hearing the gunshots, artillery begins coming directly over us toward where the shooting has occurred. Shortly thereafter, two F-4 fighter jets make air strikes dropping bombs. Heavy black smoke from the dropped ordinance marks where several Huey gun ships then begin making strafing runs. During this time we're moving cautiously because over the radios we're told that a large group of VC has been seen moving our way. Tension is rising with each step.

The soldier in line behind me is a Vietnamese soldier who is serving as our interpreter. Suddenly, he shouts excitedly, "VC, VC!" To my left about one hundred meters away, I see four Viet Cong, running with weapons. They immediately disappear into the undergrowth. We cannot fire on them because our Bravo Company is still moving to our immediate left about five hundred meters away. To fire at the VC means firing in the direction of Bravo Company. The VC often position themselves between two units with the hope that we will fire on one another. Sometimes it works.

The company commander gives the order for one of the platoons to circle right in an attempt to drive any VC toward the remaining part of the company for an ambush. We're stopped for about twenty minutes in a blocking position when suddenly the circling platoon opens fire. They spot eight small trees 'walking.' Several VC are camouflaged with these and are trying to avoid us. The platoon opens fire with M-16's and M-79 grenade launchers. At least two "trees" fall. When we reach the spot where the VC were seen, we find some discarded branches and some blood-soaked rags but no VC.

Moving in such terrain is exhausting. There's much tall grass, banana trees, sugar cane, pineapples, and undergrowth. The emotional stress of being so close to the VC and the immediate danger causes tremendous energy drain. At midday we stop for a gourmet lunch of C-rations. With my anxiety so high, I have little appetite but I eat anyway. I sit with my rear end in water. I decide not to leave a tip!

All too soon it's time to move out again. I have my first experience of crossing a deep body of water with a rope. The stream is only about seventy-five feet wide but it's too deep to walk across. One soldier unloads his gear and swims across the stream with one end of a long rope. He then ties it to a tree and each man pulls himself and his equipment across going hand over hand. We're aware that if we lose our grip on the rope, we can easily drown with boots, flak jacket, and all the equipment and ammunition we carry.

Several times during the day we stop because of artillery fire missions. We find some VC food supplies, black pajamas (VC uniforms), sandals, and other paraphernalia in some of the bunkers.

Late in the afternoon we come to a large pineapple field laced with bunkers. This is an unmanned VC complex and it's also the first dry place we find all day. We are to make this our overnight position and we begin setting up. A supply chopper brings us C-rations, water, ammunition, and additional sandbags to be filled for our defense during the night. The company commander is angry because the supplies do not include claymore mines, which are vital for night defensive positions. Claymores are anti-personnel mines that are electronically detonated and can ruin a VC's day. Arrangements are made for them to be brought in shortly by another supply chopper.

Soon, the battalion commander flies in and the decision is made that early tomorrow morning Alpha Company will do a series of eagle flights since movement is so slow. Eagle flights are five to ten Huey choppers picking up troops and dropping them a short distance away. The soldiers then sweep the area for perhaps five hundred yards and, if no contact is made with the enemy, the choppers return, pick them up, and drop them again. This process is repeated until contact with the enemy is made. The eagle flights will provide an element of surprise that today's slower movement does not have. The hope is that Alpha Company's eagle flights will flush the VC into one of the other unit's position.

Since space on the choppers is at a premium, I decide to try to get with another company if possible. I decide to catch a ride with the second re-supply chopper when it brings the claymore mines.

Suddenly, I think the world is coming to an end! Bullets begin whizzing by me in what seems like every direction. I instantaneously dive for cover in a small canal. Several bullets zip by very close to me. As I lie in the little canal, frightened like a cornered rabbit, it dawns on me that there is no sound in the world like gunshots. When you are being shot at for the first time, everything is magnified.

For five minutes, our troops return a heavy layer of M-16 and M-79 grenade fire in the direction from which the fire originated. Artillery is also called in and volley after volley impacts the tree line where the VC have been firing on us.

And then it's over almost as rapidly as it began. Verbal calls are made to see if anyone has been hit. Miraculously, no one is hurt, but this whole incident has been about as much fun as getting poked in the eye with a sharp stick!

This has been much worse than the Dong Tam mortar attacks. My vulnerability overwhelms me. I made it through this one, but what about those in the future?!

The second re-supply chopper comes in just before dark, unloads, and I catch a ride out. It's a small bubble top and due to my height, it's difficult to get strapped in. We lift off and with so many V C in the area, my immediate fear is of being shot down, but we receive no fire.

The aid boat is in a stream about a mile away. Landing is treacherous. My long legs impede the pilot's ability to maneuver the stick properly so he pulls up and we fly around again. This time on approach I hang one leg out over the right landing rail of the chopper and try to shift sideways. Even though I'm strapped into the seat, I worry that I'll slip out. A monsoon rain has now begun. Finally, we land on the second approach.

There is barely enough space for a chopper to land. In fact, this landing deck is called the smallest in the military. When loaded, a chopper's rear end sticks out over the edge of the boat. I have recently begun calling the aid boat the "USS Scarecrow." Some of the crew are not sure what to make of this name. Soon, though, the name catches on.

The pilot lifts off after dropping me off. It's too late to get to another company tonight, so I'll stay overnight on the aid boat.

Everyone is glad to see me; they heard about the firefight and have many questions. How can I tell them of the sheer terror caused by the sound of bullets cracking through the air?

My mind is on overload and stays that way throughout the night. I think back over the past few years that has brought me to this point. I entered the army last year as a twenty-five year old chaplain, the second youngest on active duty.

Almost from the beginning of my memory I sensed that I wanted to do some type of ministry and be of service to people. As I entered my high school years, I had more and more of a sense of calling but I was unclear during these early years in exactly what way I wanted to serve. My career as an army chaplain actually had its beginning in 1957 during the fall of my senior year in high school. I was blessed with a large body that helped me to be a good athlete, which in turned enabled me to be selected as an All-State football player. Numerous colleges and universities recruited me to play football. I chose Wake Forest, which helped me bridge the gap between my North Carolina backwoods upbringing, and gave me a tremendous foundation for my later ministry.

I knew that I wanted a career that would offer excitement, perhaps some travel, and would allow me to explore new horizons, and develop some level of sophistication. However, I didn't expect my travels to be to Vietnam jungles!

After college, I attended seminary for three years, pastored two small churches and joined the army reserves. As the war here heated up, the army expanded. I received orders for active duty. In June 1966 we moved to Ft. Knox, Kentucky, where I was assigned to the army reception station. Daily we received several hundred young men and it occurred to me that many of these men would be the fuel for the war. Little could I have envisioned eighteen months ago what has just happened to me. I almost became fuel myself.

What a Sunday today has been; certainly not Sunday School. It has been more like Hell.

MONDAY, AUGUST 21, 1967: For some reason, the decision is made to terminate the operation today. The battalion will be extracted and we'll return to the ships.

We finish the operation in the early afternoon. Upon arrival at the ship, I learn that a young sergeant named Wayne Merriman has stepped on a mine just before his platoon was extracted. One leg is blown off and the other is badly mangled. His survival is in doubt, and I know I must see him as soon as possible. I have gotten to know him well since I arrived.

TUESDAY, AUGUST 22, 1967: I hop a chopper headed for Dong Tam. As soon as we land, I walk to the 3rd Surg and I quickly find Wayne. He is weak, but glad to see me. His leg is gone.

"I guess you can see, Chaplain, that I left part of me in the field," he says.

I don't know how to appropriately respond. "Yeah, I see. I'm sorry," I say. At least he is alive, I think, but he looks terrible. I pray with Wayne before I leave and as I go, I speak with his nurse. She informs me that his condition is grave. He has already received seventy units of blood and still requires more.

It's now near dark. I walk across Dong Tam to my hooch to spend the night. Paul is there and is surprised to see me. I haven't taken him to live aboard the ships as I feel he might be more beneficial to me staying at Dong Tam. The battalion area is practically deserted. This is the first time I've been back to spend the night since we went aboard the ships. It's almost like a ghost town.

I grieve over Wayne's leg. I think, well, even if he survives, he'll never be able to play kick ball with his son. I am getting depressed. I find myself wanting to be back at the ship with the other soldiers. I love those guys and miss being there.

WEDNESDAY, AUGUST 23, 1967: On my way back to the airstrip, I stop by to see Wayne again. He's asleep. I'm almost relieved, then feel immediately guilty for that relief. Even as he sleeps, I see drawn lines of pain on his face. The top sheet is flat on the mattress where his missing leg should be. I say a silent prayer for Wayne.

C/5/60 is on a one day operation. Soon, word comes that the point man is killed by a Browning automatic rifle (BAR). The point man is always the first soldier out front and this is a position that is rotated among the soldiers. This is a feared position because you are the first to be seen by the enemy. The soldier who is killed is a new replacement. Few even know his name, simply referring to him as, "that new guy."

Then I learn that Ken, another young sergeant, has stepped on a mine. His foot is gone. I wish I could get to him. I counseled with him just a few days ago because he was upset when one of his men was blown up as we were leaving Dong Tam to load onto the boats. He requested my help in writing to the parents of his lost soldier. Now, Ken has been hit. Thoughts of Wayne return. My only consolation in my sadness for these two soldiers is knowing that at least they're alive. When I next visit the hospital, Wayne has lost his other leg.

I spend one night in Dong Tam and Paul is really down. He writes his wife daily, but has received only one letter from her in twenty-one days, a rather nasty one. He doesn't deserve this neglect from his wife. Neither of us are in the mood for celebration.

12:20 P.M.
Monday, August 28, 1967
Hello Sweets,
I'm glad you're so faithful about writing, Sug. If a wife doesn't write to her husband over here, it is a pretty good indication of her lack of devotion. The bulk of my counseling over here has been around letters - either the lack of them or the things that parents, wives and girlfriends say to them. I love you so much . . .

10:00 A.M.
Thursday, August 31, 1667
Hello Sweets,
Those pictures you sent are just marvelous, especially the one of Kellie on the tricycle, laughing.

3:00 P.M.
Saturday, September 2, 1967
Hello Sweets,
I had a horrible night. The mosquitoes were driving everyone crazy. 134 days until R&R!

For several days, we have been out in a holding position for the Vietnamese national elections. Before we left, we had breakfast at 11:00 P.M.! We should open a twenty-four hour Waffle House. Then, we received no mail. Plus, the mosquitoes were very bad. The only good thing was that we had no casualties except for one soldier who was bitten by a snake. Word is that here in Vietnam there are two kinds of poisonous snakes; one kills you instantly when it bites; the other, you don't die until you fall to the ground. I hate snakes.

The elections are over and at mid afternoon, we leave the area of operation to return to the ships. I arrive at the *Colleton* at 7:00 P.M. just in time for supper. The cooks act like they're doing us a favor by holding supper for us. I soon get word that some of the enlisted men may not get to eat. Along with two of the other officers, I circulate through the enlisted men's mess to make sure the troops are fed properly.

I pick up my mail after supper. Pay day. I have four letters, three tapes, a chocolate cake with cherries and nuts, a letter from mom, and three rolls of slides I'd sent to be developed before I left on operation.

THURSDAY, SEPTEMBER 7, 1967: Today, we begin an operation in the Rung Sat Special Zone, AKA, "The Jungle of Death." This is the densest combination of jungle and marsh that can be imagined. It lies between Saigon and Vung Tau and is bordered by the South China Sea. The tide rises and falls as much as fourteen feet which means that much of this swamp is under water at various times. When the tide is out there's a god-awful sea of mud. The jungle has extremely thick vegetation, entangled vines and dense undergrowth. In most of the Rung Sat, it's impossible to see more than three or four feet in any direction. This massive mangrove swamp is a sight to experience.

We're up early and I load up with Bravo Company. Breakfast is the last time I'll eat until mid afternoon. Will Davis is the company commander. He's an old captain, at least for Vietnam. He was enlisted and rose to the rank of first sergeant before going to officer candidate school. He arrived shortly after me and has been in command just a few weeks. But, this somewhat portly black officer already has the tremendous respect of the entire company. He exudes confidence but not arrogance. When he speaks, his NCOs and officers listen attentively.

We hit the beach at 9:00 A.M. and as soon as we step off the end of the ATC ramp we're up to our knees in mud. The fifteen meters from boat ramp to vegetation line takes several minutes and much expended energy. Each step involves pulling one leg from the mud while the leg in front sinks back into the mud. I am already sweaty by the time I get to firmer ground.

We move with two platoons side by side and the company head-quarters element in between. The vegetation is so thick we must literally stay on the heels of the soldier in front of us. In this enmeshed tangle of vines, bushes and thick undergrowth, getting lost is the last thing I want to happen. I could never find my way out of this mess on my own. It takes us an hour to move inland 200 meters. We're still in water and mud and the point soldiers must use machetes to cut a trail for the others to follow. This place would make a good training ground for professional mud wrestlers.

Without warning, we're hit by the VC. Small arms fire comes from several directions. I hug the mud as bullets tear through the under brush. This is not a time of mere panic; it is sheer terror. The front soldiers return fire but most of the other soldiers cannot shoot for fear of hitting our own guys just ahead. Several rocket propelled grenades and B-40 rockets come in on top of us. Our artillery forward observer begins calling in artillery and "walks" it back toward us. Artillery fragments are now flying through the brush and falling onto us. "Too close", shouts Will Davis. "Back it up! We're going to kill ourselves."

I hear someone a few feet ahead of me yell for a medic, but movement now is impossible because of the heavy fire. Bullets tearing through the underbrush make a terrible sound. Lt. Pete Roger's platoon is nearest to the VC and they're laying down a heavy volume of M-16 fire. That, along with numerous volleys of our artillery, soon suppresses the VC fire. Our artillery and helicopter gun ships are the brass knuckles of our firefights and I'm glad they're on our side. The fight ends after fifteen minutes.

We have two casualties and make arrangements to take them back down the trail we just made for evacuation to the aid boat. A dustoff in this thick undergrowth is impossible.

Will Davis orders an ammunition check. Tom Kirk carries an M-79 grenade launcher. As he's doing his check, he discovers a VC bullet has hit and passed through an M-79 round that he's carrying in his ammunition pouch.

Will gives the order to move out. Within a few meters, we learn why the VC have hit us. We come upon a huge VC base camp, supply depot and hospital. All the VC have apparently left. We find rice still cooking and many blood stained rags and blood trails leading away from the camp. Apparently they've taken all their wounded with them. We find a rice cache with approximately 5100 pounds of rice. The vegetation is so thick that I don't even see the rice until I'm less than five feet away. The VC camp contains built-up walkways, several camouflaged shelters and numerous bunkers with three foot thick walls.

The VC hospital compound has many medical supplies, most with Chinese markings. Even though the Geneva Convention prohibits destroying captured medical supplies, evacuating all these supplies is impossible in this wet hell. The order is given to destroy everything. Numerous documents are evacuated, but cases of iodine are emptied, and clothing and other materials are burned. The hands of several soldiers are red from handling the iodine, but today it is the VC who is really caught "red handed." We blow up some bunkers, but C-4 doesn't destroy most of the thick walls. As we leave, artillery is called in to attempt to blow up the rest of the camp. The hooches are also torched. The rice is emptied in the mud all around the camp to assure that it cannot be reclaimed by the VC.

The troops' morale is high. They feel good about having found and destroyed so many VC supplies in what the VC must have thought was a secure base camp.

At midday, we move out again. The heat and humidity are stifling. I drink a lot of water to avoid dehydration. We come to a stream about twenty meters wide and cross it using the nylon rope method of hand over hand. The cool water feels good to my hot body.

At 2:00 P.M., we stop for lunch. I can do without picnics like this. The food is not very good and the fancy tablecloth and napkins must have been left on the ship. I joke that it is a good thing no Moms are here to scold us for wiping our hands on our clothes. It's been a long time since we had our early morning breakfast back at the *Colleton*. I've sweated so much that I've developed a significant headache.

I eat my C-ration lunch with a civilian reporter who's with a syndicated group of United States newspapers. He has covered the war for the past two and one-half years. He tells me he's been on operations with units from up north in the DMZ to the deep south and that this is absolutely the worst and most miserable terrain he's ever encountered.

He seems puzzled at me being here, yet pleasantly surprised. He says that I must either be brave, crazy, or really love these guys for me to be here in this misery. Maybe I'm some of all three, but I certainly don't feel brave after this morning's firefight.

While we're in position finishing lunch, we hear a tremendous explosion to our right. C/5/60th is maneuvering there and someone apparently tripped a booby-trapped artillery round rigged by the VC. We learn that three are wounded and dreadfully, a fourth is dead, almost decapitated by the blast. Two of the three wounded are serious. Fortunately, they're close to a stream and are quickly evacuated, which probably saves their lives.

We move out again. Within another 200 meters, we find several hundred more pounds of rice carefully camouflaged. We dump this and spread it in the mud. The troops are really excited over finding so many VC supplies.

We're then given orders to change directions and head to an extraction point as we are to move to another small island. We're told we only have about 300 meters to travel. However, the undergrowth is so thick that we have to move about half that distance literally on hands and knees.

We get to the waterway, which is quite wide, and learn that the water is too shallow for an ATC to pick us up. Will Davis requests a Boston whale boat, a small fiberglass boat with a high speed outboard motor, for transporting us out. It's getting late and we must get to our destination before nightfall to insure proper night protection security.

While we're waiting on the whale boat, we rest. Everyone is exhausted. This Jungle of Death is worse than any one of us could ever have imagined.

Finally, the Boston whale boat arrives and transfers ten of us at a time across the stream about 250 meters to the other side. Fear wells up in me again. We're overloaded, traveling at a high rate of speed and are a perfect target for the VC. Finally, we make it to the other island where another company is already setting up night defensive positions.

Bravo Company completes the move and ATCs then pick us up and we move down stream a short distance. Several ATCs beach with us and remain for the night where Bravo Company sets up. I walk to the nearby aid boat for some APCs (a pill of aspirin, phenacetin, and caffeine, or better known as all-purpose capsules) for my headache. I'm nauseated, but I don't throw up. Doc insists that I stay on the aid boat over night until my headache eases, but I refuse. I slosh back the fifty meters to the Bravo Company HQ element, which has set up for the night.

It's now dark and I doze all night on a piece of high ground. The tide comes in but doesn't quite reach us. The night is long. The only good part is that my headache finally eases. I'm already fed up with my tour of this blasted Rung Sat!

FRIDAY, SEPTEMBER 8, 1967: After first light, we begin moving again and it's more of the same. I've concluded that trying to bottle up the VC in the Rung Sat is next to impossible. Like tying to put out a raging forest fire with a bucket—with a hole in it! Near midday, word comes that the operation will end. We are all relieved when we get word that we're going in. We make our way back to the stream and are extracted. I load up on the aid boat for the ride back to Vung Tau.

Still on the boat is the soldier killed in C/5/60th yesterday. I look at him and realize I know him. His name is Charles. He is covered with mud and blood. He looks terrible with so much facial and neck flesh and bone gone.

The pungent smell of death is overwhelming. They did not evacuate his body last night because of the danger. Still, it's not good for morale to keep bodies of dead soldiers in our presence too long. Prayer won't help Charles now. But, I pray fervently for his loved ones.

I force myself to look at Charles's distorted features and I am overcome by sadness. I wonder what impact his death will have on his family. Is he married? If so, what a young age to leave a widow. His death will keep the war going for his family for another lifetime. I'm beginning to hate war. These wonderful heroes deserve varsity letters for what they have just been through. Nothing comes close to the misery in this Jungle of Death.

A dichotomy between shipboard sailors and the infantry they're here to support remains throughout the duration of our operations. This is inevitable. Living aboard ship in such close proximity, but with drastically different missions, results in occasional friction. The ever present turf issue surfaces from time to time. Interestingly, the Mobile Riverine Force has no single commander. The 2nd Brigade has a commander and the navy has a commander. Rumor has it that there are occasional internal squabbles at this level because of inflated egos and turf issues. I have quickly learned that four distinctive forces are present within the Mobile Riverine Force.

First, there is the brigade and navy headquarters, which does all the planning for the operations. These are high ranking and powerful people. Many of them are seen by the soldiers as arrogant and, at times, condescending. These people never get their feet wet in the rice paddies and have no idea what it's like to be ambushed, lose a good buddy, be on a frightening listening post all night, or to walk knee-deep through mud in high temperature and humidity loaded down with fighting gear.

Second, navy personnel, who operate the ships, have life almost the same as the non combat crews. They often dress in khaki or work blue uniforms, which seems strange to me in a combat zone. It wouldn't have surprised me to have seen some of them wearing wing-tipped shoes. These sailors haven't the slightest idea what the infantry and river rats face day after day. Their stateside "regulations" are often interpreted by some of them as permission to harass; they do not even try to understand the combatants world.

Third are the "river rats." These are the sailors who man the armored troop carriers and monitors and live aboard their craft. The ATCs are small troop carrying boats that are heavily armed and the monitors are gunboats referred to as small, sixty foot gunboats. During times when operations aren't being conducted, their boats are tied up next to the floating pontoons, which are like large decks. The pontoons are attached to the side of the ships themselves. Interestingly, there's a "them and us" attitude that shipboard sailors have toward the river rats. At times the "river rats" aren't even allowed on the mess deck in the evening to watch what the shipboard sailors call "our movies."

Fourth are the GI's in the infantry. As one soldier said, "We're the nuts and the bolts of this war. We do more than a lion's share of the work but don't get a piss ant's share of the credit." Some of the shipboard sailors look down on them because they arrive from combat operations covered in mud. The navy is conditioned to a certain state of cleanliness, not realizing and sometimes not caring that these soldiers come in from operations where they've literally lived in mud for several days. The sailors don't have the faintest idea of what these soldiers have been through. In many cases, they're lucky just to be alive.

A bitter experience that many soldiers will take with them from this era of their lives is a mean navy chief whose job is to man a fire hose when we return from operations. The purpose is to wash the mud from the returning soldiers. He takes special delight in attempting to use the water pressure to knock soldiers off their feet. He expresses special glee in going the extra mile to antagonize these returning heroes. It's a wonder he isn't thrown overboard on some moonless night. Fortunately, this guy is the exception.

Even though there are times of acrimony between soldiers and sailors, for the most part, the marriage works out even though it's one of convenience.

SATURDAY, SEPTEMBER 9, 1967: Today is a stand down day. Immediately after breakfast, I counsel with a soldier who wants out of the field. He's become so chaffed from the past two days in the wet Rung Sat that he has difficulty walking.

I go to the hospital in Vung Tau. Wayne Merriman, the young soldier who lost both legs, has been transferred here. I'm still touched by his loss.

SUNDAY, SEPTEMBER 10, 1967: Today is my daddy's birthday. I recall when I was first alerted for active duty while in North Carolina. Barbara and I drove the forty-five miles to tell our parents of our good news. But it wasn't good news to them. Barbara's parents were quite disappointed and hurt that we'd be moving two states away, but my Pop tried very hard through his disappointment to be encouraging and upbeat. We would be taking their only grandchild a long way away from them but at that time, this was lost on us in our excitement of my new career. I miss Pop, and think about him a lot today.

A clerk from our headquarters talks to me about his father who he says is suicidal over guilt at having run another son away from home. This clerk wants emergency leave to go home. His eyes dart around as he speaks, and I don't believe him. But, it doesn't really matter; he doesn't qualify for emergency leave anyway. I hate feeling as if I have to determine if a person is being truthful.

Barbara tells me in a letter today that our parents have suggested the possibility of them going on R&R with us. Hell will freeze over first!

MONDAY, SEPTEMBER 11, 1967: We pull anchor at 4:30 A.M. and head for Dong Tam. At least 100 soldiers and sailors are waiting on the pontoon to catch the shuttle to Dong Tam. It never comes. A chopper lands on the flight deck. I scoot up there and am lucky enough to hop it over to Dong Tam.

When I arrive the PX is closed for inventory! I'm not happy! Back at the ship, I'm further annoyed because there's no mail. A boat was not sent to Dong Tam and therefore the mail won't get here until at least tomorrow.

WEDNESDAY, SEPTEMBER 13, 1967: An operation called Coronado V has begun. We have only a few troops out. We take some casualties. I'm at the fire support base and decide I must get to Dong Tam and try to meet the wounded at the hospital. I catch a ride on Monk Doty's chopper. By the time we get to the *Benewah*, it's dark. We circle over the ship for an inordinate amount of time. Normally, we fly directly onto the landing deck. I notice that the lights aren't on. The chopper buzzes the *Benewah* because the shipboard navy isn't monitoring their radios. Finally, the landing lights come on and we land. Monk is furious. I am too, as I'm eager to get over to Dong Tam to check on the wounded soldiers who've been brought in. I hope our landing didn't interrupt their movie! Stop the war while we change reels!

The flight to the 3rd Surg at Dong Tam is only four minutes from takeoff to landing. At the hospital I learn five suffer from gunshot wounds, two from fragment wounds, one has a scorpion bite, and I'm saddened to learn that two have been killed, both from Alpha Company. One of the casualties is a new man; the other one has been here for awhile. I hear that the new troop was killed by one of our own soldiers. When the firing began, apparently one of our guys panicked and his weapon was on automatic instead of semi-automatic. When the trigger was pulled, the M-16 apparently swung with a rapid fire kick and the young soldier was accidentally shot and killed.

I get back to the ship and learn that our unit has killed thirty-eight Viet Cong. But all I can think of is our guy who was killed by one of our own soldiers. I'm not angry with the soldier who did it. I'm just angry. These are KIA numbers eight and nine since my arrival. Plus, we've now had almost 100 wounded since my arrival. This is terrible.

THURSDAY, SEPTEMBER 14, 1967: We'll be leaving tomorrow and will go to a place called Snoopy's Nose.

I go back to Dong Tam and visit our guys. The war for five of the eight wounded is over as their injuries are serious enough for evacuation to Japan.

Back at the ship, I prepare my gear for tomorrow.

SATURDAY, SEPTEMBER 15, 1967: I'm eating breakfast at 2:00 A.M. We load onto the boats at 3:00 A.M. and our boat convoy leaves for the continuation of Coronado V at 4:00 A.M. I'm riding on the aid boat and catch a nap to the accompaniment of the steady hum of the diesel engines.

We are heading into the Cam Son Secret Zone along the Rach Ba Rai River where huge forces of the 514th local force and 263rd main force VC battalions have been located. The operation plan is to attempt to trap the VC in their reported positions along the Rach Ba Rai, which is a small, winding river that flows into the Mekong River about sixteen kilometers west of Dong Tam. The VC have been reported in heavy concentrations about ten kilometers up the Rach Ba Rai. Several battalions are a part of this combat operation convoying by boat, air, and land to the area of operation. The 3/60th is scheduled to be the first battalion in by boat. Following some distance behind us is another river task force transporting our sister battalion, the 3/47th Infantry, as a backup force to us.

At 7:00 A.M., when we are within about thirty minutes of the area of operations, I eat some C-rations because I'm not sure how long it'll be before I get another chance. I still don't know which company I'll go with. I'll wait until we beach to decide, since all the companies will beach together. We've just entered the Rach Ba Rai from the Mekong River. At this point, the stream is only about fifty meters wide.

The boats are fifty feet apart, moving in single file at nine miles per hour through the mist of the early morning. I heat up a can of C-rats with my normal pinch of C-4. I have on my flak vest and steel helmet since this is the same area where the fight took place two days ago and chances are the VC are still in this area.

We pass a hairpin bend in the river that is known as 'Snoopy's Nose,' because from the air and on maps, it's contour looks strikingly like Snoopy's nose from the Peanut's comic strip.

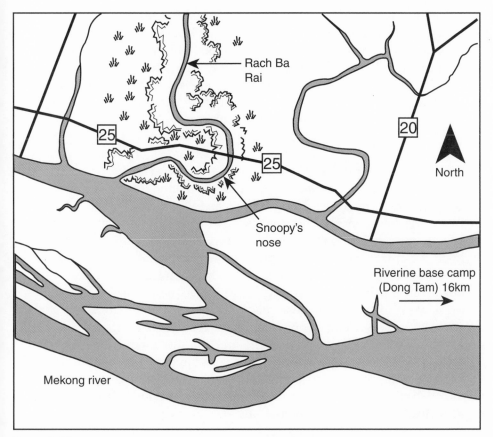

Snoopy's Nose area

At exactly 7:30 A.M., I'm standing at the front of the well deck next to the landing ramp munching on the remainder of my C-rats when suddenly, explosions begin going off everywhere in the small stream. I'm almost knocked off my feet as the aid boat swerves. I know this isn't the result of the coxswain's maneuver. Something isn't right. Someone tells me a VC rocket has hit near our fantail and exploded, apparently just below the water level, knocking our rudder loose, but not incapacitating our boat. Almost simultaneously, a rocket fired from the nearby bank on our right side sails by our bow and explodes harmlessly on the opposite bank. The navy crew swears that the first rocket explosion caused us to swerve knocking us out of the way of the second rocket's path, saving us from a direct hit.

On the radios, the lead mine sweeper's voice yells, "We've been mined!" Another boat reports being hit by recoilless rifle fire. Within seconds, both banks of the stream are erupting with fire. The unmistakable rip of enemy

AK 47 assault rifle fire, and the staccato sound of machine gun fire are interrupted time and time again by the explosions of rocket propelled grenades, recoilless rifles, and B-40 rockets. This is worse than playing dodge ball; only these balls do not bounce. They kill and maim.

Within a few seconds all boats in the ambush killing zone are returning fire with everything we have, including twenty and forty mm automatic guns, and our eighty-one mm mortars firing.

The second mine sweeper reports a direct hit, and in the next seven minutes, it takes four more direct hits that wound eight people. The boat is ordered to the rear but the crew ignores the order and remains in the battle. As more of the boats enter into the killing zone, more friendly weapons are firing at the deeply entrenched VC on both banks. The .50 caliber machine guns have not been firing because they have far ricocheting effects, and the fear is that the ricocheting could hit some of our boats. Soon the order is given to open fire with them as well.

Automatic fire from the VC is constantly beating against the hull of the boats, but it is basically harmless as the bullets bounce off the armored sides. Most of the enemy positions are within five meters of the water's edge. The ambush killing zone is approximately 1500 meters long. As the line of boats moves deeper into the ambush, the intensity of the fight grows. Some boats slow while others speed up, but each boat fires from every operable gun. There is constant firing, reloading and refiring.

In the first few moments of the initial part of the ambush, many of the navy river rats are hit. Our soldiers quickly react and enter the gun mounts themselves, not allowing the weapons to remain silent long.

Troops begin firing over the top of the bar armor with M-16s and M79 grenades. Over the deathly noise of firing I hear a sailor yell that the ATC immediately in front of us has hit a mine. Still in the front of the boat, but hunkered down below the armored sides, I rise up to peek through the hole in the ramp of the aid boat. The ATC is almost totally engulfed in flames. I grab my camera and take several pictures.

Smoke from that boat and all the firing, mixed with the morning mist, begins to create a haze over the stream as the battle rages. We begin to get calls for help as many of the ATCs and monitors are taking direct hits from the VC heavy weapons embedded on the banks of the stream. The boats are now stretched out over a distance of several hundred meters, all heavily engaged with the dug-in VC. Artillery has been called in.

The firing is so rapid that several M60 machine gun barrels burn out. While some soldiers are firing, others are rapidly tearing open new boxes of ammunition. On one boat, three M79 gunners use three cases of ammo in twenty minutes.

Early in the fight, a monitor takes a hit in the cockpit and the steering mechanism is shot away. Somehow, the boat captain is able to beach the boat while the surviving crew work frantically to repair the damage. Then the monitor rejoins the fray.

Round after round strikes ATCs and monitors. The boats at times seem like bumper cars at a carnival as they maneuver in the narrow channel. Some boat captains are jockeying for better fighting positions while other boats are temporarily out of control due to receiving direct hits.

It appears the VC are aiming at the overhead frames that hold the canvas sun cover over the well decks of the ATCs in hopes that the rockets will explode and shower the troops below with fragments. However, this tactic causes many of the rockets to simply sail harmlessly over the boats to explode on the opposite bank.

One of the first boats in the original convoy, a monitor, has radioed that it is pulling back because of on-board casualties. They are desperately asking for help from us on the aid boat. We rendezvous and the two boats pull side by side. A medic and I jump over the rail onto the monitor's deck. A navy lieutenant named Wells is the first wounded I see. He's bleeding but still talking on the radio. Then I see the coxswain who's lying still—too still. The medic finds no pulse and motions me back to check another sailor partly under the 81mm mortar. I see the sickening sight of his brains partially hanging out the left side of his head. His legs are spasmodically kicking but there is no other response. I want to pull him out from under the 81mm but I'm afraid that if I move him, his brains will completely fall out. I fight with myself over whether that matters.

My mind reels back to when I was a child in the country where we raised chickens to sell eggs. One of my chores was to gather up the eggs in a large wire basket. One day, I had about fifty eggs in the basket when I accidentally dropped it. Some of the eggs were broken and running all over the others. In my inexperience I did not know what to do for fear of breaking the other eggs. Now I have the same sensation looking at this sailor with his exposed, damaged brains oozing slowly out the side of his head.

Two other medics are now on board the monitor. Someone yells that a navy chief is in his bunk and is wounded. We look into his bunk. He's filled with lead and barely conscious. Apparently one of the very first rounds exploded near him. He's bleeding from many places on his body. It's impossible to tell how deep his wounds are since they're so numerous. The medic begins placing bandages on what looks like the worst wounds. The chief moans each time he exhales but doesn't yell or scream in his pain. His bunk is soaked in his own blood.

I see another sailor trying to help one of his boat mates. He's lying next to the wall separating the engine room from the deck of the boat. He's in a pool of blood and appears to have gone into shock. His foot and the lower part of his left leg are gone.

By now, it has been about ten minutes since I jumped from the aid boat onto this monitor. The two boats are tied together and slowly maneuvering in the stream while still firing at the VC. I notice now a third boat is pulled up on the opposite side of the aid boat. They're calling for help also as they too have several wounded. It's an ATC that was serving as a mine sweeper. I can't tell from where I am what's really happening on that boat. I just know that I have my hands full on this boat for the time being.

The forward motion of the convoy ceased about ten minutes after the ambush began. Individual boats dart back and forth, continually passing each other, some keeping to midstream while others make passes toward the bank before veering off with guns blazing.

The battle is still going on up and down the stream, and sounds of gunfire continue to fill the air. No troops have beached since we haven't reached our objective. There seems to be some chaos and indecision about whether the boats should pull back, continue the fight or attempt to move through the ambush.

Meanwhile, someone yells to me, "How do we get this guy out from under the 81mm?" This sailor is still jammed under the 81mm. I glance again at his lifeless and ashen colored face. I don't have time to feel for him. That will come later. For now, I have other wounded to tend to.

I decide to see the condition of the men from the third boat that has pulled along the other side of the aid boat. Then I hear on the radio from somewhere, "Bravo Company is coming by." Will Davis has decided to try to get his company on through the ambush to his original beaching area and get his troops on the ground and attack the VC positions on foot. They were just alerting the unwounded crew of our boats by radio not to run into them as they passed us in the small stream. Just beyond the killing zone, the platoon from that boat beaches and they form a tight perimeter, waiting for the remainder of the company to join them for a ground attack back down the river. As it turns out, the rest of the company is not able to join them.

I jump from the monitor back on to the aid boat and then onto the ATC on the opposite side of the aid boat, which has now tied up. Chaos reigns on this boat, too. The well deck looks like an unsupervised play room of hyperactive children. Several B-40 rocket rounds or recoilless rifle rounds have exploded in the well deck. Burst cans of C rations litter the floor corner to corner. The first sailor I come to is lying on his back, looking at the canvas canopy with a relatively peaceful look on his face. His chest has a hole large enough to put my fist into. As I grab a field bandage, I think of how dark it is inside of a person's chest.

A black sailor is lying nearby. He's semiconscious. He has many wounds and much of his outer flesh is torn and some is gone. I patch him as best I can and tell him, as I've told the others, that we'll get them out and to the hospital as soon as possible. He gives me a weak thumbs-up, almost as if to convince himself, not me, that he'll be okay.

At 7:58 A.M. Lieutenant Commander Dusty Rhodes, the navy task force commander, decides to pull all the boats out of the ambush kill zone and form a security zone so we can dustoff our wounded. The two mine sweepers are temporarily out of action. Rhodes decides that the fire is too heavy and the danger of mines too great to continue to run the gauntlet, plus many of the boats need replacement crews.

Thirty minutes after the fight began all boats are ordered to turn back and assemble a short distance down stream. As we pull back, four Air Force A-37's begin dropping bombs and napalm on the VC positions. One by one the boats leave the killing zone and move five hundred meters down stream to regroup.

The last boat carries the one platoon of Bravo Company, which had beached just a few moments earlier. This boat runs the gauntlet back through the 1500 meter killing zone as rockets and bullets rain heavily down. Halfway down the stream another rocket hits one of the .50 caliber machine gun mounts, killing one sailor and wounding four. But the ATC makes it through and links up with the rest of the river assault force.

Since we're now out of the ambush zone, the firing has stopped, with the exception of occasional sniper rounds, which seems relatively benign compared to what has been going on. Helicopter gun ships take up the attack from the jets. When they've completed their firing, volley after volley of artillery begins again, screaming and swishing just overhead, impacting on the VC positions.

The aid boat becomes a magnet to the other boats as they are eager to get help for their wounded. We beach, and the other boats beach as close to us as possible.

It has now been about forty-five minutes since the fight began. We must evacuate the wounded as soon as possible. The infantry has now formed a security zone on land, but they're not out very far from the boats. An occasional sniper continues to periodically fire in our direction.

By now, I am soaked in sweat and other people's blood. Even helping the walking wounded from boat to boat is hard work. Helping to transport the litter patients is especially draining. I talk to each of the wounded, tell them that everything is under control. I tell each one who I am and what is going on. I assure them that we've pulled out of the ambush zone and that they'll be dusted off soon.

I talk even to those who are unconscious, refusing to assume they cannot hear me. I assure them that they're stable, though I'm not always sure myself. I pray individually with most of the wounded. A few of the wounded become hysterical and when one begins to scream I immediately go to his stretcher and engage him in soft conversation. I hold their hands, rub their brow or head. I describe to each one what is happening since they're in no position to observe for themselves. It's almost miraculous what a calming effect this is having on each of the panicky wounded.

Meanwhile, minor fires are still burning on two of the boats. With the assistance of other crews, these fires are soon extinguished.

At 8:45 A.M. the first medevac chopper arrives and lands on the small landing deck of the *USS Scarecrow*. The wounded have been triaged now as best we can. This means we've separated the wounded into groups based on the urgency of their condition. Each chopper can only take three litter patients and three walking wounded.

I'm apprehensive as the first dustoff lands on the deck. This chopper makes a perfect target from any treeline. Those of us who are heaving each litter also make a good target, since the landing deck is considerably higher than any other parts of the beached boats. As the first dustoff leaves he takes some sniper fire after he's three to four hundred meters from the aid boat, but is apparently not hit.

As soon as one dustoff leaves, we begin maneuvering other wounded into position from the other boats to the aid boat to minimize the amount of time for the next dustoff to remain on the landing deck. I've been so busy I've lost all track of time. After forty-five minutes, the last of the wounded are finally evacuated. Scores have been wounded but only twenty-seven are dusted off. The others are patched up and deemed able to continue to function.

Typical of the walking wounded is Terry Gander, a young M-60 machine gunner from Bravo Company. As soon as the first shots were fired, Terry instinctively stood up, laid his machine gun on the side bar armor and opened fire. He immediately caught a piece of VC steel that penetrated his flak jacket, imbedding itself in his chest. His flak jacket slows the round enough that he wasn't killed. When Terry was hit, his buddy, Kenny Lancaster, caught him as he fell backward onto the well deck of the boat. Terry was patched up and elected to stay with his buddies. A hero among heroes!

While we evacuate the wounded, the navy commander is reassigning some crew members to other boats to balance the crews. Damage assessment is also made. All boats are still operational, even the ones which had been on fire. There is some structural damage, but nothing that causes any of the boats to sink or be abandoned. The crews have expended a great deal of ammunition and new boxes of ammo are opened and positioned for use in case we engage the VC again.

Command makes the decision to again run the ambush site. Damage to machine gun barrels and other weapons has been quickly repaired. Soldiers and sailors work feverishly to redistribute ammunition and other supplies.

The backup river assault group beached down stream a few thousand meters are called on for reinforcements. Commander Rhodes orders three of these boats to come upstream and replace three of the more severely damaged boats, though all are considered functional. He also orders replacement crews from that river assault group to take over for many of the wounded sailors in our assault group. This makes the boat crews again near to full strength.

Oddly, most of us are not counting on the next engagement to be as severe nor as intense as the first one, because of the constant bombardment of the VC positions up ahead by the jets, gun ships and artillery while we've been evacuating our wounded.

The infantry soldiers pulling security for our beached boats are recalled and reloaded onto the boats. This time, they are to man the onboard M-60 machine guns in the well decks. The remaining navy crews man the larger weapons.

The order is given for the boats to back off from the beached positions and regroup into convoy formation. It's now 10:00 A.M. We know where the enemy is (or at least where he was an hour or two ago) and we are going to run the ambush again, engage the enemy if he's still there, and then pass through to our area of objective beyond the ambush area. While we have been pulled back, the 5/60th has moved with their tracks overland toward the VC positions. The 3/47th is still standing by down stream. The 2/60th is being brought in by chopper.

While beached, all the ATCs have dropped their front ramps, as is the normal case, so the troops could run ashore to form security for the evacuation of the wounded. This also enables the use of the stream bank to move some of the wounded to the aid boat for evacuation. One of the ATCs raises its ramp. Underneath is a dead VC. Apparently he was on the stream bank in an alert position, his job to alert the main body upstream that we were coming. The VC must have stayed in his position in the tall grass and foliage during the fight to watch for any additional boats coming up stream to assist us. As we regrouped down stream to extract our wounded, he was still hidden in the grass. The heavy steel ramp dropped, and the unlucky VC was crushed to death. I feel for him and pray for his family.

The boats pull out into the stream and we get ready to head back into the kill zone. Even after all the casualties we've already suffered, there seems to be little fear. Perhaps we're assuming that with all of the air strikes and artillery that have blasted away at each bank of the stream, no one could survive that onslaught. Maybe we're like the allied troops in the English Channel in the invasion of Normandy during World War II who saw the heavy bombardment and assumed that the enemy had been beaten to a pulp. At any rate, we're ready to go back into that morning's terror zone. This 'no fear' is to be short lived.

While the boats are maneuvering into the proper formation for our second trip into hell, the first of sixteen additional air strikes begin. Three F4 phantom jets with their shrill, whistling screams come in and drop more bombs and napalm in the middle of the ambush zone. More artillery follows the air strikes.

All gunners are ready. Just before we reach the kill zone, the artillery is lifted. We open fire first onto the banks where the VC were dug in this morning. Immediately we begin receiving VC fire. It's like this morning's battle was put on pause and now we have hit the play button again.

This time no element of surprise exists for either side. Firepower alone will settle this fight. We slug it out, but now we have considerable more firepower as every gun is manned on every boat. Three batteries of artillery are walking shells up the river banks ahead of us and the helicopter gun ships and jets are adding their fire. In no time we are engaged all along the ambush zone. These VC are like swarms of bees that won't go away. Again radios begin immediately calling that their boats are taking hits and casualties. As before, the first boat hit is one of the lead mine sweepers. It takes two rocket direct hits. The other mine sweeper takes seven direct hits, but only three are wounded.

Within about two minutes a boat ahead begins a bizarre pattern of movement. All he says on the radio is, "We've been hit! We've been hit!" Smoke and flames pour from the boat. The aid boat is ordered to move alongside to give medical assistance. As we do, the ATC rams us sharply in the side and bounces off, almost like he's attacking us. Sailors are screaming at the boat driver demanding that he slow his boat so we can help him.

Finally, we corner him and two of our navy crewmen jump over onto the other ATC. Of the six sailors aboard, five are incapacitated with wounds and the sixth is driving the boat, though he has no experience doing so.

He is overcome by his fear and unable to realize that others are trying to help him. He is like an injured dog that growls and bites when someone tries to help him. The boat has taken several hits from B-40 rockets and the fire power, which wounded the entire crew, has blown his mind. This crew is a replacement crew who only took over a few moments ago downstream. Two medics and two sailors jump onto the ATC from that aid boat to try to get it through the killing zone so we can dust them off, but the fight is too intense now to do anything but pray for them. And us. By now we are ten minutes into this segment of the fight.

We get another panicky call that one of the ATCs loaded with a platoon of troops from Alpha Company has taken a direct hit inside their well deck and many are wounded. The aid boat pulls alongside and I step up onto the guardrail of the aid boat and spontaneously jump over onto the "wounded" ATC. My immediate thought is to help the injured soldiers if possible. I don't consider that if I fall between the two moving boats, I could drown, be cut up by the boat props, and wash downstream.

Even after the carnage of this morning, I'm not prepared for what I see as I jump the three steps down into the well deck of the ATC. A B-40 rocket explosion has penetrated the bar armor and wrecked havoc under the canvas canopy. Wounded soldiers are lying in several masses, some sprawled on top of others. Some are calm while others are panicky. I quickly begin assuring them in a loud but steady voice that help is on the way and that we'll evacuate them very quickly. Firing continues along the stream, making conversation almost impossible.

As I talk, I'm putting on field bandages as quickly as I can. Two soldiers are dead for sure. Only two of the entire twenty-nine man platoon are not wounded. Ironically, the two soldiers killed were the farthest from the explosion, and one of the two who is not wounded was only about three feet from the explosion.

Everyone wants water. How do I tell a man with his guts hanging out his side that he can't have water? Most of these guys will be in surgery shortly so they can't drink. God, it hurts not to be able to give them what they want.

It's a scene from a horror movie. Blood is everywhere. By now Doc and two other medics are aboard. When so many are wounded, where do you begin? One soldier has part of his brain hanging out through a huge hole near his ear. He is still alive and might even survive but he will probably be in a vegetative state.

Another soldier who is slightly wounded is more injured in his soul. He just looks through me as he seems to be staring out into space. Another sits in a corner simply singing hymns in a low voice, while sitting in his and other's blood.

The firing is dying down. The bunkered VC have finally been shot into near silence. I hear on the radios that the troops are to beach and begin maneuvering on the ground to fight other VC in the area. However, the dustoffs cannot occur until after the troops have secured the immediate area.

The boats have now moved a few hundred meters beyond the killing zone and we beach. We resume the process of two hours ago as boats drop their troops and then cluster around the aid boat to discharge the wounded. The dustoff choppers again begin landing on the deck of the USS *Scarecrow* and leave again as quickly as we can load them with the wounded. We evacuate not only the platoon, which has been wiped out, but also numerous others. The process again takes about forty-five minutes. I'm in constant motion, moving from one wounded to another, again assuring them that we're getting them out and offering them information on what's happening. Some ask me to contact their next of kin when I get back to the ship. Others I pray with. Some I just hold their hands.

Snipers again fire on some of the dustoffs, and again, none of the choppers are shot down. It looks as if some are hit but have little damage.

Finally, the last batch of wounded is gone. I'm absolutely exhausted. I am now able to take a drink of water and it tastes heaven-sent.

By now our three companies are extended beyond the riverbank 200 meters inland. They are in solid contact with the VC. Enemy fire is coming from different directions.

Lt. Charlie Taylor of C/5/60th has his platoon positioned but is unable to move forward due to heavy enemy fire. A VC machine gunner opens up on him and splatters him and one of his squad leaders, Tony Haag, with mud. Taylor saves his platoon from being overrun by courageously calling in artillery to within twenty-five meters of its position. Even though several of his men are wounded, the attacking VC are wiped out by his heroic action.

Kenny Lancaster from Bravo Company, who had taken over the machine gun this morning after his buddy Terry Gander was hit, is asked to search out several VC bunkers and tunnels. Small in size, Kenny routs the remaining VC and even gets a blood-soaked VC flag as a memento of the horrible events of the day. Near nightfall, fragments hit Kenny, penetrating his flak vest and imbedding into his flesh. Like Terry, he refuses to be dusted off.

I wonder what the VC are feeling. Most, if not all of those in the ambush, are either dead or wounded. They've been pounded mercilessly for several hours. I wonder how it would feel to have artillery, bombs, napalm and mini-guns zero in on you. Today those VC could not retreat.

Were they worried about their loved ones? How do they manage their fear? They certainly are brave. But dead brave men are still dead.

By now it's late in the afternoon. The aid boat is beached with the front ramp down. Shortly, through some nearby bushes, I spot a young sergeant called Egg carrying a soldier who is wounded. I run to them to help only to discover that Egg, too, has been shot in the face. It's a flesh wound, a grazing shot probably from an AK-47. He's not as concerned about himself as he is about the man he is carrying. The flesh on Egg's face is split open, but there is very little bleeding. One of the aid boat medics arrives. We are only about fifteen meters from the aid boat when the medic checks the wounded soldier and reports that he is dead. Egg breaks down. He says he was alive when he started out with him a few moments ago, dragging him toward the aid boat. He yells at his buddy, "How can you die after I have dragged and carried you this close to the aid boat?"

The Medic takes the dead soldier onto the downed ramp of the aid boat while I help Egg aboard. He refuses to be evacuated and insists on returning to his squad. He is bandaged and then returns the 100 meters to their position.

Someone tells me the dead soldier is a sergeant with nine kids.

The brigade commander has decided it's too risky for the troops to face the night disorganized. He orders contact with the VC broken, and for the three companies to pull back into a night defensive position. This will allow the remaining VC to escape with darkness, but I respect the commander's concern that we not risk additional casualties. The companies link in a semicircular position with the river. The Navy boats form the remaining part of the defensive circle.

Flares keep the area illuminated throughout the night. "Puff, the magic dragon" makes numerous hits on the areas where the VC have been engaged. "Puff" is a C-47, a slow moving twin-engine propeller aircraft specially fitted with mini-guns. Believe me, their fire can create more chaos for the enemy than Godzilla.

I eat some cold C-Rations. This is not like my mother's fried chicken but it is nourishment.

I doze off on the hard steel ribbed aid boat floor. My mind is filled with visions of burning boats, smoke, blood, torn flesh, exposed brains, and terror-filled eyes.

Throughout the night the monitors fire indiscriminately up and down the stream and out onto the opposite bank of the river as harassing fire to discourage VC movement toward us.

Shortly before 1:00 A.M., I'm startled from my fitful sleep by numerous shots from a single, small arms weapon that sounds like an M-16 rifle. It is very close. Too close. As I jump up to look over the side of the aid boat, in the faint illumination from the distant flares, I see a sailor perched on a gun mount of the ATC beached beside us. He is cursing at something or someone. As he stands in the gun mount on the fan tail of his boat changing the magazine of his M-16, he screams, "That's one less VC now because he's a dead SOB!"

It seems the VC had approached the boat quietly, swimming in the darkness. He climbed over the side of the boat, and apparently had an explosive device, meaning to throw it into that boat or our own. The sailor standing guard in the gun mount saw the VC climb aboard. He emptied an entire magazine of M-16 rounds at close range into him, blowing him backward into the stream. Thank God the VC did not fulfill his mission.

SATURDAY, SEPTEMBER. 16, 1967: Between 2:00 A.M. and 4:30 A.M., small groups of VC are observed periodically leaving the area and they are fired upon. After 4:30 A.M., no VC are sighted. The decision is made to end the operation, as it appears that the main part of the VC units have left during the night. A sweep shows approximately 250 heavily protected VC bunkers. "Charlie" was indeed dug in. He had been expecting us for sometime, as it must have taken him many days to construct that many heavily fortified bunkers.

The troops return to the beached ATCs. Their eyes tell the stress of the past twenty-four hours. Even though we've put a hurt on "Charlie," he's put one on us too. Now we must travel back down the stream through Snoopy's Nose.

We form our normal convoy and move through yesterday's killing zone at full alert. One would hardly know a ferocious battle had taken place. Now there is no smoke, loud explosions, blood, guts, soul smattering fear or chaos. But, there is the burning memory of Snoopy's Nose that will be forever seared on the minds of several hundred brave soldiers and sailors who fought for theirs and their buddies' lives. The same can be said for the 263rd VC Battalion.

All told, the 3/60th had three killed and seventy-two wounded, and the navy had four killed and sixty-one wounded, including some of the replacement crews for the second run through the ambush. It was a red-letter day, written in blood.

The VC had seventy-nine known killed and an unknown number wounded. The 263rd VC Battalion is hurt, but not out of commission. We know we will probably fight them again in the future. I hear that the press release in Saigon says the VC casualties were heavy and our casualties are light to moderate. To the families of our KIAs, there's no such thing as moderate. President Johnson keeps saying "the war is going good." It is?

Yes, Snoopy's Nose was bloodied, but this lost blood was more than "Peanuts." If swapping blood creates blood brothers, then ours is a huge family.

11:15 A.M.
September 16, 1967
Hello Sweets,
I will never forget September 15, 1967 because this was the day we went to the outskirts of hell ... what happened yesterday simply cannot be explained in words ... I have not worked so hard in a long time ...

SUNDAY, SEPTEMBER 17, 1967: The emotional fatigue most of us suffer as a result of the battle at Snoopy's Nose is significant. The soldiers and navy river rats in that battle are now bonded rather like policeman and rescue workers at the scene of an airliner crash.

The other navy, those on board the ships, have no idea what the infantry and river rats have been through. Last night, some of the snots on board the ship wouldn't allow the river rats to go onto the mess deck to watch the movie because it would "make it too crowded." Several of the river rats complained to the navy officers aboard the *Colleton*, but they didn't want to get involved.

This morning I attempt to conduct worship services. I'm refused the use of the mess decks because "The request for use must now be made forty-eight hours in advance." For crying out loud, forty-eight hours ago we were fighting for our lives at Snoopy's Nose. I'm livid at such senseless rigidity. Who do these shipboard lame brained idiots think they are? I know the guys with these attitudes are in the minority, but that doesn't reduce my frustration. I decide to complain to my brigade headquarters. I catch the shuttle to the *Benewah*, but after I arrive, I decide they are not going to intervene with the navy. They are more concerned about wrinkles in their jungle fatigues than about helping my troops.

I return to the *Colleton* and decide I'd better get away from this farce. Since I can't conduct services because the VC were so inconsiderate as to ambush us at a time when I should have been requesting to use the precious navy mess deck, I decide to go to Bear Cat to see my heroes in the hospitals. Before I leave, I have a service for the navy crews aboard the *Whitfield County*, the repair ship, and the *Askari*, a supply ship, but I can't have services for my own men. I resolve to "fix" this problem in the future. I don't know yet how I'll do it, but I know I will.

Boy, am I tired!

MONDAY, SEPTEMBER 18, 1967: At the hospitals, all these guys want to talk about is Snoopy's Nose. They're all full of questions as they were all evacuated before the battle ended. I give each one significant details about the battle.

One of the injured is Bobby Hogan from Alpha Company. He's from the Piedmont area of North Carolina and has been here only a short time. We are distant kin; some of his family had asked him to look me up when he got to Vietnam. Bobby's war is now over. He's not critical but he'll no doubt be sent back to the states.

James, the soldier who lost a portion of his brain, is here. He looks so different here in the ICU than he did in the well deck of the ATC two days ago drenched in his blood. The nurses say he makes little response. I pray in his ear not knowing if he hears me. But, God does. I tell him where he is and that soon they're going to send him back to the states. I want to cry. He's so young. I leave the ICU wanting to kick a wall. This is what war is about. I see many others including the courageous navy river rats who were wounded. These guys, all of them, are heroes!

As I leave the hospital, I think of the extremes I've seen so far. I am particularly struck by the story of a young man I will call "Branch". Three days before my arrival at Dong Tam in early July, one of the outhouses in our battalion area had been booby trapped with a claymore mine. Fortunately, it did not explode because someone detected it and the engineers were able to disarm it. It was automatically assumed that a Viet Cong had infiltrated the perimeter during the night and booby trapped the outhouse.

Our outhouses have anywhere from two to four holes. Below are cut out fifty-five gallon drums that are shoved underneath the holes to collect the human waste.

On July 23rd, a second booby trap was discovered. This time it was rigged with a US hand grenade and was designed so that as the lid was raised, the pin would be extracted from the grenade causing it to explode. Fortunately, it too malfunctioned. By now, many are wondering if the perpetrator is really a VC or perhaps a demented GI.

I had counseled on three occasions with Branch, a strange and troubled young man. I was so concerned that I alerted the new company commander, Captain Joe Jenkins, and First Sergeant Trump. Branch is polite and good-looking but obviously not well-centered emotionally. He has steely, blue eyes that appear to look through you at times. He is more than a half bubble off plumb.

Several men later see Branch in a dead run leaving the outhouse. After about fifteen meters, he either fell or dove to the ground. Then came the huge explosion in the outhouse. The blown up outhouse was missing its roof, and the sides were splintered. Branch was quickly apprehended and secured. Now it's apparent who the booby trapper was.

We breathe a collective sigh of relief; at least we know the VC aren't infiltrating during the night. After Branch's arrest, the explosions stop.

Being 12,000 miles from home in the midst of a combat zone where life is so uncertain, it seems so ironic that there are always enemies from within. Many ask why Branch did this awful deed. When persons who may appear normal are placed in situations of stress, their insanity sometimes surfaces. I believe this was the case of Branch. He was quickly sent to the stockade at Long Binh that was known as LBJ, for Long Binh Jail.

So, there I was, going from visiting wounded heroes to the discovery of a young man's mental sickness. It's hard to have compassion for him. But, outhouse bomber or not, he still is a child of God and I must minister to him.

TUESDAY, SEPTEMBER 19, 1967: I'm up early and fly back to Dong Tam and visit with the four wounded still at the 3rd Surgical Hospital.

Returning to the *Colleton*, a young, distressed sergeant wants to talk with me. He has received two letters from well meaning family members informing him that his wife is cheating on him back in Oklahoma. He's crushed. He's usually a happy-go-lucky guy, but now he's quiet and sullen. I listen to him. But, there's precious little I can do except to let him know I care.

What his family members expect him to do here about his wife's running around is beyond me. Perhaps they wrote out of frustration and/or inability to do anything about the wife. Yet, where there is broken commitment, there are broken hearts. It's bad enough to have to dodge VC bullets, but it's just as bad to be wounded by the unfaithful love of your life.

WEDNESDAY, SEPTEMBER 20, 1967: Last night a brigade staff officer called. A reporter and photographer for *Life Magazine* wants to know what a chaplain in the Mobile River Force (MRF) does. They want to go out with Bravo Company tomorrow and ask that I go with them. I've already decided to go with C/5/60th. I tell the staff officer that if they want to see what I do, they will have to do so by way of C/5/60th air assault because that's where I'll be. He's not happy. He tells me that if I don't go out with them I could miss the opportunity to get my picture in *Life Magazine*. As far as I'm concerned, the reporter can just return to the states. Though I'm normally a compliant and easygoing person, I decide I'm not going to tap dance for the press nor the staff officer. I know this won't earn me a Christmas card from him, but I'm set to go with C 5/60th and that's that.

Dick Botela is the commander of Charlie Company. He's slowly earning the respect of his men. He's an older officer like Will Davis, in Bravo Company. Dick and I are fast becoming good friends. I'm on the first flight into the landing zone (LZ). I'm not sure I like that. It's early morning. We form at the nearby Dong Tam air strip in ten groups of six for the ten helicopters that will pick us up. As an experiment some Vietnamese "Kit Carson Scouts" are going with us on this operation. These are former VC who have come over to the Vietnamese government side by way of the Chieu Hoi program. If a VC wishes to switch sides, he can get a safe passage card, or he can just turn himself in to the Vietnamese authorities. The safe passage cards are normally dropped like confetti by our aircraft into areas known to be infested by VC.

This is the first time the Kit Carson scouts have been with us. I wonder if we can trust these guys. They have antiquated M-1 rifles, which were WWII weapons. The scouts look like mere kids, wearing tattered uniforms.

This will be my first air assault. Most of these guys haven't made combat air assaults either since many of them have joined the unit in the past month or so.

We're in staggered groups of six in ten different areas up and down the runway. The choppers land simultaneously and the noise is painfully loud.

We're quickly loaded and lift off the runway. We make a huge circle around Dong Tam and the formation heads across the My Tho river south. We rise to about a thousand feet. The chopper doors are open and the crew gunners on either side of the aircraft are at the ready with their M-60 machine guns. One of the door gunners gives me a funny look. He sees the camouflaged cross on my left collar and is obviously surprised to see me with an infantry squad. Then he mouths, "Where's your weapon?" I just smile and shrug my shoulders. He smiles and mouths the Vietnamese phrase, "You Dinky Dow," (literally, "Dien Cai Dau") meaning, "You're crazy," while pointing at me and using his index finger for quick circling motions around his ear. I shake my head 'yes,' smile back at him, and repeat his sign language. We grin at each other stupidly.

Seventy five feet away it looks odd to see other soldiers in the choppers flying parallel beside me in formation. One soldier I know recognizes me, waves and I salute him. He laughs and gives me a British salute in return. One of his squad buddies sees him do this and gives him the finger, unaware that he's joking around with me in an adjoining chopper. The soldier who waved points to me in my chopper and points to his collar, obviously telling his buddy not to do that because the chaplain is watching him seventy-five feet away. I find the whole exchange quite humorous.

Artillery is softening up the landing zone (LZ) and will cease fire a few seconds before we arrive. My mind goes back to the first time I flew. I was a senior in high school and, as a result of having been selected as an All State tackle, I was recruited to play football at several colleges and universities, including The Citadel in Charleston, S.C. They flew me from Charlotte to Columbia and then to Charleston for a wonderful weekend in January 1958. For a seventeen-year-old country boy, that first flight was something. Even though I eventually decided to attend Wake Forest, the trip to the Citadel was the genesis for my thinking of a ministry in the military. That first flight was scary, but then there was no chance we'd get shot at. Not true, here.

At 200 feet, two gun ships fly past us rapidly, their mini-guns blazing. As soon as they pass us, the door gunners open up with their machine guns. Our forward speed is considerably slower now and we're very low. The gun ships make a run in the opposite direction, this time firing rockets that still make a loud noise even over the wop wop wop of the choppers.

We're landing in a free fire zone that is southwest of Ben Tre, known as a hot bed of VC. We're now only a few feet from jumping out and our firing has ceased. One of the door gunners yells to us that the formation has received some ground fire. My adrenaline kicks in and I really want to make a quick exit. At ten feet off the ground the choppers throw their noses into the air and their tails down for rapid slowing. At five feet we all jump to the ground, run a few feet in the rice paddy water, and hit the deck prone. The choppers accelerate by dropping their noses and raising their tails, then move rapidly along the rice paddies. They rise quickly to clear the nearby tree line, then they're gone. The overwhelming noise of the chopper blades for the past minutes immediately ceases and our voices return to a normal level. I feel like a teacher of hyperactive children five minutes after the final bell has sounded and there is finally peace and quiet. But I know there is no peace here in the rice paddies.

The command group organizes, we rise from the wet rice paddies and begin moving out to what we hope is the safety of a nearby tree line. It must be secured because the rest of the company will be arriving shortly.

The cool water from the rice paddies is no longer cool and I soon break into a sweat. It's now just past 9:00 A.M. Fifteen minutes later the rest of the company arrives and their landing is uneventful. We move out again.

Almost immediately we come to a small village that has the unmistakable odor of all Delta villages. Someone comments that the smell would offend a buzzard. We discover what appears to be a Vietnamese country store. The Kit Carson scouts quickly determine that it's a VC supply house. There are far more supplies here than are needed to support just the local population. The "store" has many bushels of sweet potatoes. I recall that when I was a kid, we always grew sweet potatoes at home. My older cousin got a job driving a truck and he took his first trip to Charlotte, North Carolina and stopped to eat lunch in a diner. He decided to be brave and order something off the menu that would be different from the food he'd grown up on. He saw listed on the menu "candied yams" and ordered some, thinking that perhaps it was some exotic foreign cuisine. As he later told the story, without seeing any humor in it, he said, "Candied yams are nothing but blasted sweet potatoes and I've eaten them all my life."

I think of this, oddly, as we torch the VC store.

We move out again and the going is rough. Since this area is infested with VC, we fear that the trail is booby trapped. We maneuver off, parallel to the heavily traveled trail. The mud and water impedes our progress.

Several times in the next two hours we take some sniper fire. Each time we hit the deck and take what cover we can. We call in several volleys of artillery to the area where the fire originates. Then we move out again.

Bravo Company has beached nearby, having arrived by boat on a nearby stream, and is moving about 500 meters to our left. We can't see them because of the heavy foliage. The two companies are moving parallel. Then, at noon, the VC attempt their usual ploy.

The VC fire on us. They are positioned between Bravo and Charlie Companies. They fire and then hunker down into their "spider holes" or bunkers while both companies fire in the direction of the receiving fire, unwittingly firing on each other.

This tactic works for about ten seconds. Both companies spontaneously lay down a heavy volume of fire. Dick Botello and Will Davis realize the trick and call an immediate cease fire. Fortunately, none of us are hit, but it's a close call.

We move out again. At about 1:00 P.M., we stop and some of us eat C-rations. Two of the Kit Carson scouts decide we need some fresh coconut milk with our food. Almost as quick as lightning two of them climb up two different coconut trees. With each having tied their ankles together, they move like monkeys. They quickly disappear from sight as they climb about seventy-five feet high. They yell and we scatter below as they began dropping coconuts. As quickly as they went up they now come back down.

I now see why VC snipers who tie themselves to trees are so difficult to spot; we know exactly where these scouts are and we still have trouble seeing them.

After coming down, the scouts get a machete and, with the precision of a skilled butcher, they chop the ends off the coconuts and pass the coconut milk around to us, receiving many smiles and nods.

The scouts then catch a chicken, ring its neck, build a fire and begin to cook it for lunch. However, before they can finish, the order is given to move out. Much to their disappointment, they must leave the half-cooked chicken behind.

We come to a small building beside a canal that, like most of the structures we come to, we search. We find two males in their mid-twenties. This is very unusual; non-VC males are usually gone by the time we get near them. It's assumed that these are VC. One of our scouts is trying to get one of the detainees to talk while the other scout takes the second one a few feet down the trail to do likewise.

He talks to the captured man in a rapid voice, then slaps him suddenly and so hard it startles me. He then takes a knife and places it to his throat. Dick and I move forward, thinking he's going to cut the VC's throat. My heart is pounding; I don't want to be witness to murder. Our Vietnamese interpreter quickly assures us that the scout won't cut his throat; he just wants the VC to think he will, because the VC are terrified of being cut. Nevertheless, I'm not going to allow neither this man nor anyone else to be executed if I can stop it. The morality of war is no different in this situation than anywhere else.

The scout then blindfolds the VC. Apparently he's told that his head is going to be cut off if he doesn't talk. He begins chattering like an auctioneer.

The interpreter tells Dick that many VC are in this area and gives the local VC unit's name and the strength of these units. That and other valuable intelligence probably keeps us from walking into a supposed ambush that has been set up one kilometer up the trail from us.

We set up in a temporary blocking force. While we're waiting, all of a sudden a large tree falls, startling us. There's been no explosion and no reason for this tree to topple. I look at its roots and discover that they have simply rotted away. After everything we've been through, who would imagine a falling tree could ambush us? The heat is stifling. Several of the guys jokingly ask me to pray for rain to cool things down. Water in the canteens is warm.

We're all relaxed when another sniper opens up on us. He apparently has come through some nearby banana trees, and picked a position from which to open fire. I dive into the small crater left by the trunk of the fallen tree. At the same time, our artillery forward observer does the same thing. We scramble for cover and begin to snicker like two little kids fighting over a blanket.

I realize how far I've come in managing my feelings over the past few weeks. Seconds ago, I was petrified. Now I am laughing while being shot at! I don't discount the danger, only note the irony.

We suppress the sniper fire with our own fire and move out. The artillery has stopped up ahead. The heat is very bad, the worst I've experienced in a couple of weeks.

Soon, we begin preparing for our night defensive positions. Resupply is brought in by helicopter including water, ammunition and claymore mines.

The interpreter says many of the area signs nailed to palm trees are VC signs. We set up for the night in an area that includes three isolated hooches. Only women are in the area. We ask where the men are. One young woman in her mid-twenties says her husband is dead. She shows us a picture of him, but for all we know, he could have been one of the snipers earlier in the day.

Our defensive perimeter is now set. I'm exhausted. Before dark, I heat some C-rations. They taste good, but I torture myself by thinking of deviled eggs, black-eyed peas with chopped onion and corn bread. Then the rains come, hard, and the dirt turns to mud. It's now cool. The air is fresh. I sleep in the middle hooch on the packed dirt floor. At least I'm dry. Most of the soldiers are positioned with no cover.

An M-60 machine gun is set up and two soldiers are ready to fire at any moment throughout the night. This machine gun is only a few feet from where I sleep. Their field of fire is over a small canal into a wood line about forty meters away. Fortunately we aren't attacked, but throughout the night, the VC periodically harasses us as they fire several random explosive devices into our positions. Tony Norman, a lieutenant who was on the same plane with me from the States, receives one of our own malfunctioned flares that comes in on top of his position. He's fortunate not to be seriously burned. Poor Tony has already had his eardrum burst in an earlier encounter.

At 2:00 A.M., I'm again awakened by an incoming rocket propelled grenade, which explodes next to a sleeping soldier. He never knows what hit him as it lands next to his head. Even if he had his steel helmet on, he still would have been killed because the grenade landed so close.

After each RPG, artillery is called in, but it's nearly impossible to know the exact origin of the fire. We fire anyhow.

THURSDAY, SEPTEMBER 21, 1967: At first light, I begin moving around. I'm tired. The hard floor was not exactly my idea of comfort. The main trail area is about 100 meters from our night positions. Five soldiers halfway there have gathered and are pointing down into the small canal. I approach them and they excitedly tell me about a body in the water. I assume they are joking, but a male Vietnamese is indeed lying face down in the water, fully clothed. I'm puzzled because yesterday afternoon we passed by this very spot and no one saw him. I wonder if the VC have dumped his body there during the night and perhaps have booby-trapped the body, thinking we might retrieve it this morning. Lt. Charlie Taylor comes up and I mention the possibility that the body could be booby-trapped. Normally, VC bodies are checked for identification, documents and weapons. This morning the decision is to leave the body in place. His friends will find him soon enough; it is just not worth the risk.

We move out. The heat is overpowering and draining. We stop for some C-rations. Those crazy Kit Carson scouts somehow catch three fish, build a fire, and begin to cook them whole, head and all. Before they have time to eat, the order is given to move out. They are disappointed again at not being able to finish their lunch.

I move up and down the column of soldiers. They've picked up the theme that I must pray for rain to cool things off. My response to each one who says 'pray for rain' is to say, "Ok, I just need two or three hours and then it'll rain."

At 4:00 P.M. the rains come. Everywhere I go in the next hour or so, the guys are bragging that I came through for them with the cool rain. Even soaking wet, everyone is jovial.

All three companies are to rendezvous one kilometer ahead and be extracted. We keep moving down the 'hardball' trail that now has become slick because of the rain.

The command elements of the three companies gather in a small opening. Having landed nearby, Lieutenant Colonel Monk Doty and Captain Jordan, the artillery liaison, walk up. Monk seems surprised to see me. Some of the other officers tell him that I've done my job by bringing the rain to cool everything down. This brings another chuckle. One company has three captured VC, including a female. Women VC can kill just as easily as the men can.

Even though the troops are all around us in a hold position, we decide that standing in this small clearing of no more than a one-half acre makes us an inviting target should any VC snipers be in the trees watching us. We move to a more concealed two-hooch area, while strategy for extraction is discussed.

The boats are in a nearby stream and we're to move another one-half kilometer to the stream and return to the ships. One of Alpha Company platoons, led by Lieutenant Ira Owens, will remain to provide rear security for our extraction.

Water is everywhere. It's still raining and the soldiers are delighted that we're going in. We move quickly to the stream bank. The tide is in and this is a difficult extraction. We walk neck deep into the stream, surrounded by small trees and dense foliage. The boats can't get close enough for a normal extraction. I realize how hazardous this is. We walk through the water gingerly as one step into an unseen hole can be disastrous. We crawl up onto the down ramp of the ATCs and soon the boats are backing out.

Ira Owen's platoon is suddenly hit! We're no more than two hundred meters from them. They're ordered to move to the river for quick extraction as artillery is called in to suppress the VC fire. Fortunately, the platoon takes no casualties.

The VC were all around us in the small opening where we had a strategy meeting and we didn't even know it. As the three companies left, the VC waited to attack the smaller element. Their efforts at concealment are masterful. We are always vulnerable.

FRIDAY, SEPTEMBER 22, 1967: I go to Dong Tam to visit some wounded at the hospital. Returning to the *Colleton*, I wait an hour and fifteen minutes for the shuttle boat. The *Colleton* is only three-quarters of a mile away in the middle of the river. In fact, I can see it. But it may as well have been a hundred miles away since the darn shuttle boat wasn't run.

SATURDAY, SEPTEMBER 23, 1967: Late in the day Bravo Company has another soldier killed. Life is becoming more uncertain daily.

6:25 P.M.
Sunday, September 24, 1967
Hello Sweetheart,
You have mentioned the possibility of me calling you. I just haven't had the time to go and wait in line a half day or so. I went today but there were 12 guys ahead of me; at least we have tapes, which are a life saver . . .

Monday 11:30 P.M.
25 Sept 1967
Hello Sweets,

I took a nap this afternoon and dreamed that Grey had two brothers! All three were triplets. I was thrilled to death. I sure do miss the kids and their growing up. I feel good that you're their mother and that they're well cared for. I'll make up for lost time when I get home.

TUESDAY, SEPTEMBER 26, 1967: I have two memorial services today, one for Sgt. Loftin from Alpha Company and Houston from Bravo Company. I must be careful not to get too routine about these wonderful guys dying.

I have done a lot of counseling. Several talk of wanting out of the field. Others have problems at home. Another has a problem with his back. Another is homesick. I tell myself not to become too cynical. I must keep caring and loving these guys, even when they irritate me by trying to manipulate.

CHAPTER THREE

September 27, 1967–November 2, 1967

WEDNESDAY, SEPTEMBER 27, 1967: We leave at 1:00 A.M. on another operation. It's a very dark night with no moon. I'm riding on the aid boat. No one sleeps because of what happened at Snoopy's Nose twelve days ago. Plus, we're heading to the Ben Tre Canal where the VC are known to be heavily fortified.

We get to the canal at daybreak. Artillery proceeds us. All guns on the boats are manned and pointed directly at the banks. If the VC ambush us, it won't take but about two seconds to return fire.

The now dreaded event occurs again. Sounds of heavy weapons break the early-morning boredom. Two ATCs are hit just to our front. We're told that both boats have several casualties.

We move quickly out of the VC kill zone and pull alongside the first boat and tie up to it. I jump over and find a dead sailor full of shell fragments. A round has gone directly into the coxswain's area, blowing the man up. Blood and bits of flesh are scattered all over the boat. We find an eyeball under the .50 caliber machine gun mount. It's no different in the well deck; a round went off in there also. A sailor is hurt very badly but he will survive.

By now, the second boat that was hit is on the other side of the aid boat. We quickly move all the wounded onto the aid boat deck, although this makes us inviting targets for other VC along the canal banks. We're too busy trying to stabilize the five wounded soldiers to be preoccupied with our own safety. Moving them from one boat to the aid boat is difficult because all three boats are tied together and moving at full speed and the stream is small. Our objective is the artillery fire support base up ahead because that will be a safer location to dustoff these wounded sailors than the landing deck of the USS *Scarecrow*.

Two medics and I move the three dead sailors. Two, including the blown up coxswain, are mangled. We have no body bags so we use ponchos to cover them. It's not good for the others to see the gruesome results of enemy fire. It's not good for me to see it either. Wrapping their bodies and manhandling them over the side and onto the aid boat covers me with their blood and body fluids. I find myself angry; at war, death and such needless loss; I wish some of the politicians could see this.

Then I see a sailor sitting in the corner of the well deck, a vacant expression on his face. I lead him to the side, he moves as if he is sleep-walking. I tell Doc he also needs to be medevaced. I get him settled in the well deck of the aid boat away from the physically wounded and dead. As we move down stream, I then spend time talking to three of the injured who are conscious.

We get to the fire support base. Two dustoffs are already on the way. We move the five wounded to a small clearing about thirty meters inland of the stream bank. Then I remember the sailor with the vacant look. I run back to the aid boat to find that he hasn't moved in the fifteen minutes since I put him there. I almost have to force him to the dustoff. He's not resisting, but he's nearly completely immobilized. I know his buddies flesh will heal and their bones can mend, but will his emotional wounds ever heal?

Another chopper arrives in a few minutes for the three dead sailors. We have them laid out in the same small clearing. Just as the chopper touches down, the prop wash blows the poncho off one of the dead. It's the coxswain with the entire left side of his head gone. The chopper door gunner, who's only ten feet away, turns his head away quickly. He looks like he's seen a ghost. He gags but doesn't puke. We quickly load the dead onto the chopper and I pat the leg of the door gunner and give him the thumbs up just as the chopper lifts off. It is the beginning of the last trip for these heroic river rats.

By now, the remaining crew has washed the blood and bile away from the boats. It's almost as if nothing has happened. Had a tragedy like this occurred in the states, things would have come to an immediate halt as order was restored and feelings dealt with. Empathy would pour in from every imaginable source. Not so here. There's no time. This in itself is tragic. We have to survive. Another fight may occur at any minute. Energy is now focused on what may happen and not on what has just happened a few minutes ago.

We arrive at the new area of operation in fifteen minutes. The troops beach. Even though the stream is lined for many kilometers with VC bunkers, no more shots are fired today. We set up night defensive positions. No snipers fire on us.

THURSDAY, SEPTEMBER 28, 1967: At mid-afternoon the order is given to terminate this operation. We reach the ships at 10:30 P.M. It takes forever to unload. I'm exhausted and impatient. Tomorrow I turn twenty-seven. Yes, LBJ, "The war is going good".

I've lived to see another birthday.

7:30 P.M.
Friday, September 29, 1967
Hello Barbara Sue,
I don't feel too good. Probably a cold. We now have $1300.00 saved in the class "S" allotment. I have $250.00 in the safe in my room and I'll put another $200.00 in Class "S". I'm getting a 5.6% raise in October. It's not costing me much to live; I probably didn't spend more than $10.00 this month. It was real sweet of Kellie to want to send the leaf to me. I sure do miss the kids . . . and you, of course.

FRIDAY, SEPTEMBER 29, 1967: Today, I'm twenty-seven years old. No one here knows. Barbara, Mother and Daddy have sent a few things. But, with whom can I celebrate? Here, birthdays are nothing special. Each day that I live is like a birthday; I don't die. Stateside, a soldier would get the day off in most assignments. To take the day off here means nothing. My birthday is just another day of my 365.

If I were at home, Barbara would make a big deal of it. She always does. She has so much love to give. She'd have me a cake and several presents. She'd have people over and we'd celebrate. Here I don't even mention it. I don't feel badly; I just don't feel. Maybe I've seen too many die in the past two weeks. The loss of an eye, someone's brains scrambled, and torn flesh seem far more important than my birthday.

I've seen more death and destruction in the past few weeks than most people see in a lifetime; and I have this horrible feeling that the worst is yet to come.

Happy Birthday, Jim?

SATURDAY, SEPTEMBER 30, 1967: We leave early this morning on another operation near Ben Tre. I'm coming down with a cold so I stay on board the aid boat. I get word that Alpha Company has a KIA, a young buck sergeant I'll refer to as 'K'. A sniper shot him while he was crossing a bamboo foot bridge. I hate these blasted bridges. But I hate a lot of other things about this war, too.

We move to a pick-up point. Two soldiers have taken K's body to the stream bank and we load it into the well deck. He's already in a body bag. He's recently been transferred here from the 4/47th, one of our two sister battalions.

Since all the battalion personnel arrived at the same time, division HQ instituted an infusion program of moving soldiers around to avoid too many from the same unit rotating back to the States at the same time. But at the rate we've been taking casualties over the past two months, none of the original guys will be left to rotate. The VC are instituting their own infusion program on us by systematically shooting us.

As I look at K, I think that he didn't even die in the presence of his close buddies. But then I wonder, does it really matter? K died just a few minutes after he'd been shot. He fell into the water from the foot bridge, but the tide was out and he was pulled out of the water in just a few seconds. I see that he only has a small entry wound, but I don't turn him over to see what kind of exit wound he has. It doesn't matter. He's dead.

Later, Shorty, one of the river rat crew whom I've gotten to know quite well, talks to me. "Chaplain," he says, "I could never look at a dead man as calmly as you do."

"Inside I don't feel calm at all," I tell him. We talk for a little while and I can tell that K's body being on the boat bothers Shorty. It reminds us all of how close death is all the time. "Shorty, don't worry. As short as you are, and as tall as I am, we'll both survive. That's the long and short of it." We grin, but even to my own ears, my attempt at humor sounds empty.

Soon, the rains come. The winds blow. This is not a normal monsoon. It's more like a front is moving in. The air is cool. I'm glad I'm on the boat tonight instead of trying to "sleep" in a rice paddy. Then, I feel guilty. I'm here and the troops are out there. But, my guilt is somewhat assuaged by the thought of my coming down with whatever I've caught. I don't need to be wet and cold tonight.

SUNDAY, OCTOBER 1, 1967: Soon after daybreak, Shorty approaches me again. He's still bothered by K's dead body. He tells me he had night-mares all night. He seems a little relieved when I tell him that the body will be evacuated before long.

He tells me again that he admires the calm approach with which I deal with the dead. After listening to Shorty's feedback I realize that maybe God has given me some special abilities to operate in crisis situations. I've never really thought about it before, but perhaps I do have this special gift.

The operation ends and we go in. I still feel awful, physically and emo-tionally, for K's family, for Shorty, and for myself.

10:30 A.M.
Sunday, October 1, 1967
Hello Sweets,

Can you believe that I've already started on my 4th month? It'll be Christmas before we know it . . .

MONDAY, OCTOBER 2, 1967: I make arrangements for two Jewish soldiers to attend Holy Day services in Saigon. I receive some birthday fudge in the mail. It's all busted up and crumbly, which is about the way I feel.

TUESDAY, OCTOBER 3, 1967: Today I conduct the memorial service for K. He hadn't been in the unit long enough to make friends.

The sergeant whose wife is running around on him in Oklahoma wants to talk again.

WEDNESDAY, OCTOBER 4, 1967: The operation scheduled to begin today has been delayed for twenty-four hours. The sergeant whose wife has 'hot pants' comes back and we talk more. He really is sad and frustrated about her.

5:00 P.M.
Wednesday, October 4, 1967
Hello Sweets,
I hope Grey hasn't bothered you too much with his cutting teeth. You sound in your letter like he's getting on your nerves. I guess you have a lot of frustrations in having to carry on the household by yourself, but you're doing a good job and I'm proud of you. I'm still eating the crumbs of the fudge.

THURSDAY, OCTOBER 5, 1967: I prepare my gear and get ready for today's operation. It's only been a month and one-half since my first ground operation in Ben Luc. So much has happened to me. We'll visit the Cam Son Secret Zone again today. This is back in the general area of Snoopy's Nose, near Cai Lai. This is a bad area, but none of us talk about that. I'm flying in with Alpha Company. Charlie Company has already been picked up and inserted, and now the choppers have returned to pick us up. I'm in the first lift. After we're inserted, the second half of Alpha Company will be brought in.

From the air, the land looks so peaceful. The rice paddies, foliage and streams make a beautiful picture. We make a wide turn. The chopper doors are open, as always. The door gunners are vigilant. Because of the rushing air, no one dares to spit because it would surely hit the door gunner. Troopers legs are dangling from every aircraft. As we begin to descend, I get butterflies. Who knows what will be down there? Going into any LZ is like playing Russian Roulette.

When we descend to about 500 feet, I realize something is amiss. The radio operator in front of me is talking excitedly into his radio. He yells to the other six on our chopper that Charlie Company is in contact with the VC. The soldier next to me is a new replacement. He's pale, and the expression on his young, zit-covered face says he'd like to run. I pat his boot and mouth to him over the 'wop wop wop' of the Huey rotor blades that things will be okay. I'm shaking inside.

We're going in 800 meters from Charlie Company. The gun ships are working over the LZ with their mini-guns. They report that they're receiving fire. A hot landing zone! What a rotten deal. If Charlie Company wasn't in their fight, the command decision would probably be to drop a kilometer or so away from the hot LZ. But we must go in and help Charlie Company.

At one hundred feet, my mind is going one hundred miles per hour. What have I gotten myself into? Why couldn't I have stayed behind on this operation? My personal feelings about ministering to these wonderful guys are in direct conflict with my will to survive. The choppers stay in formation. These "slick" pilots know what they're doing. They must be frightened, too, but they aren't showing it as they furiously work their dials and knobs. I scan the horizon as if I could see the VC. All I see is some smoke.

We descend quickly and at five feet we all jump off. Until now, there has been no VC fire. Now the sickening sound of rifle fire is coming at us. I make a low dash to the nearest rice paddy dike with bullets zooming by like hawks diving after chickens. I dive low and remain prone next to the dike. Bullets are flying in every direction. I fear one of the rear choppers may be hit, crash and explode on top of us. Fortunately, all the choppers are now airborne. Several are hit but none are shot down.

The squad I'm with is in the direct line of fire from the tree line 150 meters away. Someone shouts, "We're on the wrong side of the dike!" We roll over the small dike to the opposite side. My heart is beating wildly like a dozen pile drivers; I hug the mud and water. I can't see anything around me except the rice stalks, which are only inches from my face. How quickly one loses perspective. Only thirty seconds ago, I could survey the landscape from the descending chopper, now I see absolutely nothing. I can only hear the continual sounds of VC AK 47 rifle shots zinging *very* low over our heads. I don't know where the rest of the company is, but I don't dare raise my head and look.

I hear the company commander's voice on a nearby platoon radio telling all elements to stay down and don't move. Then, almost as an afterthought, he says that if they begin dropping mortars on us, we may have to get up and run in attack formation to the nearest tree line. Mortars! I hadn't even thought about that.

Artillery whistles low overhead and impacts on the nearby tree line. Thank God it's *our* artillery. Charlie Company reports their contact with the VC has declined.

I'm scared. I'd dig a hole if I could. This stuff is supposed to only happen in the movies.

The shooting has now slowed, but we're all still pinned down. It's been ten minutes since we've been inserted into this hot landing zone. I'm oblivious to the fact that I'm lying in water. I just wish I could get lower.

The platoons are doing a verbal wound check by calling out each soldier's name for a situation report. Miraculously, no one has been hit. The remainder of Alpha Company isn't to be inserted until this area is secured.

Just when I'm beginning to feel a little less tense, out of nowhere, a VC machine gunner suddenly opens up again. I'm immediately sprinkled with chunks of mud. Dirt goes down my back. In a split second, I go from a feeling of relative relief to absolute and sheer terror. A thousand thoughts cascade on my mind instantly. How thick is the dike? Will the bullets penetrate? I was in such a hurry to take cover as I jumped off the chopper that I don't even remember how large the dike is. Some dikes are a couple of feet thick; others are as little as ten inches thick. Oh, God, please let this dike be a thick one. I flash on an image of Barbara and the kids at my funeral.

For the first time in my life I wish I were small. I am absolutely petrified. The gunner has fired only three or four quick bursts at me but it seems as if he fired at me for an eternity.

"Is anyone hit?" an officer named Joe Van Cycle yells.

"Not over here," someone shouts.

"The chaplain's over there. The VC were shooting at him."

"Chaplain, are you OK?"

"I'm OK." My voice is so strained I can barely get out the words.

"Everyone stay down," Joe yells. "Charlie may still have you in his sights."

The order is given for everyone to stay put until artillery is brought in again. Artillery is immediate and furious over the nearby tree line where the firing has originated. Relief floods me as I listen to the 'Kaw-hump' sounds of our artillery. After another fifteen minutes, the artillery stops.

In the meantime, Charlie Company has maneuvered to the tree line at a right angle to the VC's tree line. They'll cover us when we're ready to move out of our LZ. God, I wish I could stay here until dark. Will I have the courage to stand up and run? Does the VC machine gunner still have us in his sights and is he waiting for us to move? I'll know in a few minutes.

I feel so vulnerable.

Lieutenant Joe Van Cycle, one of the platoon leaders, swears that the machine gun that opened up on me was a .50 caliber machine gun. But I know that can't be. Had it been a .50 caliber, the rounds would have torn through the dike as if it were Jell-O, pulverizing me in the bargain. But, regardless, being targeted in the open and being helpless feels like being thrown in a lions den.

An hour has gone by since insertion into the landing zone. I'm still frightened but no longer panicky. Like a snake, I've slithered up to a PFC in the mud just ahead of me and we're talking. But, our conversation isn't about being pinned down in an open rice paddy. It's small talk, as if we talk about nonsense, we can deny the predicament we're in.

The order is given to gather gear and prepare to get up and move out in five minutes. I have everything with me that I loaded up with. Soon, the company commander yells in his deep voice that on the count of three, we'll all get up and run for the tree line where Charlie Company is located about 100 meters away. I'm immediately petrified again. Will I have the guts to get up and be exposed to the VC who may still be in place and have me in his sights? I'm afraid to move afraid I won't be *able* to. I could stay here in this mud for weeks—just don't make me get up!

When I hear the commander shout, "One, Two, Three: Move! Move! Move!" I force myself to get up. I fully expect to be shot at. I break into a dead run toward the tree line. My heart is pounding. In college, as a football tackle, I was one of the slower players on the team. Today, I could have been a running back, even with the gear I am carrying.

After about thirty meters, we've heard no shots. We all slow from a dead run to a fast walk. Glee is on all of our faces; we have, quite literally, dodged another bullet. We don't know where the VC are, but as long as they're not shooting, we don't care.

We make it to the tree line and pass through a few of Charlie Company's positions that have been covering us. We move safely another 100 meters and stop to regroup. The second half of the company is now inbound and lands without incident. One of the soldiers smiles at me, "Chaplain, that was some kind of crap out there, wasn't it?"

I manage to hide my terror behind my grin, but am acutely aware that grins don't stop bullets.

I feel exhilarated. It's a miracle no one is wounded or killed, but our emotions and fear have been severely assaulted. Having extracted us from that horrible predicament, I'm surprised at my feelings. If exhilaration comes from being on the edge of extreme danger, then our high is legitimate.

Our feelings rapidly change to more sober thoughts. We still have to maneuver to our objective. This is VC land. We've fought him here several times in the last few weeks and this his own back yard, the Cam Son Secret Zone. Our job now will be to try to find the VC again and kill them.

As we move out, I'm thinking about the courage it took for us all to move out of that rice paddy. I'm so proud of these guys. They're nineteen and twenty years old. Yet they have just shown more courage in the past hour than the average person will show in a lifetime.

We now move out. Every turn on the trail is a prime opportunity for the VC to ambush us. Streams and foliage are everywhere. The heat is stifling. We stop for some quick lunch. I'm glad because I'm developing a headache, but the C-rations taste terrible. Soon we move out again, passing through the same area where Alpha Company was in the fight on the thirteenth of September and had two soldiers killed.

It happens again! All hell breaks loose. The VC attack us from our rear! The squad I'm with all dive into the small stream next to the trail for cover. Bullets are zinging through the trees like swarms of bees on the attack. Everyone is returning fire. The VC are where we've just been! Apparently they were there all along. They're such masters of deception and camouflage that we didn't see any of them. They're so disciplined that they waited for us to pass through their positions and then simply attack us from the rear.

The firing continues for three minutes and the company commander gives the order to cease fire. We must determine the location of all our positions lest we fire on our own.

The squad I'm with is outside and in front of what has now become the company fighting perimeter. Since we were the follow element, when we were hit from behind we became the front. We're about twenty-five meters from the main company. The six of us in this squad knee walk and crawl through the stream water and mud back to the main body. We're able to stay low and don't dare rise above the banks of the stream. Once we've rejoined the main body of the company, the artillery forward observer is checking coordinates to bring in artillery. His counterpart at the fire support base thinks he's confused and tells him his coordinates are where we were just located. The forward observer yells to him, "That's right! Charlie's there now and firing on us."

I want a cigarette and so does PFC Tim Doty. All of his are wet from having crawled though the stream to safety a few minutes ago. I give him a Camel.

Tim is from West Virginia. He's a likable guy; loud, in an innocent kind of way. Everyone teases Tim about being from West Virginia. Tim always takes the teasing well.

I light Tim's Camel and he tells several others hunkered down in the canal that since the cigarette is from the chaplain, it's a "Holy Smoke."

During the lull in firing, while we're smoking, a Mexican-American platoon sergeant tires of lying in the small stream, stands up to lean against a tree on the bank. As he casually smokes, a single AK-47 round comes blasting into our position and tears into one of the tree limbs about five feet above his head. His reaction is to simply look up at the tree as if the noise is nothing more than a squirrel. Several men yell to him to get down. He responds by sticking his middle finger up and pointing it in the direction from where the VC bullet came.

This sergeant is in his mid-thirty's, old for a platoon sergeant these days. He tells us, "If it's your time to get it, you'll get it and if not, you won't." This fatalistic attitude is very poor theology and reflects a kind of predestined attitude that people have begun to voice here in Vietnam. My own theology is that God helps those who help themselves and the rest of us are helping ourselves by staying low and, hopefully, out of harm's way. If there's nothing you can do about your destiny, then one would never buckle a seat belt, have a fire alarm or get a medical checkup.

It's not brave to needlessly expose oneself to the enemy in a foolhardy way. Though many of the men believe that when your number's up, it's up, bullets don't know this. It is better to err on the side of safety than to be killed because of faulty theology that gives no power to the God-given position of the right of self-determination. Rather, it gives all the power to the VC.

About six more quick VC rounds again come in and all of our positions open fire for two "mad minutes." Then the artillery begins coming in. An hour goes by and we take no additional VC fire. It's late afternoon now and the order is given to secure the company perimeter, as we will remain overnight in our current positions. As usual, we joke. Someone talks about stopping smoking when he returns home. My standard line is, "anyone can stop smoking, but it takes a *man* to face cancer."

Sergeant David Hershberger, a squad leader and one of the men who was with me in the canal when we were hit, thanks me for being here. It makes me feel good. I leave their position and move the forty meters over to the company command post to spend the night.

The guys in the headquarters element are glad to see me. It seems like days since we were all pinned down this morning, and now it's like a reunion. Being under fire bonds people together. We have a lot of opportunities to bond these days and I'm not sure I like that.

The headquarters element is setting up around an abandoned hooch with the typical dried mud bunker. I drop my gear just outside the hooch. A resupply chopper is due here momentarily. I'm too exhausted to be greatly concerned about the chopper as it comes in and hovers just over the palm trees, wiggling its way downward into a narrow clearing.

At the sound of several loud pops, I immediately think it's a machine gun and we all hit the ground, but it's the rotor blades of the descending chopper, maybe thirty meters away, hitting the outer branches of a palm tree. I expect the chopper to turn on its side and crash, but thank God it doesn't. The chances these pilots take to get us resupplied with food, water, and ammunition are incredible.

The chopper is quickly gone and all is quiet now. Not much daylight is left. There's only time to eat a few C-rations. We fill our canteens with newly resupplied water. Abruptly, one of the soldiers begins cursing a blue streak and shouting that the water is laced with fuel oil.

I sip from my own canteen and discover he's right. Since it's now dark, we'll have to spend the night without fresh water. Some Dong Tam supply specialist apparently filled the wrong can with water. We all grumble and complain, but there's nothing we can do about it.

I dig a shallow hole near a hooch and place two VC mats from the hooch in it to sleep on. My eight inch "hole" may offer a little protection should we get hit during the night, but not much. I have a night toddy of hot chocolate using borrowed water from one of the radio operators who has a spare canteen of uncontaminated water.

I lie down in my hole and I'm only there for a second when I feel it— water is beginning to seep into my "bed". I roll over onto the higher ground for the night.

Now the Vietnamese national bird, mosquitoes, appear out of nowhere! My repellent seems to do little good and I swat and scratch incessantly. I wonder if the VC have somehow trained the mosquitoes to attack us. Some five star hotel this is!

Just after dark I hear several M-16 shots in the distance. It comes from Bravo Company's position about 500 meters to our right. In a little while, I hear that they've had a KIA. A soldier had gone out to set up a claymore mine just at dark. As he was walking back to his position, a soldier in the next position saw him, panicked, and thinking he's a VC, fires a few rounds. His buddy is dead in ten seconds. What a waste. Which side does this KIA go under, our body count or the VC's? But after what we went through today, can anyone blame a nineteen-year-old infantryman for being too quick on the trigger? Now, his buddy is dead, soon to be zipped into a body bag for his last flight home. Some mother and father will get their son in a sterile casket to bury in a few days. Another good soldier is dead and the shooter will have nightmares about this for as long as he lives. Yes, Lyndon, the war is going well.

Throughout the night the VC harass us. Every thirty minutes or so, an explosive device is fired into our positions. Fortunately, no one else is wounded. It's as if the VC just want us to know that they know we're here. This makes for a long, miserable, scary night.

One of the radio operators is lying next to me. We look through an opening in the canopy up into the starlit sky. It reminds me of the summer nights of my childhood when I'd lie on my back at night in my yard and star gaze.

At 9:00 P.M. we see a distant light moving rapidly through the sky and I realize it is a satellite, the first one I've ever seen. I fantasize about catching a ride on it and being dropped off at home.

My tired mind reflects on today's events. Did God really call me to minister here? Someone once said, "It's never as bad as you think." I disagree. It is as bad as I think, and they really are out to get me; the VC and these mosquitoes. I should have white hair by morning. After the past few weeks, and especially today, I've earned it.

FRIDAY, OCTOBER 6, 1967: At first light, we begin breaking our night positions. Our resupply chopper comes in with fresh, clean water. I have C-ration fruit cocktail from a can and fruitcake that tastes as if it was made shortly after Lincoln's assassination. I'm still wet and I feel lousy. I'm really feeling cynical this morning. That's what a "good night's rest" does for you.

We begin moving out after destroying and burning the hooches. We move 1000 meters when we get a frantic call to prepare to be lifted out by helicopter. An observation chopper has spotted over 100 VC with weapons. The 3/60th is to surround them. A big fight seems to be shaping up. Oh, goody, goody! We haven't had a firefight in several hours now.

We're to go into the area again in two lifts of choppers. Charlie Company will go in first on one side of a major tree line where the VC have been spotted. Bravo will go into the opposite side of the tree line, then Alpha will move in behind Charlie Company.

The choppers come in. I'm glad for the noise from the choppers to blot out the sound of my teeth chattering. Yesterday, we went into the hot landing zone not knowing in advance the VC were there. Today, we're going in knowing full well they're there. We land and hit the rice paddy deck and then the choppers are gone. The only shots I hear are in the far distance. We move out to surround the area where the VC were spotted. I hope it is a mirage. It isn't.

It's 9:00 A.M. We group and prepare to move into battle. As I'm lying on the ground, I put my keys down to look for something in my pocket. Artillery is now coming in heavy on the objective ahead. We move out and I forget my keys. I wish there was some way that I could've booby-trapped them.

As Charlie Company moves out ahead of us, I hear shots.

The firing is coming from an element of VC in a bunker inside a hooch. A platoon leader, a lieutenant named Vic, and some of his soldiers try to flush the VC out by throwing a grenade into the bunker. The VC roll it out. Another grenade is tossed in, and then out it comes, exploding as harmless as the first one, yards away from the hooch. One of the VC fires through the grass wall of the hooch. Vic is hit and falls to the ground. Another soldier is shot. Several VC dash from the bunker with AK 47's blazing. As Vic lies seriously wounded on the ground, he throws a hand grenade and kills three of the VC. The other soldiers kill the remaining VC, but Vic is badly wounded. The grenade tossed by this brave and likable guy has saved lives. The irony is that Vic was to leave tomorrow for R&R. Come to think of it, he will get R&R, but not rest and recuperation, more like resuscitation and recovery.

We get Vic and the other wounded soldiers away as the artillery stops only long enough for the dustoff flight to come in and leave. We move through some undergrowth to within 100 meters of the tree line and stop for forty-five minutes as artillery continues to blast away in the trees where the VC were spotted earlier. Then we move again.

As the first platoon moves out, the VC open up from everywhere. Bullets are zigzagging in every direction. As I hug the ground it's impossible to know from which direction the main fire is originating. All I know for certain is that I am terrified.

Someone yells that there must be at least a hundred VC just on our side of the tree line. We realize that they must have patiently waited through the volley of artillery, not firing on us until the artillery lifted and we were within easy range of their weapons.

Bravo Company is also catching it on the other side of the tree line. A chopper is shot down on their position. I'm hugging the ground and glance over to find myself beside David Hershberger, the squad leader from the canal, again.

He yells to me over the loud sounds of the battle field, "Chaplain, you are everywhere."

The VC are hitting us from three sides. They're even in the trees. Artillery is coming in again onto the VC positions. We're very close to where the artillery is exploding but the fire is too heavy for us to pull back. Fragments are raining onto us. A three inch piece of jagged steel suddenly plows into the mud six inches from my right leg. I pivot on my stomach and use a plastic C-ration spoon to dig out the fragment as a souvenir.

The first platoon pulls back on their stomachs. They've been shot up pretty badly with several wounded. The fight rages all afternoon. An hour before dark we're ordered to pull back. There is an open area between the platoons and another line of foliage to our right rear. We must run through that clearing to reach cover. I lope with the other soldiers through the mud into our new position, with the VC shooting at us continuously.

We have several who are wounded and at least two KIAs. When we pull back, one of the KIAs is left in position. It's too risky to evacuate the body now. He'll be recovered tomorrow morning.

We are now regrouped. I help Lieutenant Joe Van Cycle carry some of the wounded to an area where we believe a dustoff can land. The rains come just before dark. I talk to the wounded by crawling from one to the other. Finally, the Air Force bombers drop napalm and 500 pound bombs onto the tree line. Elsewhere this would be scary because they're so close. But they're dropping their ordinance on the VC positions and this seems to comfort us all.

Then another soldier named Jason is shot. I've counseled with him several times in the past. He wants to be a professional singer and entertainer when he returns to the real world. Two of his buddies drag him to join the rest of the wounded. Jason is shot in the throat, but he can still talk.

"Will I sing again Chaplain?" he asks.

I tell him he will, but of course I don't know that. I tell him that, at least, we're still alive and that he'll be out of here on a dustoff in a little while. He's shivering from trauma.

Night has come and the shooting has finally come to a halt.

A bunkered hooch becomes the Alpha Company command post with Charlie Company next to us about fifty meters away. Shortly after nightfall, we move the wounded again to the command post. One dead body is left outside covered with a poncho. The other body remains in place where he died about 100 meters away.

Brad is one of the wounded and he's in excruciating pain. It's agony for him not to scream, but he doesn't want to risk identifying our position in case the VC attempt to attack us tonight. I give him an unopened can of C-rations and tell him to squeeze it as hard as he can when he feels the urge to yell. I tell him it's like injured cowboys biting the bullet in the wild west.

Finally the dustoff chopper arrives. I help load the wounded. We evacuate six WIA's. The dead body remains with us, as there's no room on the chopper.

Bravo Company, who is still on the opposite side of the tree line, is able to get their wounded out also. I hear the count for the day; Alpha has had two KIA's and six WIA's; Bravo has four KIA's and seven WIA's; and Charlie Company has had only two WIA's.

I'm getting used to torn flesh, blood and guts. What a terrible realization. I'm still wet and miserable. A soldier known as Little Al offers me some C-ration hot chocolate. I've seen him countless times over the past few months. His fear is always present. He's now a radio operator. He's such a tiny guy, not much larger than the VC. The large radio on his back seems out of place. He is only eighteen.

The night is mosquito-free. I doze with Little Al Harris on one side of me and a company medic on the other side. We use a small rice paddy dike as a pillow and the lower two-thirds of our bodies are in water.

SATURDAY, OCTOBER 7, 1967: At daybreak, two Vietnamese civilians come to our command post and say they live about 1000 meters away and that, during the night, the VC left the area in what appeared to be single file. They add that the VC were carrying many dead and wounded with them, and that it took over an hour for the several hundred VC to pass by.

I hope these two Vietnamese civilians are right. I wonder if the VC are still in the tree line. Maybe they're just setting us up and wanting us to walk into an ambush. We'll know soon because Patron 6 (LTC Doty) is now ordering Alpha and Charlie Companies to prepare to assault the tree line in one hour.

A volunteer patrol goes to retrieve the body left in position yesterday. The dead soldier was a new man named Ted.

Alpha and Charlie Companies prepare to take the tree line where so many VC were embedded just a few hours ago. Both companies are on line in a straight horizontal line. I'm with the headquarters element, walking ten meters behind the advancing line. As we walk into the clearing I feel exposed and vulnerable.

Thankfully, no VC are here. The tree line is all mud bunkers and splintered trees. Some bunkers have been blown up by direct artillery hits. The area is obliterated and I wonder how the surviving VC could have withstood such bombardment. In my own way I admire their dedication. Death is death regardless of which side you're on.

The dog tracker teams discover some residual VC ammunition and other equipment. The VC have carefully wrapped the equipment in plastic and placed it in small streams, obviously planning to retrieve it after we leave the area. I can only imagine what they took out with them during their night retreat.

Patron 6 says, "Prepare for another air assault."

Come on Monk, give us a break, I think. Three days in a row? We quickly group for air extraction. We're airborne again in seconds. Most of the VC have gone, but a few have not as several snipers still remain and are taking pot shots at us as we ascend. Fortunately, they are poor shots. Nevertheless, the sounds send fear rippling through me.

We descend quickly into a huge open rice paddy. We assault a nearby tree line and the only encounter we have are five water buffalo that are giving us the evil eye. If they get mad, they can be a real danger. We decide to go around the animals.

We move to a well-worn trail. I'm still with Alpha Company. Shortly, we hear firing close by. Some VC have positioned themselves between Bravo and Charlie Companies and fire in both directions hoping to get us to fire on one another. Three more from Bravo Company are wounded in this short firefight.

We set up a blocking force. I rest on a crude wooden bed in a nearby hooch. Then the good news comes to move out toward the river to be extracted. Two hours before dark, we reach the river and soon the boats arrive for extraction. Fatigue is an understatement, but the VC are gone and so are we.

So much has happened in the past three days that I feel like I've aged three years. Maybe I have.

SUNDAY, OCTOBER 8, 1967: I'm up early for services because today is Sunday. This is the only day a preacher works, or at least that's what some folks back in the States believe.

I'm eager to get to Dong Tam to check on our wounded. At the 3rd Surg, the nurse tells me that Vic is critical, but awake and alert. Surprisingly, he's not too down about his R&R. Maybe it is the morphine. Vic is a hero and I tell him so. He seems happy but a little embarrassed. I think he doesn't realize how near death he is. I leave and check on the other wounded, coming away glad that they will make it.

Then I walk to the Dong Tam chapel, and my jaw drops when I see an old friend! Bert Kirby is sitting there. We embrace. I can't believe it! I'm so excited. Bert was a pastor just across the river in Rockingham, North Carolina when I was living in Lilesville, North Carolina. We became great pals and grew even closer in the army reserves.

Bert is several years older than I am. He tells me it's been less than two weeks since he, his wife Margaret, and another mutual friend visited my wife, Barbara, in Albemarle, North Carolina. Bert was on leave there before coming to Vietnam and they all made a tape to me. On this tape, Bert said laughingly that wherever he was assigned, he did not want any part of the Mekong Delta and the 9th Infantry Division. Well, here he is!

He's been in Dong Tam only two hours and has a million questions. He looks to me for guidance as if I'm some grizzled veteran who has all the answers. The division chaplain has told him he'll be at Dong Tam for a little while and, eventually, will be assigned to a battalion out of Bear Cat. I well remember how I felt just ninety days ago when I first arrived. Lord, that seems so long ago. I've grown up so much in these three months.

I make sure Bert knows where all the vital facilities around my hooch are such as the latrine, mess hall, shower and the bunker. At late afternoon it's time to return to the ship. I leave feeling somehow I should protect Bert. At 11:00 P.M. we learn that Dong Tam is being mortared. I think of Bert and hope he's in the bunker. Can he find it in the dark? What rotten luck to be in a mortar attack the very first night at Dong Tam. The VC aren't very considerate of newcomers or to us crusty old veterans who've been here three months.

MONDAY, OCTOBER 9, 1967: I'm out early to get a shuttle boat to Dong Tam; must get to the Long Binh and Saigon hospitals.

TUESDAY, OCT 10, 1967: I hitch a ride to Long Binh. Among the six I visit is Sgt. 'Egg", who was shot in the face at Snoopy's Nose. He's progressing well. He wants all the 3/60th news, as do the other guys. By the time I leave, I've told the same news over and over.

Brad now is much better. We reflect together what he experienced three days ago. He'll be going to Japan and then to the states to recover. Roy is critical; he was shot in the chest. I wonder if he will make it; looks bad. Jason tells me he has no damage to his larynx. He was shot in the throat and the shoulder. When we talked three nights ago, after he was shot, I wasn't even aware that he'd been shot in the shoulder, too. He'll sing again and I rejoice with him.

Kenny Lancaster is here! He was wounded at Snoopy's Nose three weeks ago. He tells me that he was hit again five days ago, which was the day of my "hot landing zone" experience. A recoilless rifle round exploded on the dike and blew him several feet into the air. He's a radio operator and landed on his radio, addled and battered. He has a severe foot wound, has almost lost two toes and has three fragments lodged next to his spine. His field radio is mangled but probably saved his life.

At Bear Cat, I treat myself to a MARS phone conversation to Barbara. The connection is poor but I hear her lovely voice live for the first time in three months.

9:15 P.M.
Tuesday, October 10, 1967
Hello Babes,
Talking to you today made me a little sad for the first time in a long time.
All my love,
You know Who

WEDNESDAY, OCTOBER 11, 1967: The ships have now moved to Vung Tau in preparation for another Rung Sat operation. After the last few operations, the Rung Sat will be somewhat of a relief. This makes me laugh cynically. The Jungle of Death will be a relief? We'll see.

A new eight day operation has begun and is designed for small unit ambushes at night. I decide to stay aboard ship and catch up on some long neglected things such as sermon preparation, correspondence and reports. I'll go out in a day or two.

FRIDAY, OCTOBER 13, 1967: Friday the 13th, my lucky day. The operation is called off. Another day of rest.

SATURDAY, OCTOBER 14, 1967: Today is memorial service day. Since the operation ended prematurely, I have the service for Alpha Company for two of their KIAs and another for four from Bravo Company. We leave tomorrow for another Rung Sat operation.

A new Spanish speaking soldier knows little English and doesn't want to go to the field. He has a concern that if orders are given, he won't understand and will not know what to do. I wonder if a hillbilly would have the same problem if his platoon leader were from Boston.

Two soldiers are having trouble at home. Another has a police record and has just received a Dear John letter. According to him, he has a long rap sheet. He's the umpteenth soldier who has received such a letter. The next worst thing to this is getting no mail at all.

I am discovering that it is not unusual for young enlisted men frequently want out of the field because of their fears of combat and death. This fear can cause a soldier to risk being court-martialed, ridiculed and even kicked out of the army. These extremes are expected, occasionally, from some of the enlisted men. However, we have two officers who also succumb to their fears.

In *The Wizard of Oz*, the Wizard is a loud and boisterous bully. When exposed, though, he's a scared and vulnerable little boy in a man's body. The Wizard's use of intimidation keeps people away so that, hopefully, his flaws will not be exposed. Our Wizard is an officer in 3/60th with a habit of talking loud and gruff to his soldiers. He patronizes them by calling them "Son" and most of his soldiers quickly learn to dislike him.

In one recent and memorable battle, the battalion commander told the Wizard to relocate his soldiers. The Wizard said, "No, I'm returning to the boats." He disobeyed a direct order and chickened out in a time of battle. The command and control monitor pulled up to where the Wizard was loading his troops and our S-3 (operations officer) had an animated conversation with him. After this "persuasion" the Wizard reluctantly took his troops back ashore.

A few days later, back at the ship, the Wizard spent a lot of time talking with me. It's obvious he's terrified. I feel both sorry and contempt for him. Condescending remarks abound throughout the 3/60th about his quitting under fire.

Inside, this man who wants to be seen as macho is another very scared little boy. Perhaps I'm the only one who sees this part of him. We later learn that the Wizard coerces someone under him to put him in for the Silver Star for the battle from which he quit. This really angers some of his officer peers.

Then there is The Ghost. I see him hunkered down in the corner of the aid boat. His platoon has just been hit hard, and the battle is continuing. Several are wounded and the non-wounded are merged into another platoon. The Ghost, who's the lieutenant platoon leader, has left the nearby position of his soldiers and has come to the aid boat.

"What are you doing here?" I ask him, thinking maybe he, too, has been wounded.

"Since the platoon's been all shot up, I can't help them anyway." He mutters, not looking directly at me. It's apparent that his fear has overcome him.

A few weeks after this incident, we go into a semi hot landing zone. On the ground, I hear someone curse and say, "That SOB Ghost Lieutenant stayed on the chopper." The Ghost told his platoon sergeant just before touchdown that he was having stomach problems and that he needed to go in. Then, he stayed on the chopper.

Someone else says, "He has stomach problems all right - no guts."

The feelings and behaviors of these two men caused others to look down on them. It is proof that an officer's rank is no shield against terror.

11:50 P.M.
Saturday, October 14, 1967
Hello Sweets,
How does the 3rd or 4th of January sound for R&R? My new brigade chaplain wants to take his beginning Jan 18th because his wife is in school and will be on break then. We both shouldn't be gone at the same time because that would leave only one protestant chaplain for the entire brigade . . . I can't believe that Christmas is just two months away. We will be in Hawaii before we know it. Everyone says it's the best week they have ever spent.

SUNDAY, OCTOBER 15, 1967: For a change, we leave for an operation at midday instead of midnight. This operation is to be small platoon-sized ambush operations in several locations of the Rung Sat. We have received many new troop replacements over the past couple of weeks, and this operation in part is to orient them to small unit operations.

MONDAY, OCTOBER 16, 1967: During the day troops are congregated at the fire support base. Some sleep; others swim. A passerby would think that we were having a picnic, except there's no grill to warm our C-rations, which are about as appealing as eating grub worms.

TUESDAY, OCTOBER 17, 1967: We end the operation and head in. I suddenly have a strange burning sensation in my eyes and nose. Everyone on the aid boat is hollering, "Gas, gas!" No one has gas masks. I run to the side of the boat and reach into the water to wet my handkerchief and hold it over my eyes and nose. Someone motions me into the boat's engine room. Two sailors and one army medic are already there seeking safety from the gas.

We can't figure out the origin of the gas. Then we learn it was dropped from one of our planes to harass the VC. We're harassed more than they are. Finally, after about ten minutes, we cruise out of the gas zone.

WEDNESDAY, OCTOBER 18, 1967: Mail call brings a letter from Ted's father.

Ted's body was one of two we left in the field overnight when we couldn't evacuate them until the next morning. I remember examining his injury and seeing that the entry wound to his head was very small and the exit wound, to my surprise, was also relatively small.

What is it like to lose a son? When the dreaded visit to one's home by a uniformed officer and a chaplain occurs to tell you your boy has been killed 12, 000 miles away, only those who have been on the receiving end of that information can understand the shock and anguish it brings.

How does one process the shock and anger of losing a son, whether to cancer, a car accident, a drug overdose or from a VC bullet? Grief causes us to respond in different ways. This father obviously loved his son dearly, and he processes his grief by going on the attack.

He writes letters to me, to the company commander, the division commander and who knows how many others. The essence of all his letters are, "Why was my son, a 'green' troop, on the front line?" In broken English, he writes that he's a member of the American Legion, he knows his Ohio senator and he has ways of "finding things out."

As I read his letter, my heart immediately goes out to him in his pain. I imagine how I would feel if I lost my son Grey. His frustration and anguish gushes forth in his letter. He wants answers, although answers will never be enough to assuage his pain and grief.

The company commander and I meet with the battalion commander, and we all agree that we should respond to this grieving father. Of course, when Ted died, we all sent the normal official letters of condolence as is required.

I again write to Ted's father that his son died a hero. I explain that Ted took over a machine gun from a wounded buddy. When he raised up to cock the M-60, a single VC bullet caught him in the head and he died instantly.

Ted was like all new troops; here to replace other troops, who have been killed, wounded or rotated out. Every soldier is "green." There's no way to ease into combat. It's like taking a bath; you get wet. Ted's death would be no less painful if he'd been here for months.

Ted, Sr. expresses his pain via letters and a desire to "get to the bottom of this," as if a crime has been committed. War *is* a crime. When people kill people, it is criminal.

FRIDAY, OCTOBER 20, 1967: Carl tells me that his girlfriend is pregnant. I'm not sure if I believe him. He wants leave to go home and marry her.

Yet, there's something believable about him. Maybe if my daughter Kellie were pregnant, and the father wanted leave to go home and get married, "to give the baby a name," I'd want someone to 'go to bat' too. I tell Carl the documentation he must get from the states in order to have a chance of leave. I send him on his way wondering if he'll follow through.

Later in the day, Carl's cousin, David, also in 3/60th, comes to me with essentially the same tale. This seems rather too coincidental to me, but I keep my cool. I don't challenge David or let on that I believe that he and Carl are taking me for a ride. I only repeat what I've told Carl about documentation. I think, well, Lois Lane was pretty dumb not to see through Clark Kent, but I am no Lois Lane.

I'm surprised. They both get documentation, both go home and marry their pregnant girlfriends and both return. Carl, in fact, becomes a gung-ho troop and takes a great deal of pride in being a machine gunner. So much for Lois Lane. Maybe Superman is real after all.

SATURDAY, OCTOBER 21, 1967: Yesterday the ships moved back to the Soi Rap area below Saigon. Today, we begin another operation. I'm with Bravo Company. We move about 1500 meters and come to a wet, gooey, sticky gunk called mud. We sink knee deep with each step. The hot sun at midmorning, the high humidity, the loads we're carrying and the thick mud makes for serious energy depletion.

Will, the company commander, calls me by radio to the HQ element. I can tell by his voice that he is madder than a wet setting hen. A new man I'll call Oscar has told him he wants to quit. How do you quit in the middle of mud? Will, livid, says, "Either you continue to hump with us or we leave you behind." He wants me to talk with Oscar

Oscar is nineteen, out of shape and looks like he's ready to cry. He's not sure if Will is serious about leaving him behind. I tell Oscar that I'll help him through the mud. I take his weapon and some of his gear so that all he has to do is move himself through the mud.

With each step, I help pull him out of the knee deep mud. We're all struggling. The tide is out and this makes it even worse. Oscar is huffing and puffing like an old steam locomotive. I imagine instead of saying, "I think I can, I think I can," he is thinking, "I know I can't, I know I can't." I feel sorry for him. I keep talking to him trying to encourage him by reminding him that we'll soon be to higher ground. This reminds me of once when I was a kid, one of our mules got loose from the pasture, went into the woods, became entangled in a thicket of vines and couldn't get out. It took several men to finally get that old mule freed.

Finally, we reach high and solid ground. Will talks to Oscar, not as a threatening boss, but as a consoling father.

"I knew you could do it," he tells Oscar, "Keep up the good work."

SUNDAY, OCTOBER 22, 1967: Vietnamese elections are to be held again. A cease-fire is to go into effect at noon today. Our objective is to set up and stay in one place but not maneuver during the cease fire.

We set up at the edge of another small village. A former Buddhist pagoda becomes our command post. All three companies are linked in the village. The day is a lazy one of drying out for most of the troops. This is a vast contrast from yesterday's mud. The villagers are congenial and friendly to us.

A beautiful little girl of about ten takes a special liking to me. Her grandfather calls her "ti ti Ba", which means little girl. She has a lovely temperament. She knows a little English and I talk to her periodically throughout the afternoon. I have fantasies of adopting her and taking her home to the states out of this mess. I miss my own little Kellie more than ever.

Joe Jenkins, the commander of Echo Company, and I have become good friends. We take an entire case of C-ration meals and empty the meat cans into a large pot borrowed from one of the mamasans. We build a small fire under the pot, add dried onions, some hot sauce and bring the "mulligan stew" to a simmer. We invite the Vietnamese from the hooch to eat with us. This is different from their fish heads and rice. What would they think of fried chicken, mashed potatoes, black-eyed peas, collard greens and cornbread? What would I think about it? But, the stew is very tasty. They giggle as they eat it and we offer them chocolate, peanut butter and other sundries from the C-rations.

Joe and I talk about July 25th when he came under fire for the first time. Being a reconnaissance company, some of them were on a mission on some small Vietnamese river boats up the canal called Route 66 when they were ambushed. They took several casualties. As Joe was calling on the radio for artillery during the ambush, he was screaming so loudly into his radio transmitter that no one could understand where he was or what he wanted.

Joe told me, "Chaplain, they wanted me to speak calmly when people were trying to kill me! Hell, this isn't a movie. This crap's for real. How could I speak calmly when those SOBs were trying to send me to the hereafter?" Joe is volatile but always keeps things in perspective. He's a neat guy.

After dinner, the Vietnamese offer us some rice alcohol and Vietnamese cigarettes. I try some of both and they each burn like the homemade white lightnin' my cousin and I sampled when I was a small boy. We drank it straight and thought we were going to die on the spot. I didn't take a second drink of the moonshine and I don't take a second drink of this rice alcohol.

The day has been lazy. Boots dry in the sun. I could take more of this. No fighting, snipers, air assaults, ambushes or booby traps. Days like today, without firefights, are about like R&R. Well, not quite. I tell myself to enjoy this down time while it lasts, because it won't.

MONDAY, OCTOBER 23, 1967: The elections are over. We move out and hump inland for 300 meters. Then, we come to more mud as we cross a huge but shallow canal. The tide is out and in no time we're in waist-deep mud; mucky gunk again. Mothers complain of a little dirt. What would they say now about their sons, caked in mud from armpits downward?

We cross several canals by way of the narrow footbridges constructed out of reeds. What a trip! Balancing on these is hard. This is worse than a wing walker on a biplane during an ice storm. The handrails are very shaky and only about ankle high. After three or four guys have crossed, the narrow reeds become covered with mud. Thankfully none of the hated little bridges are booby trapped today.

We stop for awhile and rest. Bravo Company's lead platoon is next to a small swamp. They ask for permission to fire. They've spotted a rather large snake in the water and want to kill it. Permission is granted and I hear several single shots and a lot of laughing. I investigate.

"You guys shoot the bull better than you can shoot a snake," Lieutenant Ball, the platoon leader (called Curve Ball) teases.

"Let the chaplain have a shot," says a soldier.

"Chaplain," says Curve Ball. "Show them how to kill a snake."

Several soldiers hand me their M-16s. I haven't fired a weapon since I "qualified" at Ft. Knox in April. I take the nearest M-16.

"Where's ole Lucifer?" I ask.

Then, I see the snake, click off the M-16 safety, take quick aim and fire off one round. Mud, water, and pieces of snake explode high above the water.

The whole platoon cheers as if I'd just scored the winning touchdown in the Super Bowl. For the next several days they call me, "Chaplain, The Snake Killer." They tell me that the next time we get into a firefight, they want me to do the shooting.

Soon, the temporary frolicking is over. We move out rapidly and even Oscar is hustling. Morale is good because we're no longer in mud, the VC aren't trying to kill us and we're going to be extracted.

As the troops are loading onto the boats, our new brigade commander, Col. Bert David, lands his chopper nearby and Will, Dick Botello and I have a conversation with him. I like this new brigade commander's easy-going way.

I'm not certain how Col. David found out about the snake so quickly, but he has already heard and, with a twinkle in his eye, congratulates me on being such a good shot.

10:20 P.M.
Monday, October 23, 1967
Hello Sweets,
I'm pretty tired; walking in the mud and sleeping on hard ground does that . . .

TUESDAY, OCTOBER 24, 1967: The ships move back to Vung Tau. We'll have two days off and then we're back to the Rung Sat for a three day operation. After then, we'll off load back to Dong Tam.

WEDNESDAY OCTOBER 25, 1967: I have lunch at the hospital with a physician who wants to talk about war, which he's very much against. He feels pulled in one direction by being a pacifist in a combat zone and in another way by treating those who're wounded in war. I want to tell him, "Who's not against war?" but that would be inappropriate. Besides, I think he just wants me to listen, not comment. A person who needs to talk and be heard is seldom be in a position to hear. Since I'm a good listener, I do what I'm good at. This is his agenda, not mine.

THURSDAY, OCTOBER 26, 1967: The operation is delayed for twenty-four hours. Hurrah! Another day of rest.

10:20 P.M.
Thursday, October 26, 1967
Hello Sweets,
This will be short . . . I haven't gotten to sleep yet and it's less than 4 hours 'til I have to get up for the operation. You asked about Bobby Hogan. I know him well. He got in country about the same time I did. He was on that boat that got wiped out.

FRIDAY, OCTOBER 27, 1967: I leave with Alpha Company. Ira Owens, a lieutenant with much field experience, is the new acting company commander. He's quiet and unassuming. I've chosen to go on this operation with Alpha Company because of their transition.

We beach and the going is rough; same old Rung Sat. We see the sun in few places because of the foliage. At midmorning we stop and form a blocking force. Much of our movement is on hands and knees through this miserable swamp.

We move out again crossing several canals. This is always "fun." At 5:00 P.M., we begin setting up our night positions. Everything is wet and it's obvious that high tide tonight will get us all. I begin building a nest for myself by tearing 100 or so small branches and making a pile. I know there'll be little or no sleep tonight.

It's dark now. I've just eaten some C-rations. I'm still wet and miserable. The Vietnamese national birds are coming to life; mosquitoes are everywhere. I cover my exposed body with my repellent and this helps some. At 10:00 P.M., I can tell the tide is gradually coming up. It's pitch black. Squad positions are close by but no one can see anyone else. The VC don't come. But the high waters do. Inch by inch, the water level rises. I hear the sounds of playful crabs as they come in with the dirty water.

As I lie on my bed of broken and piled branches, sleep is only a wishful thought. After 11:00 P.M., the water is around my feet and for the next several hours, I'm alone with my thoughts in the dark swamp. Night discipline is crucial; no sounds can be made, lest enemy sneaking up be given our locations. Our positions tonight won't be given away by any of us talking in our sleep because no one can sleep.

At 1:00 A.M., I want to smoke. The only safe way to smoke is hunkered down and completely covered by my poncho to block any light escaping from a match or lighted cigarette. I carefully drape the poncho over myself in a squatted position with my rear in the water. I am looking forward to the pleasure of having my smoke. My lighter has been broken the past several days so I have to use C-ration matches. I discover they are wet! No smoke tonight.

SATURDAY, OCTOBER 28, 1967: I spend the time now trying to calculate today's day and date. Best I can figure, it is October 28th. One year ago today, I was promoted to captain at Ft. Knox! That was my first active duty promotion. That's 'high cotton.' So, what am I doing here in a wet, scary swamp with no dry matches? There ain't no cotton here. Big deal. Here, privates and captains are all alike - we're all miserable.

At 4:00 A.M., the tide begins to recede. Then, it's first light and time to rise and shine. I settle for my C-rations instead of a breakfast buffet.

I circulate to the various positions in our small perimeter. I try to be jovial and encouraging to the tired and old looking kids. After resupply, we have another tough day moving through the swamp. The times we can move standing up instead of on hands and knees are scarce. We stop numerous times, cross countless canals, but we don't find the VC.

It's getting late, and we haven't reached our anticipated position to remain overnight yet. The tide is out so the Boston whale boat cannot reach us for resupply. We move to another canal where the water is thought to be deeper. To get there, we move through knee deep mud for several hundred meters. Fatigue is overcoming many of the guys. No one is joking. Tension is showing on all our faces. Supplies must be ferried by hand the last 100 meters because the water is still too shallow for the whale boat to maneuver close to us.

We set a very tight perimeter of not more than fifty meters in diameter. For a company position, this is very small. Twenty minutes after we stop it is pitch dark. No one has time to eat before dark as night defensive positions and potential fields of fire must always be established should we be hit during the night. I bend over four small saplings, tie them together with my belt, and figure that somehow, I can use the trunk of them as my "pillow" while using the body of the four as my mattress.

After dark, when there's time to eat, no one can even see what's written on the C-ration cans, so we just open C-rations pot luck, not knowing and, being so exhausted, not caring what delicacies are inside. We can't use our normal pinch of C-4 plastic explosive to heat our cans because even a small flame could give away our positions. The cold C-rations taste like wet sawdust.

High tide is at 2:20 A.M., so I know that if I sleep, I must do it soon. A few soldiers tie their ponchos to trees and make themselves a hammock. I don't dare try such an engineering feat.

I'm exhausted. It's been two days of wet, muddy hell and no rest. I'm lying on my four sapling bed, and all that comes are the crabs with the creeping in of the tide. First, water oozes into my already-wet boots, then it fills my pants. This is like lying in a bath tub with my clothes on. I'd like to pull the plug on this stinking Rung Sat bath tub. Then we could all go home.

Night discipline is tough when we're so exhausted. Even though we're no more than five feet apart, none of us can speak. The water is now knee deep. I'm hoping that the tide doesn't bring snakes. But, I'm almost too tired to care.

Suddenly, I hear a loud noise to my right followed by whispered cursing and more whispers of, "Be quiet, be quiet." A soldier has fallen out of his poncho hammock into the knee deep water.

Everyone must stand in place. If someone must move, it's literally at a snail's pace. Periodically, I hear whispered cursing. No one sleeps. Talk about being lonesome in a crowd.

The water eventually reaches my waist, which is almost chest high for some of the guys. Will morning ever get here? Each moment is agony. I play mental games. I fantasize about home. I replay football games I played in high school and college. I speculate where old teammates are and what they might be doing. I limit my mental images to positive thoughts. Time moves like cold molasses on a winter morning.

My bones ache I'm so tired. I stand . . . and stand . . . and stand. I periodically drape my poncho over my head and smoke. Pure delight. After wet matches last night I've made sure I have plenty of dry matches for tonight. One thing is for sure; we don't have to worry about setting the woods on fire.

At 3:30 A.M., a soldier who has been on edge for several days finally breaks. He suddenly begins cursing loudly and flailing around in the water as if he is striking at some unknown enemy. His explosion frightens many of us because no one knows what is going on. A sergeant and another man grab him and order him quiet, and in his temporary psychotic state he tries to hit them. He strikes one of them on the steel helmet, almost breaking his fingers.

After ninety seconds of his thrashing, he stops, as quickly as he began. Ira Owens has sloshed his way the few meters to his position and calls for me. I wade to their location, which is about twenty meters away.

I know the panicked soldier, having talked with him several times before. Even in non-combat situations, it has been obvious to me that he isn't bound too tightly. I'm surprised he hasn't broken before now. I gently invite him under my poncho for a smoke and he agrees. I light his cigarette and begin whispering to him. He settles down quickly. The only glimpse I have of him is under the light of my match. When he takes a drag off his cigarette, his face is drawn and tired and older looking than his twenty years, older looking than it was only two days ago. I ask him about home, family, school and anything else I can think of as we stay hunkered under my poncho, smoking.

We stay here for perhaps an hour. The water is now gradually receding as the tide slowly moves out. As soon as either of us finishes one cigarette, I light another. It's not that I want another smoke, but the only way I can really read his face in the darkness is when I strike a match. With each lighted match, I can see that he is getting more relaxed.

I stay with him until first light, assuring him throughout the ordeal that light will come before long and we'll be out of the night. By first light, he's whispering apologies for "acting like a baby." I assure him that it's okay.

SUNDAY, OCTOBER 29, 1967: Morning is finally here and we move out to be extracted. As we move, I keep asking the soldiers if they remembered to make their beds. Everyone thinks this is funny. This is the first time there's been any laughter in two days.

We're extracted, only to move to another larger island where we move inland. I'm wondering if we can take a 3rd day like the past two. Fortunately, the terrain here is not as bad.

Then, the good news we've been waiting for the past three days comes: "Prepare to move out for extraction." This energizes everyone. We get to the waterway, pop a purple smoke grenade so the boats will see where we are, we load and move out for the ships. The operation is over at last.

Purple smoke! Purple has a Biblical symbolism of royalty. Royalty never experienced what we have for the past three days. I do wish some of the politicians who keep this war going could, though. Regardless of what they think of themselves, they aren't royalty.

MONDAY, OCTOBER 30, 1967: There's some talk that the navy ships will soon go to Subic Bay in the Philippines for about six weeks of repairs. Sounds like an extended Christmas vacation to me. If they leave, we'll be doing riverine operations out of Dong Tam until they return. The river rats, of course, will stay here.

It seems like half the soldiers want to talk to me today, so my desperately needed rest will have to wait. We're moving to Dong Tam Wednesday with plans to off load on Thursday and Friday.

7:00 P.M.
Monday, October 30, 1967
Hello Sweets,
I plan to do some Christmas shopping when I get to Dong Tam at the PX and send the rest of the money for R&R fund. I think I'll talk to the brigade chaplain and tell him I'm putting in for R&R for the 8th or 9th of January. It isn't long off, is it? Take it easy, greasy. You are the greatest.

TUESDAY, OCTOBER 31, 1967: In the evening, we go to the Vung Tau officers club for a party for the original officers who came over with the 3/60th. The party is a whopper. There are steaks, farewell speeches and much booze. Most everyone is blown away by the end of the evening. Though I'm happy they're going home, I'm guiltily sad for me. I've just finished four months, although it seems like a lifetime. I still have eight months to go. I'm jealous.

It takes an hour for the shuttle boat to reach the *Colleton* and all the drunks are in a singing mood. Several are so drunk they must be carried aboard. As much as I like these guys, as a non-drinker, I've never had much patience with those who over-indulge. They always seem to want to talk religion with me, but when sober, that is the furthest thing from their minds.

WEDNESDAY, NOVEMBER 1, 1967: Today the ships leave Vung Tau and head for Dong Tam. The trip takes until mid-afternoon. We encounter some very rough water in the South China Sea. The navy says we have about ten foot seas. The ship becomes 'puke city.'

Once anchored, I have to wait an hour and half on the pontoon for the shuttle boat to take us to Dong Tam. The Great Wall of China could be built in the time it takes to wait on these shuttle boats. Dong Tam was mortared again last night. I join several other officers at the Dong Tam officer's club for another round of partying. It's a good time. Then LTC Doty, Joe Jenkins, Floyd Buch, a few others and I go to the navy officers club at Dong Tam.

When it's time to return to the ship, we meet the pre-arranged army Boston whale boat operator. It's 10: 00 P.M., raining very hard and the wind is blowing. It's darker than a bat cave. I'm uneasy about heading out into the My Tho River in such a small boat and no lights in this storm. The boat is only sixteen feet long and five of us are aboard.

By the time we get to the river, we hit three foot waves. None of us has life jackets. I am frightened because the ships have no lights, the rain is coming down in buckets, the wind is blowing what seems like gale force and none of us, whale boat driver included, knows where we're going.

I'm afraid that we'll be swamped by the waves. If this happens, there's no way any of us can possibly be saved. No one would even know we're missing until in the morning. I pray, hard.

We cruise at a slow speed for what seems like an eternity. Tension is high, as are our pucker factors! Then we see it! The huge silhouette of a large black ship. We're no more than fifty feet from it when we spot it. The good news is that this is a ship. The bad news is that this is the *Benewah*, not the *Colleton*. We pull alongside the pontoon and a sailor points us in the direction of the *Colleton*. We set out again in the dark.

Being the little green uniformed homing pigeons that we are, we ride the river waves directly to the *Colleton*. It's sweet relief.

THURSDAY, NOVEMBER 2, 1967: The scared lieutenant moving out of my room is an interesting study. Floyd Buch has already moved out but he forgot to take a fifth of Seagram's 7 that he had secretly stashed away. Tommy, the Medical Service Corps lieutenant who is also one of my room-mates, is petrified when he learns that Floyd has left the booze here. Remembering the hassle over booze when we moved aboard three months ago has him spooked, and Tommy is a very sheltered guy. He is scared that the navy will be displeased if they learn of the booze. I tell him I'll take it and I quickly stash it in my bag. I figure I can use it for future trading material should I need to.

"Relax, Tommy, what will the navy do, make us stay on board? If push comes to shove, I'll tell them it is communion wine." Tommy's lower jaw drops in disbelief.

I finally get to Dong Tam and unpack. I'm not in my hooch ten minutes when guys begin coming by for counseling. A support soldier has been on R&R for seven days and wants to marry a girl he met there. When a G.I. is away from women very long, their infatuation is often mistaken for true love.

A big talking, lying and alcohol-dependent senior medic stops by. He's drunk, so I tell him I'll see him later, and fortunately he leaves.

We've been doing riverine operations for three months and we're now back to Dong Tam. What a difference three months makes.

CHAPTER FOUR

November 3, 1967–December 31, 1967

FRIDAY, NOVEMBER 3, 1967: Paul, my former assistant, has rotated back to the real world and a new Paul (Cherkas) is now my assistant. He's from Rhode Island and I already like him a lot. I tease Paul about Rhode Island, saying it is neither a road nor an island.

Today is adjustment day for everyone. Now that we're all back in Dong Tam, most of the troops are new enough that on arrival they went directly to the boats, and thus are not very familiar with Dong Tam. The rest of us are rather like high school guys who've been away at college for a while and now are back home for the summer.

SUNDAY, NOVEMBER 5, 1967: At 3:00 A.M., the mortar siren goes off indicating that we're under a mortar attack. The siren is a new addition. In July, everyone just yelled as we ran to the bunkers. Unfortunately, the siren goes off about three minutes after we're in the bunkers. This is mortar attack number eight that I've been in since my arrival. Tonight we receive thirty-nine rounds.

I am feeling terrible today because of a soldier named Jim. He, like so many others, came to me several days ago wanting to change his military occupation specialty (MOS) because his father was ill. I learned that Jim already had received several Article 15s, an administrative punishment usually resulting in a small fine, reduction in rank, and/or extra duty. Jim's Article 15s are for several infractions.

It's not my nature to be harsh, but I do confront Jim about the Article 15s and his using his father's illness as a reason to get out of the field. Later, Jim comes to me again and wants emergency leave. His father is still sick. I explain that the American Red Cross must verify the emergency and that it must be a life or death issue in order for leave to be granted. I explain all the steps that must be taken. In a few days, Jim is killed in combat. He was a less than desirable soldier, yet, he died in combat. What more can any man give than his life, regardless of his character, behavior, or values?

As I reflect on Jim, I realize he wanted from me something I couldn't give and that was for him to get out of the field and go home. What I could have given, but didn't, was perhaps more compassion and empathy. I do feel terrible about this. I can't second guess myself. I do the best I can. I must move on.

TUESDAY, NOVEMBER 7, 1967: We fill sand bags for my hooch and when we're finished for the evening, I'm soaked with sweat. I head to the shower point, looking forward to a nice refreshing shower. But, it's broken and won't be repaired until some time tomorrow. When working, this shower is a wonderful experience compared to previously having to use a bucket punched with holes that is hung overhead on a crossbar. Tonight, I sleep dirty and sweaty, but at least I am not sleeping in the field.

> *10:00 P.M.*
> *Tuesday, November 7, 1967*
> *Hello Sweets,*
> *I got your package today finally. The oatmeal cookies are still good. The glazed pecans are delicious. It's getting closer and closer to the time for R&R; I can't believe that I'll be able to see you the children in 2 months.*

THURSDAY, NOVEMBER 9, 1967: What a day! Or rather, what a night and day. At 1:00 A.M., the mortars came in again. This time, the trusted siren goes off five minutes after the first round hits. So much for timing. We're long since in the bunkers when the "warning" is sounded. Then again, maybe last night's late alarm was just an early warning for tonight.

Our road runner tracks have been ambushed. The dustoffs begin arriving. I see too many familiar faces. David Hershberger has fragment wounds to his shoulder and burst ear drums. I've been in several fire fights with David, including the day on October 5th that we landed in the hot LZ. It looks like David will be okay and will fight again. A new second lieutenant has been shot in the knee.

A new PFC, 'Reggy', has some gruesome-looking wounds. Sections of tissue have been blown from his jaw and his leg is injured badly. His face looks like it has been in a meat grinder. Some plastic surgeon will earn his pay patching up these wounds. Reggy can barely talk and I wonder if his jaw is broken. It appears some teeth and other tissue from his mouth are missing as well. All told, nine from Alpha Company are wounded, as well as two supporting personnel from other units.

We also have two KIAs. This road runner operation is costly for such a short fight. In addition to the one track that's completely taken over by the VC, another is hit by a B-40 rocket and is burned.

I get back from the hospital just in time for breakfast. Numerous soldiers question me about the details. They have come to know that I usually have more information than anyone else does, since I can access both the tactical operations center and hospital sources.

Paul and I had planned to go to the orphanage this morning, but since I've been awake since shortly after midnight, we decide we need sleep. I sleep in my own sweat as the morning heat begins to build. Minutes after falling to sleep my field phone rings again, informing me that we have still another dustoff coming in. I get up and head back to the hospital

Two wounded from division headquarters in Bear Cat are brought in. One of the wounded tells me that he was in a two and one-half ton truck bringing supplies to Dong Tam from Saigon when he hit a mine halfway between My Tho and Dong Tam. I realize that could have easily been Paul and me. We'd have been on that stretch of road heading to the orphanage at just about the same time as the truck.

In early afternoon, two calls come in from the berm on the west bank of Dong Tam. The report is that a grenade has exploded. Three soldiers were manning one of the bunkers. Two apparently had left their duty to visit a nearby cat house across Route 66, and I don't mean for a veterinarian visit. While they were gone, a VC sneaked up and threw a grenade into the bunker. The soldier who stayed in the bunker later says that the VC threw it in, it was a dud and the VC threw another grenade and that one exploded. This soldier claims he slept through both grenades; yeah, and I believe in the tooth fairy.

One soldier was wounded because the other two weren't on guard, and the man inside was either sleeping or not being vigilant while on guard. All three will be disciplined via court martial. This attack came in mid-afternoon in broad daylight. The VC are getting much more aggressive and brave.

Then, late afternoon, reports come in that the VC are periodically taking potshots at vehicles between Dong Tam and My Tho. This is particularly bothersome, because that's the only road in and out of Dong Tam. This environment around Dong Tam has changed for the worst since my arrival.

9:15 A.M.
Thursday, November 9, 1967
Hello Sug,
I'm pretty tired this morning. Unless things get to improving, I'm going to request reassignment after I get R&R. If it sounds like I'm disgusted, I am. I guess I am just tired because there's been only one night I've gotten any decent sleep since I got off the ship. It does me good to pop off at times. I received a letter today you wrote at the beauty shop. Are you curly now? I

can't believe Kellie will be 3 tomorrow. I wish I could be there but I'll make up for lost time. Three years ago, I was a happy man when I first saw that little girl. I was just as thrilled when I saw that fat little boy, too. I don't guess you ever get over the thrill of seeing your child for the first time. It's just 60 days 'til you know what. I've already been here 135 days. In just over a month, I'll be under 200 days to go. Take it easy, greasy.

I wonder about the powers that make strategy in this war. President Johnson knows more about pulling the ears of his beagles than he does of the reality of this war. I see the vast increase of VC activity in the Delta in the past three or four months and I wonder why so few combat troops are here. We have three battalions in the Mobile Riverine Force and only two other infantry battalions in the entire Delta. Only five infantry battalions in an area with one third of the Vietnamese population, and the VC activity is dramatically increasing. This makes no sense to me.

Long Binh, Bear Cat, Vung Tau, and numerous other places where headquarters are located are loaded with thousands of troops who have no idea what this war is really about. Yet, we have many infantry battalions protecting those areas that have had little or no VC activity in a long time. It seems like a tremendous waste of manpower.

We've had twenty-seven killed since my arrival. Furthermore, when some of our troops go to Bear Cat or Long Binh on military business, they are continually being given DR's, disciplinary requests, by MPs for such things as improper insignias and dirty uniforms. A DR is similar to a misdemeanor infraction in the civilian world. Additionally, many non-commissioned officers there seem to enjoy harassing our troops. If some of these clerks and jerks came down here and had to dodge bullets, rockets and booby traps, and wallow in the mud like my men do, they'd react drastically differently. I'm convinced they have no idea what's going on in the field.

I'm disgusted. A part of me screams from inside, "This isn't fair!!" How can our strategic leaders make decisions based on "position papers" and use body counts to measure the success of the war effort? I don't know about 'body counts.' What I do know is that every one of our dead American bodies counts—to their parents, wives, children and girlfriends. I sense a huge disconnection between our war and the war in Saigon, Long Binh, Bear Cat, and Washington. Politicians are out of touch with the impact of the real war.

FRIDAY, NOVEMBER 10, 1967: Today is Kellie's third birthday. I'm a little down, but I make a vow that if I make it out of here alive, I'll celebrate her fourth birthday with her.

SATURDAY, NOVEMBER 11, 1967: Butch Hartson is a lieutenant forward observer (FO) for the artillery and a really nice guy. An FO is a very important part to the infantry. He goes on the ground with us on combat operations, and when artillery is needed, he radios in. He relates the coordinates of our location, where he wants the artillery to impact, the kind of ordinance (high explosive, white phosphorus, etc), as well as how much artillery. The FO faces the same dangers as the infantryman.

Butch looks like he's about fifteen years old. He's been in country for about three months. The toll of combat distress has yet to age his youthful face. We discussed baptism as a means to reflect his decision to become a Christian. He decided that, if at all possible, he'd like to be baptized in Vietnam. We made plans for the baptism to be today in the turning basin.

Paul, Butch, three of his friends and I walk to the turning basin and I baptize him in the same murky waters that we've sloshed through together many times. This time, however, his baptism symbolizes Butch's new life in Christ. I'm thrilled for him.

We walk the 100 yards back to the hooch area to change out of our wet clothes. After I finish changing, the hospital calls and tells me we have casualties coming shortly. A mine has exploded on a MEDCAP. This is where our medical and civil affairs personnel go into a village to offer assistance to the local civilians, and this is where Paul and I would have been if not for Butch's baptism. Echo Company is pulling security for the MEDCAP and several are wounded, and we have at least one KIA.

Shortly after arriving at the hospital, four wounded soldiers are brought in, all with fragment wounds from the booby trap. Their blood covered fatigues are quickly cut away and discarded. The field bandages are removed so the trauma team can examine their wounds.

These guys are eager to talk about what has just happened. They tell me that everything was calm and that they were just relaxing around the perimeter of the village. Doc and his medics were setting up to do the MEDCAP when, suddenly, there was one loud explosion and they were all wounded. It apparently was a command detonated mine.

The dustoff has also brought the body of a KIA. I've been so busy with the four wounded that I haven't inquired who he is. The body bag is lying on the ground just outside the ward. I go out, unzip it, and am horrified to see that it's Second Lieutenant Stiver. He was new to the unit but I had spoken with him on several occasions. He was a caring lieutenant, eager to take care of his soldiers.

His face is so pale it hardly even looks like him. I move his arms to check his blood-covered dog tag to make absolutely sure it's him. When I move his arms, his left arm moves too easily. I hadn't noticed that it's almost completely detached from his body. A large fragment has all but severed his arm between his shoulder and elbow. Doc later tells me that he was only a few meters from Stiver and there was absolutely nothing he could do to help him.

I'm alone with Stiver's body. I feel a sense of rage boiling up in me. I can't take his death! He seems so alone here in the open air. His body is waiting for transportation to Saigon for graves registration and then back to his grieving family. It all is too final, too quick. He chose to live a good life. He didn't get a chance to choose how to die.

As I stand here, I realize that had I not baptized Butch Hartson a little while ago, I'd have been on the MEDCAP, too. A part of me is sorry I wasn't there. A bigger part of me is relieved. When you die, you need someone you like with you. Yet, Stiver died so rapidly that it wouldn't have mattered. Perhaps it would have mattered to me, though.

I know that in a few hours his family will get the awful news. I hurt for them already. Their lives will change forever. That's what death does, especially death like this, so far from home. I silently pray for his family.

I stay with Stiver for perhaps five minutes, mesmerized. Butch's baptism and Stiver's death are such a stark contrast. It's not fair. I hate it. But I must go on.

With the blast at the MEDCAP, Bravo Company is quickly summoned and is moved rapidly to sweep the tree line near where we took this morning's casualties. These guys aren't too happy about the quick move out but, like all combat operations, they don't have a vote.

I hear five guys are coming in early, wounded by another booby trap. I hop back to the hospital to meet their dustoff. They all have fragment wounds. Curve Ball, a platoon leader lieutenant, was hit in the thigh. Another got it in the leg, still another is wounded in his rear end. His pride is hurt more than his butt!

SUNDAY, NOVEMBER 12, 1967: My buddy Joe Jenkins tells me he wants to talk. As a black company commander of Echo Company, he was distressed to learn that a specialist 4 in his unit is a member of the KKK, or at least that's what Joe was told. The specialist has three K's marked on his camouflaged helmet cover. Joe is angry. He fantasizes about what he'd like to do to Mr. KKK and his fantasies aren't nice. Joe fears someone could easily be "accidentally" shot, and considers transferring the man out.

He settles down after we've talked for a while and decides that since paddy strength, the number of soldiers on an operation, has fast become an important issue, even an alleged KKK member is still an additional soldier in the field against the real enemy, the VC. Joe confronts the soldier and tells him to remove that crap from his helmet cover and to never display, comment, or behave as a member of the KKK again, else the consequences will be the worst ass-whipping he's ever had.

TUESDAY, NOVEMBER 14, 1967: Shortly after the September 15th ambush at Snoopy's Nose, I was informed that I would be recommended for a Bronze Star with "V" device for valor. I didn't know exactly what that meant. I've only been in the army for sixteen months, but I know that the Bronze Star Medal is a significant award. I guess back then, it didn't quite sink in.

It's now time for the awards ceremony. Several enlisted men and a few officers, including Doc, and Will Davis, also get awards. I'm honored to get the award, but a little mystified because I'm convinced that many of the soldiers are more deserving of this than I am.

I wish Barbara could have been here to share the ceremony, but then think, no, I wouldn't want her here in this god-forsaken place. I try to make a tape to her, but my recorder has been broken for two or three weeks and I haven't had time to get anyone to fix it. I know nothing about mechanical things—in fact, to me a sledgehammer is a precision instrument. I can barely wind my watch! Tapes are my lifeline to my loves.

When I hit the sack, I'm proud of my Bronze Star.

8:20 P.M.
Tuesday, November14, 1967
Hello Sweets
Did you know that you're married to a war hero? According to the citation, I'm a real hero. Ha! The citation was blown a bit out of proportion. The award for the Army Commendation Medal with "V" device for valor hasn't gotten back yet. I was put in for it for the battle on Oct 6th. Mother told me about Kellie picking the 2 morning glories for her and Daddy. How I miss her, miss watching her and Grey grow.

WEDNESDAY, NOVEMBER 15, 1967: I have the memorial service for Lt. Stiver. He was only here long enough to get killed.

I have a discussion with a soldier named Chuck. He's a relatively new soldier who doesn't think he should go to the field. He claims to be a member of the Jehovah's Witness group. They can be non-combatants if they can prove they're a member. I question him as to how he went through basic training and advanced individual training as a Jehovah's Witness. He tells me that he was converted while on leave prior to coming to Vietnam.

Convenient, I think. I explain the documentation necessary and he says he'll get that and meanwhile assumes he won't have to go into the field. I tell him that his commander is likely to send him to the field until he gets the documentation. He looks devastated.

Next, I talk with Tim. We were together when we were hit from the rear last month and we shared a "Holy smoke." I've seen him many times since. He feels guilty that his buddy was killed a few days ago. I can tell he is experiencing combat fatigue and decide to go to bat for him. He's been in the field for an extended period of time. I will try to get him reassigned.

We're scheduled to do another MEDCAP in nearby Vinh Kim today. C/3/60 is pulling security. The population is about 2000 and 1999 of these are children, it seems.

Just before noon, the Cao Dai (pronounced cow die) elder sends word to Paul and me that he'd be honored to have us attend their noonday service and join him for tea to follow. The US Army captain, an advisor to the local Army of the Republic of Vietnam (ARVN), is also invited. Paul and I accept the invitation.

As I'm walking to the temple, which is about 200 meters to the middle of the village, one of the soldiers asks me where I am going. I say, "To a Cao Dai service."

Looking puzzled, he says quite seriously, "How did the cow die"?

I stop long enough to explain what I know about the Cao Dai religion. He seems relieved that I don't have to conduct a funeral for a cow.

The Cao Dai is a relatively new religion that began in the local area and has now spread to other parts of Vietnam. It's a combination of Hinduism, Buddhism, Catholicism, Taoism and Shinto.

The small temple is very colorful with a prominent "eye" representing the primary vision of God looking over his children. One person plays a drum, another plays what looks like bongo drums, another has cymbals and another has a strange looking stringed instrument that makes a whining noise. The temple has many candles and the priests wear colorful robes.

I remove my boots and am ushered to a place of honor. Indeed, I do feel honored and the Vietnamese worshipers seem honored to have me.

After the service, we move to an annex where we're given some Vietnamese tea for refreshments. The annex has numerous porthole type openings which are low enough to the ground to see in from the outside. I'm surprised to see hundreds of kids and local women are observing us. They seem gratified to have a view of American "celebrities." We finish tea with some wonderful French bread that is a special treat. Paul and I shake hands with everyone, bow and are bowed to graciously. We leave and walk the short distance back to where the MEDCAP is being conducted.

We fly back to Dong Tam. Just as we left the MEDCAP, Charlie Company engaged in a firefight with some local VC. One soldier has a gunshot wound in the thigh. Another is more seriously wounded with a gun shot through the neck and another through the shoulder. He's hurt badly but they tell me he will probably survive.

THURSDAY, NOVEMBER 16, 1967: Today, I get a call from the hospital. Lt. Tony Normand has been brought in.

Most lieutenants are assigned to a line platoon soon after arrival. Tony was the exception. He was assigned as executive officer of Echo Company working for Joe Jenkins for the first couple of months. They made a good pair. Joe is extroverted and gung-ho. Tony is an organizer.

Tony came over with me on the same plane from the real world. We met in Oakland, processed at the 90th Replacement in Long Binh, went to Bear Cat and then ended up in the same battalion. Coming into the unit at the same time provides us some extra glue for bonding. I like Tony. He's down to earth, bright, and aware of what goes on around him. Also, Tony's father is a minister in Alabama, another link for us.

Tony's already known as Bad Luck Tony. First, in July, an explosion damaged his eardrums when he and Joe were on a reconnaissance mission with some RVN navy boats and were ambushed. Later, when he jumped into a drainage ditch during a fire fight, a rat bit Tony. This meant rabies shots. When the medic gave him his first shot in the stomach, the poor guy fainted, leaving the needle in Tony's stomach. Tony had to finish the injection himself. Then, he had a flare land next to him in the field a few weeks ago. The chances of a spent flare hurting you are all but unheard of, yet, it happened to Tony.

He's now assigned as the company commander in C/5/60, which left us last week to rejoin the 5/60th, and they left on operation yesterday morning. Prior to leaving, Tony had stopped by to see me.

Today, luck wasn't with Tony again. They were on patrol in an area called the Plain of Reeds when a VC in hiding with an AK-47 must have decided to perform a one man ambush. Tony discovered him, but the VC opened fire on him before Tony had a chance to react. He received eight bullet wounds; two in his arms, one in his leg and five in his torso. The medic said he had fallen in water and shouted, "I'm hit, don't let me drown." Tony was very close to death when he was dusted off to the 3rd Surg Hospital.

I arrive at the hospital and am shocked. Tony looks awful. He drifts in and out of consciousness. His blood pressure fluctuates wildly and the surgeons rush him into surgery.

I feel absolute rage at the VC. In the past, I've been angry, but this time it feels personal. Tony is my friend and it looks as if he will die. They tell me his surgery will take several hours.

When I return to my hooch, Lt. 'Capable' is there. Capable was recently given a field grade Article 15 and $300.00 fine, which is all but unheard of for an officer. He was drunk and AWOL overnight in My Tho, which was extremely risky. Capable is overweight and known to run his mouth. Now, he wants to talk. I don't. I want just a few moments to myself to grieve for Tony. Nevertheless I spend an hour listening to Capable's bewilderment about why the command is so upset with him. Internally, I'm in turmoil. Three hundred meters away, Tony is fighting for his life. Here in my hooch, I'm barely capable of listening to Lt. 'Capable.' I feel so torn. I'm here to minister to all, I know, regardless of my personal feelings. As I listen to 'Capable' talk, I try very hard not to let my true feelings show. I'm probably the only one who can or will listen to him. He finally leaves, giving me time to catch my emotional breath.

No sooner is 'Capable' gone than I see Ben coming. He suffers from low self-esteem. As washed out as I am, I muster up the emotional energy to interact with him for forty-five minutes, all the while wondering if Tony is still alive. When Ben leaves, I call the hospital. Tony is still in surgery.

It's long after dark and I need time to myself. I walk around for awhile. Everywhere I walk, I see someone who wants to talk. Usually, I cherish this type of interaction with the troops. But not tonight. I go to the motor pool, find my Jeep and just sit there for awhile. I pray for Tony.

FRIDAY, NOVEMBER 17, 1967: I go to the hospital. Tony has made it through the night. He's been cut open from Adams apple to pelvis and side to side. He has lost a kidney, spleen and part of his liver. He's awake but barely. He only has the energy to speak two or three words at a time. I just sit with him for a while, holding his hand. I'm not sure he'll make it.

In the afternoon, I return to the hospital, but Tony's asleep. In the evening, he sends word for me to come see him. He wants me to write Claudia, his wife. He wants her to know that he'll be okay. I don't exactly tell her that, but I do assure her that he has the best care available in Vietnam. Tony can still barely talk. He's frightened, and cries a little. Inside, I'm crying too. On the outside, I shed no tears. Perhaps I should.

Joe Jenkins sees Tony later and reports how uncomfortable he is with Tony's environment. Of course, he's hooked up to every imaginable tube known to medicine. The only thing Joe could think to say to Tony was, "Do you want a cigarette?"

Late afternoon today, I play basketball with the troops. During the game, I only think about playing and winning. I don't think of the hospital, or Tony, or the two KIAs yesterday, or the other wounded who are trying to recover. When the game is over, one of the soldiers tells me I was playing like a workhorse. I pray Tony's luck will turn.

9:30 P.M.
Friday, November 17, 1967
Hello Sweetheart,
I finally was able to find something today for Christmas presents for you and the kids. I went to the Vietnamese gift shop on post and got the kids each a pair of Vietnamese style PJs. I also bought 2 pieces of cloth with tigers on them to hang on the kid's walls. I won't tell you what I sent to you.

10:05 P.M.
Saturday, November 18, 1967
Hello Sweets,
Still no recorder. It is only seven or eight weeks now until you know what!! R&R! Thanksgiving is just next week. I'll try to borrow a recorder tomorrow and make some tapes.

6:10
Monday, November 20, 1967
Hello Sweets,
I bought a new recorder today - a Sony for $22.00. I just hope the speeds jive with yours.

TUESDAY, NOVEMBER 21, 1967: I fly to Bear Cat and visit the hospitals again. Reggy, whose jaw is messed up, is still here. He can speak only through clenched jaws. Benny had his leg removed and he's not accepting it too well. Nor am I. I take a letter to Wayne from his Thai girlfriend. He's absolutely delighted.

WEDNESDAY, NOVEMBER 22, 1967: I'm glad to get "home" so I can try out my new recorder. Then, I'm devastated. The tape is too fast. I can't figure out what is wrong. For weeks now, I've had nothing but trouble with recording and that's my lifeline to Barbara. Then, I discover another "part" in the recorder box. I put that on the recorder in place of another part and that changes the current from 60cc to 50cc, making the sound perfect. I'm elated with my new found mechanical ability. I fixed this without the use of a sledgehammer!

THURSDAY, NOVEMBER 23, 1967: For as long as I can remember, and until I left home, the ritual of Thanksgiving Day was hog killing time for my father. He has always prided himself on being able to raise good cattle, chickens, vegetables and fruit. Pop, however, was always proudest of his hogs.

Being a mill worker, he was always off work Thursday and Friday of Thanksgiving week. Since it was also cold enough to keep the meat from spoiling, Thanksgiving day was the day, year after year, that we killed hogs. From early morning before daylight, we did the whole works. We boiled the water in a huge black vat with fire underneath, shot the hog, delicately shaved off all the hair, completely dressed, cut up and processed the meat, including doing our own sugar curing of the hams. Friday morning after, we always had pork brains and eggs for breakfast, along with fresh sausage. What a treat!

As I get up this morning, I wonder if Pop has killed hogs today. Man, I miss the tradition. As I shave, I long for Thanksgiving at home instead of here in Vietnam. I guess I also long for my Pop.

However, today I have a busy day. We're bringing the My Tho orphans to Dong Tam for the first time. We've planned a big party for them with lots of food, games and entertainment.

We send a chopper to pick up Pastor Ha and his family and send several two and one-half ton trucks to get the orphans. We have a wonderful Thanksgiving day worship service, traditional Thanksgiving meal and then entertainment for the kids. In mid afternoon, we take the kids back to My Tho. They are filled with American turkey, dressing, all the trimmings, gifts, and we hope, a lifetime of memories of this day. I take a photo of Pastor Ha's family and a good time is had by all; except Echo Company, who is out on defensive patrol.

I get the all too familiar call that Echo Company has encountered another mine booby trap and casualties will be coming into the hospital via dustoffs. Four wounded are flown in, all with fragment wounds. Then, they unload the bodies! We have three KIAs!

What is worse, is that two of these dead soldiers had a very unique relationship that dates back to their basic training. One lived near their basic training camp and he and the other took weekend passes and visited his home. The buddy fell in love with his friend's sister. Their visits continued through advanced individual training and they both received orders to Vietnam together. Just before leaving for Vietnam, the sister and the friend became engaged.

Upon arriving in Vietnam, these two buddies requested assignment together and they ended up in the same division, brigade, battalion, company, platoon and squad together. They were fast friends, and now one VC mine has ended both their lives and one young woman has lost her brother and her fiancé all with one blast in a dirty war 12,000 miles away. This had the makings of a movie love story. Now, it's a horror story.

FRIDAY, NOVEMBER 24 1967: I see the four who were in yesterday's booby trap. They're still shaken knowing that three buddies were killed.

MONDAY, NOVEMBER 27, 1967: Today's memorial service for Wallace, Simpson and Daugherty, the three soldiers killed on Thanksgiving day, is especially difficult for me because I keep thinking about one sad young woman in the states who has lost a brother and a fiance.

Joe Jenkins schedules a company party later in the afternoon to help neutralize the feelings of loss for his soldiers. It's quite a party. One soldier there has a motto that is also mine. He periodically yells out, quite proudly, "If'n you ain't country, you ain't." He's proud of being from the country and so am I. I haven't always been, though. When I was in college, most of my football teammates were from large cities up north. I thought of these guys as somehow being superior to me because I was, "from the country."

The party has much food, booze, volleyball, and it is good for the troops to unwind. Not too far underneath our fun are the feelings of what this morning's memorial service represented; that we are all very mortal and only one blast away from injury or death.

TUESDAY, NOVEMBER 28, 1967: I go to My Tho and talk with Pastor Ha about a Christmas party we want to give for the kids. We visit his church, which is being renovated. It's a beautiful little church with pink highlights, and he obviously is thrilled to show it to us. Much of our service offerings have been given to help finance their renovations. He has really become a good friend. He's so courageous in what he's attempting to do in his little pink church; living out the gospel in action.

WEDNESDAY, NOVEMBER 29, 1967: Just before I left Dong Tam yesterday, I learned that 'Branch,' the outhouse terrorist of four months ago, is still in LBJ. We'd been told that he'd already been sent to Leavenworth. It's been several weeks since I've seen him, thinking he was no longer here. I don't want to, but I go by to see him. He's been sentenced to twelve years in prison. Still, I feel sorry for him. He's obviously a sick man. I hope he'll get help when he gets to Leavenworth. But, at least he cannot hurt my guys again.

THURSDAY, NOVEMBER 30, 1967: Battalion commanders in combat have very heavy stress. Command is limited to six months and one reason is stress. Not the kind of stress that the infantry soldier has in being shot at and subjected to booby traps, but the kind of stress that goes with being responsible for the lives and welfare of so many young men. Decisions made for combat operations can cost lives, and do, almost daily. Many of us on the ground see Patron 6 as safe and secure flying 2000 feet above us. It's easy to say that he's got a "pie" job compared to humping on the ground. Having the responsibility of so many on one's hands and conscience, though, can't be pie.

The other reason that command is limited to six months is that, career wise, combat command is a very important ticket to have punched. Junior lieutenant colonels want very badly to get a battalion commander job in combat. If he does well, he increases his potential for promotion to colonel and maybe general officer.

Battalion commander, Monk Doty, has met the limit to the amount of stress he can take. His command time is up today. He's ready to return to the world. Monk has decided to retire shortly, which surprises some of us.

John Hill will be the new battalion commander. Rumor has it that he'll be a "kick ass, take names" kind of commander. Some of the infantry officers have heard of him. Many commanders come in and "act bad" to get attention away from their predecessor and get focus on them. The intimidation of juniors is an effective device to get attention and devotion. Fear is a motivator, especially for career officers and NCOs. My fear is that LTC Hill will use fear as a motivator.

The ceremony is a typical change of command. The commanding general from division is here, troops are in formation, brief speeches are delivered and then it's over. A brief reception is held in the mess hall and then Monk leaves for the airstrip. I'm sad to see Monk leave. I've never had a boss change in the army before, so this is a new experience for me.

After dinner, we have the first staff meeting with LTC Hill. I'm still not sure I'll like him. He sounds gruff. I try to reserve my judgement of him for the time being. I'm not sure what kind of "King of the Hill" he'll be.

FRIDAY, DECEMBER. 1, 1967: When I awake this morning and realize it's a new month, I'm exhilarated to know that when the next month begins, it will be R&R month!

We've scheduled a memorial service for Homer Middleton from Bravo Company who was killed two days ago. I brief LTC Hill about the service. This is the first we've had together and he seems a little nervous about his role. I tell him what to say and assure him that I'll take care of the rest. All goes well.

MONDAY, DECEMBER 4, 1967: I council with a new man today. Jose wants out of the field and says he has diaphragm trouble and can't eat. He's built like an Olympic weight lifter, but his muscles won't do him much good here. The VC are not sumo wrestlers. All he needs to do is shoot, not arm wrestle.

Then there is Richard, who has had ten Article 15s and one court martial. Sounds like he has been in court more than Perry Mason.

Then I counsel again with Chuck, the 'conscientious objector.' He's a persistent guy. He certainly doesn't believe it's, "better dead than red." He's doing all he can to avoid field duty. This is the umpteenth time I have counseled with him and I'm getting pretty irritated with him.

TUESDAY, DECEMBER 5, 1967: Today, I've agreed to have a memorial service for Vernon of the 43rd Scout Dog Platoon. This platoon is one of several separate units here at Dong Tam that provide combat support for the Mobile Riverine Force. Their scout dogs are trained to sniff out ammunition, weapons and VC hiding in bunkers. We haven't used them much because the Delta is generally bad terrain for dogs. However, they do help us in perimeter operations, and that's where Vernon was killed last Thursday.

The unit has no chaplain assigned, of course, because chaplains are only assigned to battalion level and above. Before the memorial service I spend some time in their area. I'm impressed that the dogs are also protected by sand bags. With the increase of mortar attacks in the past few months, it makes me feel good that these animals are protected as best as can be. I love dogs and miss my childhood dog, King. He went everywhere with me; fishing, swimming, and on bicycle rides. He was always there.

The 43rd Platoon members are grieving the loss of their buddy and one of their dogs. In the memorial service, I acknowledge the loss of Vernon's dog, also named King, as if he too were a soldier, which in a way he was. After the service, and in days ahead, many of these guys tell me how much they appreciate my acknowledgment of the loss of King.

Thanks King! Both of you.

WEDNESDAY, DECEMBER 6, 1967: I have my first official conference with the King of the Hill today. He wants feedback from me on troop morale and how the wounded are doing in the hospitals. He wants me to be an extra set of eyes and ears. Of course, that's what I was to Monk

Doty, so this won't be new. I do appreciate the King wanting this from me, and I sense that this is the start of our good relationship.

THURSDAY, DECEMBER 7, 1967: Pearl Harbor day! As I wake, I think of Hawaii. I'll be there next month! I can't wait for R&R.

> *6:40 P.M.*
> *Thursday, December 7, 1967*
> *Hello Sweets,*
> *I took a short nap today and dreamed that I had a three day pass and went home. It was crazy. I caught a plane to California, and another to Charlotte, then a bus to Albemarle. I ran home from the bus station. I still had on fatigues and my steel helmet.*

SUNDAY, DECEMBER 10, 1967: When I return to my hooch after conducting services, I notice a flurry of excitement a short distance away. Echo Company has been on a road runner operation overnight, and as they came in a little while ago, Joe Jenkins brought us a surprise; a very dead VC. He was killed when he walked into their ambush during the road runner operation.

Joe thought it would be good for morale to bring a dead VC into camp; sort of a trophy. Joe wants to have his photo made with his foot propped up on the dead VC's chest in a victory pose with his AR-15 weapon pointed skyward and a big smile on his face.

This isn't some sort of African safari where a kill is displayed. This violates the Geneva Convention rules of warfare about displaying and being disrespectful to the dead. Word has quickly spread around the base camp. Many support soldiers who have never seen a "real live VC," come to see. It's amazing how rapidly the news traveled. Soldiers are coming from all directions.

The King of the Hill also hears about it and comes out of the battalion operations center so angry that his blood vessels in his neck look ready to burst. He calls Joe aside and in no uncertain terms tells him that he must return the dead VC immediately.

Embarrassed by the King's tail chewing, Joe gets one of his sergeants and some of his men to take the body back. The sergeant, unsure of exactly what to do, decides to take the dead VC to My Tho, where he locates the civilian hospital. He pulls up to the front door, dumps the body out at the front door, and speeds away. His action brings a severe lecture from the U. S. Embassy in Saigon regarding the proper care and respect of the dead. Later in the day at a staff meeting, the King refers to the dead VC as the "village idiot" because he stupidly walked into Joe's ambush.

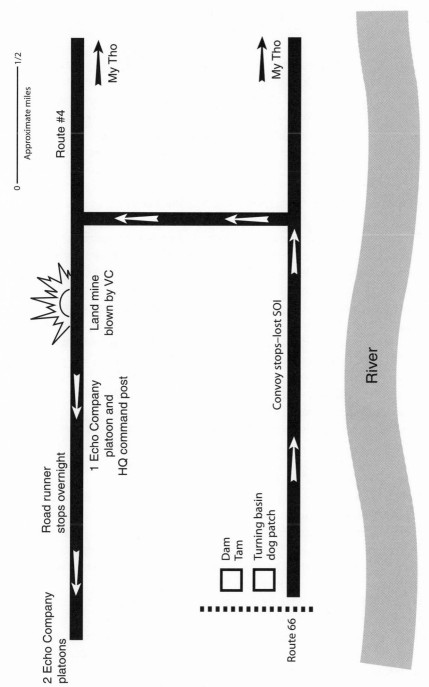

Route #4

My Tho

My Tho

Land mine
blown by VC

1 Echo Company
platoon and
HQ command post

Convoy stops–lost SOI

Road runner
stops overnight

2 Echo Company
platoons

Dam
Tam

Turning basin
dog patch

Route 66

River

Echo Company's Road Runner Operation, December 10, 1967

Sunday night I can't decide if I am crazy, eager for excitement, or just foolhardy. I've agreed to go with Echo Company on their next road runner operation. Until now, my policy has been to go out only on combat operations that involve the entire battalion. However, tonight is an exception. Maybe I feel sorry for Joe for getting kicked around today by the King of the Hill. Paul, my assistant, is ecstatic. He's wanted to go out for several weeks, but there's been no need for him to go. The risks have been too great. I tell him we're going tonight and he grins from ear to ear like a baseball player who has sat on the bench all year and now he has a chance to go into the game.

I check out a .45 pistol. This is the first time I've carried a weapon since the Ben Luc operation in August. It seems like a hundred years ago. The battalion S-2 asks to go out also, and will ride with me.

Time to move out. We have four armored personnel carriers, a couple of two and one-half ton trucks with two platoons of troops for ambush operations and several Jeeps, including one with a recoilless rifle mounted on top. We move through Dog Patch, our nickname for the village just past the gate, and up the road toward My Tho. We keep forty meters between each vehicle.

Suddenly we stop. Phil, one of the platoon leaders, has lost his copy of the Signal Operating Instructions (SOI). If the VC get this, it's like a public advertisement of how to find out what we're going to do tonight. Finally, Phil finds the SOI. This will keep the King of the Hill from jumping on Echo two times in the same day. We move out again.

We cut across to Highway #4 southwest of My Tho, which we call VC alley. I tell Paul, "If we get hit, keep moving, don't stop." I have his M-16 and the S-2 has his M-16. We know many VC are in this area.

In a tree line just off the road I spot two males I believe to be VC. They have what look like weapons, but I can't be sure. The entire convoy gets through this area without incident.

A report comes in over the radio that the road has been blown up behind us. I look back and 500 meters to our rear, a huge column of dust and smoke is rising to the sky. When we reverse our trek tomorrow, we'll see the huge crater that is the result of the VC blowing the road. It is as if they intentionally waited for us to pass before detonating the mine, and in so doing, to give us the message that, "We can get you anytime we want." I'm betting that the two males I thought were VC are the ones who detonated the mine. I don't understand why they didn't blow up one of our tracks, because our entire convoy passed directly over the unexploded mine.

We go to a bridge, drop off two platoons who'll set up ambushes and then we go back up Highway 4 for a kilometer or two. We set a very narrow defense alongside the road so we can be ready to move out to help either of the ambush platoons should they get hit.

It's near dark and Vietnamese civilians are fast moving out of the area. They know the VC are here and don't want to be caught in any cross fire. This is the same area where Joe Jenkins's "village idiot" was killed last night.

We waste time in the twilight. Joe and I eat some C rations. He tells me that last night the VC was totally unaware of his men's presence. He was walking up a trail with his AK-47 slung to his shoulder. The outpost soldier spotted him with his starlight scope, alerted the nearby ambush fire team by radio and the VC was dead by the time he hit the ground, after ten M-16 rounds struck him.

Joe chuckles a little now over the reaction of the King. It wasn't funny this morning when he was getting his tail chewed out. Sitting on this road in VC land isn't funny either. Dark has now arrived. The road surface is still warm from the day's hot sun. We all talk in hushed tones. If we were back in the real world, we would build a campfire and have a wiener roast. But this is no picnic. The VC are everywhere. They could hit us tonight. Our LPs (listening posts) are 100 meters to our right and left of Highway 4.

There's a curfew for the Vietnamese between sunset and first light. Therefore, any movement is automatically considered VC movement and will be fired upon.

At 9:00 P.M., the S-2 calls into the operations center. He's told that Vietnamese intelligence has just indicated that two VC divisions are to meet in the exact location we're presently at. This is just unheard of. Nevertheless, Joe orders a 100 per cent alert. Where would the VC divisions come from? Where are they now? Paul is quiet. I know the alert has frightened him. I finger my .45. What good would it do if we're attacked? It would be nothing more than a pea shooter against a pride of hungry lions.

We have at our position only one 106mm recoilless rifle that is mounted on a Jeep and two tracks with a .50 caliber machine gun each. We have less than one platoon of troops at our site. How could such a small group hold off two divisions? I don't believe that two VC divisions are in the area. But, who am I to question the military intelligence?

Joe orders the other platoons down the road to link up and form a two platoon defensive position for their own safety. There's no enemy contact thus far. I'm painfully aware of how much more vulnerable we are on a road runner than in other combat configurations.

Then, the listening post (LP) to our left radios in that he hears a noise. The recoilless rifle lines up to fire. The LP is told to fire one round of M-79 toward the noise, after which the recoilless will fire a high explosive round. The nervous LP fires too soon! The recoilless is not ready. Joe curses, but under his breath. Now the LP has given his position away and the recoilless hasn't fired yet. If the noise is from the VC, they'll leave before the recoilless can fire.

Just then, the recoilless fires and the Jeep rapidly moves thirty meters away. This prohibits the VC from firing where the flash from the back blast occurs. We receive no fire. We don't know if we hit anything, and we don't know what the noise was. We stay awake the rest of the night. Nothing happens. Thank God.

I'm glad to see the first faint glow of light from the east. Morning has broken, or is getting ready to. Everyone is sleepy. Civilian traffic begins. Deciding to nap, I lie down between two of the Jeeps parked on the roadway. The Vietnamese passing by think I'm dead. When a track driver heats up some morning coffee, I get up. The soldiers joke about me being the chaplain who arose from the dead.

At 8:00 A.M., Joe gives the order to load up. We're going home. Somewhat apprehensively, we go back toward My Tho, see the crater from yesterday's mine, cut over toward Dog Patch, and then into Dong Tam. We bring no VC trophies today. We unload, and soon Paul and I hit the sack, just as the morning heat begins to sear the inside of our hooch. I sweat in my sleep.

The next day I meet with a soldier who wants leave to be with his wife when she has his baby; as if all of them don't want leave, for one reason or another. Larry, another HQ troop, got drunk and was late for his shift in the tactical operations center which is the largest bunker around. I have little patience for a man who can't get to work because he's drunk, yet I know he, too, needs my help.

I give so much of my attention to the field troops. I find myself somewhat resentful, though, of soldiers who work in secure areas of the staff. Ludicrously, I feel they shouldn't have problems since they don't get shot at or risk stepping on a booby trapped mine. Today, as on all days when I'm not in the field, I have a steady stream of non-combat soldiers with problems. I also have a deadline to complete a newspaper article for *Stars and Stripes*. Yawn! I am not interested in the mundane task.

SUNDAY, DECEMBER 17, 1967: A headquarters sergeant comes for counsel. He's in a weird triangle. Before coming to Vietnam he had an affair and then broke it off because he wanted to make it work with his wife. But, he sent his "affair" a Christmas card and now she wants back. She's threatening to contact his wife if he doesn't resume the relationship with her. He doesn't know what to do about her blackmail.

I leave mid afternoon for Bear Cat.

MONDAY, DECEMBER 18, 1967: One soldier in the hospital has a broken jaw as a result of a fist fight with another soldier. As a reply to "muchas gracias," he told a Latino soldier, "muchas scratcho my ass." He got more than a scratch. He's all wired up and is embarrassed for being here for non-combat injuries. I guess boys are boys, and fist fights happen even in a combat zone.

After returning from Saigon, I spend a considerable amount of time after dinner talking with the King of the Hill. He laments to me that our paddy strength is steadily dropping. Obviously, the more soldiers we have who are fit to go on combat operations, the better chance we have of overcoming the enemy when contact is established. Recently, replacement personnel for those killed and wounded have been slower in arriving, which keeps our paddy strength down.

I suspect the King wants me to be his conscience. He's still getting his feet wet as the new battalion commander, and his job is to win battles while keeping the big picture in mind. In doing so, he can easily overlook individual needs and he knows that. I appreciate our budding partnership.

I leave our conference feeling sorry for the King because I sense he'll have to be the "bad guy" in his job as commander.

WEDNESDAY, DECEMBER 20, 1967: We load cookies, cake, Kool Aid and ice cream packed in ice for the party and convoy to the orphanage in three vehicles. The kids know we're coming and as soon as we arrive at the gate, they mob us. Pastor Ha has to shoo them away so we can get our vehicles into the small school and orphanage compound. All the kids want to be held and I have sometimes three or four at a time on my shoulders and in my arms.

Before we return to Dong Tam, Pastor Ha wants us again to see the recently completed renovation of his church. He's so proud of his little pink church.

On the drive back to Dong Tam, I have a warm feeling for these kids. Yet, it is tinged with sadness; these kids face such an uncertain future. I think of Kellie and Grey and am grateful they're safe with their mother.

FRIDAY, DECEMBER 22, 1967: Santa's not coming but the Chief of Chaplains is. He's Frank Sampson, a Roman Catholic priest. He was a prisoner of war (POW) in WW II having volunteered to stay behind with his wounded soldiers. He spent the remainder of the war in a German POW camp. I have the utmost respect for him, just knowing what he did for his soldiers who were wounded and being left to the mercy of the Nazi soldiers. He must have loved his soldiers the same way I love these guys.

Most of the area chaplains are to meet him at the Dong Tam chapel. Sampson is a two star general, which, to me, is up near God somewhere.

We meet in the chapel. He addresses us and tells us of what a great job we're doing. He says Westy (Gen. Westmoreland, the USARV Commander) has told him that he wouldn't trade this group of chaplains now in Vietnam for any the Chief could offer.

It's not until now that I learn that Westy previously had no respect for and even was antagonistic toward chaplains. He had seen no need for chaplains in the army at all. The chief says that Westy has changed his opinion of the value of chaplains because of our dedication and the good job we're all doing

I'm skeptical. Maybe crusty old Westy is so involved in this war and it's such a series of blunders in the strategic and diplomatic area that he won't consider getting the clergy on his wrong side. Stateside, many clergy are against the war and some are quite vocal about it. Since this has become a war of sides, maybe Westy just wants everyone he can possibly get on his side.

Or maybe Sampson just wants to boost our morale. Mine could use a little boost. Whatever the case, Sampson's remarks work. I leave the meeting feeling a little more appreciated, although I know the brass traveling with Sampson know little of what it's like just one kilometer away during combat operations.

We go to one of the mess halls for lunch. It's supposed to be the chaplains and their commanders, but, mine isn't here. The King of the Hill is directing our operation. That's where my men are. I should be there also.

Sampson leaves. Harv, my brigade chaplain, is ecstatic that things have gone so well. He's been here about a month. I notice that he even spit-shined his boots for the brass. But, this is his battle and today he has won. I don't dislike Harv, but he irritates me. Just before Sampson arrived, I noticed Harv giving me the once over, trying to be discreet, and obviously hoping I'd look presentable.

Another of my soldiers has been dusted off, shot through the arm. He and the others could tell Harv and the other brass what the war is really like: the mud, booby traps, bullets, ambushes, walking point, no sleep, scared stiff with each slight night sound; all this while being homesick and shot at almost every day of your nineteen-year-old life. That's what the real war is about, not spit shined boots, pressed jungle fatigues, fancy speeches and luncheons with the brass. The soldiers view the brass as having the attitude of, "If I want your opinion, I'll give it too you." They wonder if the brass even have a sense of humor.

SATURDAY, DECEMBER 23, 1967: A truce will be in effect for Christmas, which is only two days away. Today, the Dong Tam post personnel bring some of the kids from a nearby Catholic orphanage onto post for a Christmas party. On the way, the VC blow a command detonated mine under the two and one-half ton Army truck transporting the children. One fifteen year old girl is killed and several other orphans are injured.

SUNDAY, DECEMBER 24, 1967: As any child, Christmas Eve was always exciting for me. This year, Christmas Eve is different. I'm up at 12:15 A.M. in order to leave on the operation with Bravo Company. The operation plan is for Alpha, Charlie and Echo Companies to set up near Ben Tre at a crossroads canal and wait out the truce there. Bravo Company is to provide defense for the artillery up stream. My plan is to go in with them, spend most of the Christmas Eve with the men, then relocate and spend the rest of Christmas Eve and Christmas day with the other companies who'd be set up close by.

We load up and move out at 1:30 A.M. The other companies won't leave until after day break. I'm getting excited because I know that I'll be leaving for R&R in less than two weeks. I can't wait. I spend the dark hours of our ride down the river fantasizing about what it'll be like in Hawaii with Barbara and the kids.

After beaching and setting up, I make my rounds. I intentionally talk about Christmas, since it's on everyone's mind. It's good therapy. I ask guys where they were last Christmas Eve and they all seem eager to tell where they were and what they did. Almost none of them were in the army. They lighten up when I ask them where they'll be and what they'll be doing next Christmas Eve. I fear many of them will never see next Christmas.

By 8:00 A.M., the artillery has anchored their barges and set their guns for firing. They begin prep fires to soften the LZ for Alpha, Charlie and Echo Companies, which are soon to beach down stream. I'm hoping the VC don't want to fight during Christmas. For a wife or parent to receive word about their husband or son being killed would destroy their Christmas, not only for this year, but for each Christmas to come.

We get word that Alpha Company, which has just beached, is in contact! The artillery begins firing missions for them and then the VC break contact.

It's time for the service. We're muddy. No white shirts, ties, high heels or stained glass windows in church today. I hope there will be no blood stains either. It's a warm feeling reflecting on God's intervention in life through Jesus Christ. Sometimes, though, it's hard to see or evaluate how or when his intervention comes to this god forsaken place.

Soldiers of all faiths attend the service, as usual, including several Catholics and one Jew. They all take communion. War and the daily threat of death is a great equalizer.

I now move to the artillery barges to have another service. After wading waist deep out to the barge, I set up the altar next to a 105mm howitzer.

I must begin preparing to get from here to the area of operations. I see a chopper in the distance coming our way when suddenly I hear a soldier curse and yell, "Damn, that chopper's going down!" I watch as the pilot does an auto rotation with his rotor blades. The chopper hits the rice paddy hard about 400 meters away, but doesn't explode. None of us have heard any gunfire, so we're unsure what brought the chopper down. We hear that the pilot had a power outage and was forced to bring the crippled craft down immediately. Fortunately, he was close enough to us that a platoon of Bravo Company quickly moved to secure a perimeter around the chopper. For this crew, their Christmas gift is having an in-flight emergency in a location where help is readily available.

I catch a ride in Col. David's chopper as he is going to the aid boat. We lift off and quickly get to the area of operations, which is a mass of smoke down below, mostly from our artillery. As I look down from the chopper at 1000 feet, I wonder how many VC are in the area.

The VC begin firing at us. I wait to hear metal hit metal. But, thank God, it doesn't happen. We're not hit.

We land on the aid boat and I'm dropped off at Echo Company's position. Joe Jenkins, the company commander, describes how rough the terrain was that they moved through earlier in the day to get here. Part of the time, water was neck deep but the King of the Hill kept urging them to move faster. Joe is angry at the King for not understanding the limitation of movement.

The truce scheduled to begin at 6:00 P.M. has now begun. Soon it'll be dark. It's time for chow and my only brother, Gerald, has sent me a Hickory Farms package of canned ham, pumpernickel bread, cheeses and dip. As I eat, my thoughts go back to the years as we were growing up. I've always looked up to and admired Gerald. Being two and a half years older than me, he blazed a trail for me to follow. It was he who encouraged me to attend Albemarle High School to play football instead of remaining in the small county school where I had no future. There, sports changed my life and opened educational doors that I never would have known otherwise. Without Gerald's encouragement to develop my God-given athletic talent, I doubt I'd ever have gone to college.

Later, when I was in college, Gerald encouraged me as an athlete. As I eat my Christmas goodies, I regret that in 1960, because of preseason football camp at Wake Forest, I wasn't able to be in Gerald's wedding. Now, even at 12,000 miles away on this Christmas Eve, I suddenly feel very close to Gerald and am aware of how very much I miss him. I'm beside a small hooch and four other soldiers are nearby eating their C-rations. I share my present with them and comment that this is a part of what we have to look forward to when we return to the real world.

As if on cue, the VC from the nearby tree line open fire on us. We all scramble for cover. I dive behind a large cistern. The remainder of my Christmas goodies are scattered and spilled as the first shots come in. Glad for safety, I nevertheless hate the VC for interrupting my meal and destroying my gifts that are now splattered in the mud around the edge of the rice paddy.

Bullets come fast and furious. As they pierce the thatched hooch, they sound like a kid running through a corn field, breaking the stalks. My mind momentarily flashes back to when I was five. Gerald, who was seven, and our cousin, Johnny Barnhart, who was eight, and I decided we wanted to play war. We went to a corn field adjacent to our property. We pretended that we were tanks and innocently stomped down several rows of corn.

It's strange that this image is flashing through my mind as the VC bullets are whizzing by. That war was play, this one is not.

The truce that began only a few moments ago is over, and here we are as all hell breaks loose. The soldiers are now firing toward the tree line and several boats on the canal are plastering it with their .50 caliber machine guns. After a few minutes, the incoming VC fire stops, but the boats continue to fire. Joe requests artillery fire but the command group says, "No, we're in a truce." Joe is beside himself. He screams at me, "The VC fired, we fired and those SOBs at the operation center won't let us have artillery. I wish they were in the tree line so we could fire on them."

Abruptly the firing stops and it is very quiet. The quacking of a few nearby ducks seems strange. No one has been hit, thank God.

I decide to pick a small hooch in which to sleep. Only two hooches are within our perimeter. It's dark now and quiet. My mind wanders. How I miss Barbara. This is my first Christmas ever without her. I hope I never have to spend another Christmas away from my family.

Deciding to switch off these negative thoughts, I find an empty C-ration can, C-ration sugar, chocolate mix, a book of matches and get a pinch of C-4 to heat the water. The hot chocolate really isn't as good as pecan pie and ice cream, which is what I would be having at home, but it's good, nevertheless.

Mostly, we're all quiet and into ourselves and our inner thoughts. Not long before I'm ready to attempt sleep, I become aware that some chickens are roosting nearby. Now and then, they squawk quietly. I wonder if this evening is anything like the one Joseph and Mary spent in the stable when Jesus was born. Mary and Joseph were dry and so am I, at least for now. They were a long way from home, doing something they had to do, but not necessarily wanting to do. So am I. Jesus was born into an uncertain world. Now, almost 2000 years later, the uncertainty continues. He is the Prince of Peace; inner peace in my life. I long for peace in this place. Maybe soon. I finally doze off, not too peacefully, but sleep nevertheless. Some Christmas Eve!

MONDAY, DECEMBER 25, 1967: I am startled awake at 1:00 A.M. from an incoming round of some explosive device. It's just one round, and no one is wounded. We return no fire because no one knows where the round originated.

I get up early and have a Christmas breakfast of C-rations. What I wouldn't give for some pancakes, eggs and sausage. I begin scouting around for a location to have a service. Dry space is limited and I finally decide to have the soldiers sit on a nearby rice paddy dike while I stand calf deep in the paddy water and mud.

I finish the service, leave and take the short boat ride over to Charlie Company. Our battalion is set up in a corner of Ben Tre and, unlike the past, there are a number of civilian Vietnamese nearby. I guess they know there's a truce and trust there'll be no firefights today. After what happened yesterday afternoon, I'm not so trusting.

Charlie Company is set up near a little school with many larger than normal trees that block the excruciating heat from the sun. It reminds me somewhat of a large country setting for a family reunion with dinner on the grounds.

I make my normal rounds in the defensive positions with the soldiers. Surprisingly, most appear to be in good spirits. Perhaps that's because of not having to maneuver today through the mud, rice paddies and swamps.

I conduct the Christmas service on the steps of the school. Then, the hot chow arrives by chopper from Dong Tam. It tastes good. C-rations get old in a hurry.

An old man, very sick, is brought to our area. He looks like he's not long for this world, and I say a short, silent prayer for him.

Arriving at Alpha Company's position, Frank Pina, the company commander, is his usual nervous self. Holes are dug into the hard ground and overhead camouflage has been built with bush limbs.

I decide to go outside the perimeter for a short break, and I warn the guys not to shoot me when I return. I'm only half joking. Some soldiers have been mistakenly shot for this before. I only go a few feet beyond the perimeter and relieve myself behind some nipi palm.

While outside the perimeter, I notice a small gazebo-type shelter that would make a good location for the service. We adjust our perimeter and I set up my small altar with my back to the in coming trail. During the service, my voice is the only sound in the quiet shade of the nipi palms. Suddenly, there are a chorus of clicks as guys simultaneously switch their M-16s from safety to ready. Several soldiers drop down on one knee in firing positions and the others aim past me toward the trail to my rear ready to send someone to his funeral. I stop in mid sentence. Then everyone else hits the deck and so do I.

An old papasan, about seventy and dressed in white, has walked up the trail to within about thirty meters of where I'm standing. He looks in our direction with somewhat of a confused look on his face and then slowly turns and walks in the opposite direction. He'll never know how close he came to getting thirty M-16 rounds fired into him.

The truce ends today at 6:00 P.M. and most of the guys are cutting foliage to further camouflage their positions. In case of a ground attack tonight, this will keep the VC from seeing our positions.

As I make my rounds, most of the soldiers talk about the service and how we all instinctively reacted. I tell them that the old papasan was really a Vietnamese Santa Claus, but they scared him away and now they're going to have to wait another year to get their presents. I try not to think that some of these men may never see next Christmas.

As the sun sets, some of the guys have small transistor radios and listen to AFRN play Christmas music. I realize this is the first time in my life that I'm glad Christmas is over.

At 10:00 P.M., two people are spotted outside the perimeter through a starlight scope. They're in the same location where we held the Christmas service a few hours ago. An E-5 volunteers to sneak the few meters down the trail to do a one person reconnaissance of the area. Off goes the sergeant. His bravery astounds me.

Suddenly, the VC open fire from the direction the sergeant has gone. Bullets are zinging by from several directions. We can't return fire because no one is sure where the sergeant is and we can't risk killing him. Everyone holds their fire momentarily. A loud explosion is followed immediately by another one. The firing ceases and within a few more seconds, the sergeant crawls back to our perimeter to report to Captain Pina what happened.

As the sergeant was sneaking down the trail, at least two VC opened fire on him and he was caught in a cross fire. He dove for protection and tossed a grenade at one of the VC. He saw the VC fall, threw his second grenade, and then began rapidly crawling back to the perimeter because he had no more grenades.

This E-5 then asks for and is granted permission to crawl the few meters back down the trail to recon the area again. He returns in a few more moments and whispers that the VC he killed is gone. He swears the VC was dead a few moments before when he threw the grenade. Probably the VC removed the body as they left the area. He tells us that his pucker factor was so high, he could have picked up coconuts with his cheeks!

All is quiet now. My mind now wanders to next Christmas.

At 2:00 A.M., there's one huge explosion just outside the perimeter. Good night, Rudolph.

TUESDAY, DECEMBER 26, 1967: The dew hangs heavy as first light begins to appear. We're all more relaxed than we were at twilight because then we were expecting to be attacked.

I realize that as of today, I'm half way through my tour! Hallelujah! Praise the Lord! I want to shout. Also, in just a few more days, I'll be on R&R.

It's 6:10 A.M. and the truce is over. Now, it's back to the war, as if the past thirty-six hours hasn't been like war. I make my rounds. We're extracted and head to Dong Tam. Many times during the day, I remind myself that I'm halfway through my 365! The rest will be down hill. My morale is high.

Echo Company has a party. Several of the guys break out guitars and some sing. At 10:00 P.M., I hit the sack.

At 1:00 A.M., twelve rounds of VC mortars come into Dong Tam.

THURSDAY, DECEMBER 28, 1967: Little Al Harris comes to see me again. At eighteen, he's a newlywed. But, we're all newly weds or nearly-deads. Christmas has this kid, who has a kid of his own, quite scared, and he remains very homesick. Me too.

FRIDAY, DECEMBER 29, 1967: Today, we return to the Cam Son Secret zone. This place gives me the creeps. In fact, the whole Mekong Delta gives me the creeps. We're set to embark at 1:00 P.M. At 11:30 A.M., Big Smith comes and wants to talk. He's been to see me several times over the past few months. He talks on and on about his problems at home. His wife has written to me before about Smith not writing to her. Smith is a big, sullen soldier who's seething with hostility. Today, he reports his mother has beaten up his wife, who is employed in a state hospital for the mentally ill. Sounds like the whole family might end up as patients there in the future. Yet, he still refuses to write to his wife.

I want to be of help to him, but I have an operation to go on in a few moments. I finally have to tell Big Smith that I have to go. Looking somewhat rejected, he finally leaves. If he had talked another three minutes, I would have been left behind.

Paul wants to go on this operation with me, and I agree. It's fine with Frank Pina, because he wants as many bodies in the field as he can get. That's live bodies.

We beach, move fifteen hundred meters in and spot six VC and open fire on them as they run into the tree line. We receive no return fire. The rule of this war is that any male fifteen to forty-five is to be detained. We always assume that if a male runs, he's VC. Vietnamese males here have no rights. But, who does in this war?.

It's now one hour before dark and we set our night perimeter. We set up the command post (CP) at a hooch on the edge of the village. As soon as the mamasan sees that we're setting up for the night, she "di di maus" (leaves quickly). Dark is almost here and I eat. Cold C-rations certainly don't taste like my mother's chicken and dumplings.

A squad has captured a Vietnamese male who has no ID and we assume he's a VC. The detainee is tied to a tree around the corner from the hooch. Frank directs the artillery forward observer, his NCO and their radio operator to guard him through the night. He'll be evacuated tomorrow morning.

A soft but somehow forceful curse from Frank awakens me from my doze. "Why did you let him escape?" It's 10:00 P.M. and Frank is chewing out two guys whose identity I can't make out in the dark. The forward observer NCO had left the prisoner to step around the corner of the hooch to talk to his radio operator. He swears he was there for not more than three or four minutes. During this time, the prisoner managed to extract himself from his bonds and quietly and quickly "di di maus" to his freedom. This could be serious if the VC tells his friends of our exact location. They can zero in on us. Frank knows this and orders an increased alert for the remainder of the night for all positions.

The E-5 feels badly. He's only nineteen. I tell him that it'll be okay. "Worse things have happened than this," I add, and that seems to help his embarrassment.

He stretches out on the ground beside me and I invite him under my poncho for a smoke. As I light his cigarette, the brief flickering of light reflects the sadness on his young, mud covered face. As we finish our smokes, I tell him that I know he didn't let the VC loose on purpose and Frank knows that, too. "Let's sleep it off and you'll feel better at first light."

SATURDAY, DECEMBER 30, 1967: I cover myself with my poncho. It is cool and I want to warm up. I doze off again at 1:00 A.M. I wake at 1:15 A.M. soaked in sweat. The poncho does not allow movement of air around my body. It is still cool, but I'm wet now and I recall my mother always warned me about getting chilled while wet. My thoughts are, "It'll just be my luck to get pneumonia and not be able to go on R&R".

I'm awakened again a 2:30 A.M. The King of the Hill is trying to call Bravo Company and cannot get them on the radio. He's angry; very angry. Bravo Company is about 500 meters down the trail from us. Capt. Jim McDonald, the new company commander, is liable to pay a high price for this later. The King asks Frank to try to raise them on his radio, but he, too, is unsuccessful. The King assumes the entire Bravo Company command element is asleep. He's ranting on the radio and tells Frank he's going to order an artillery marking round near their position to awaken them. The round comes streaking over head and its loud explosion not only awakens the sleeping Bravo Company command post, it awakens half the people in the Mekong Delta. Eventually I doze off again.

I awaken just before first light. I try hard to think what day it is. It's Saturday and back in the real world, it would be a lazy day to watch football bowl games on TV.

The dew hangs heavy in the air. Light comes gradually and the smell of hooch smoke slowly drifts over the little hamlet. Then, a few meters down the trail, someone yells, "Medic, medic!" I haven't heard any gunfire or explosions and I'm puzzled. Yet there's considerable concern in the voices of two or three other soldiers who are also calling out. I run a few steps in the direction of the commotion.

An old papasan is carrying a little girl of about five years old in his arms. She looks like a rag doll, but rag dolls don't bleed like this. Limp, she looks unconscious. The papasan, who's probably her grandfather, seems as if his soul has been destroyed. The little girl's entire face is covered with blood soaked bandages.

The medic, who has been in country just a few days, slowly begins to carefully unwrap the bandage from the girl's face. Even though unconscious, the little girl whimpers softly. This new medic is not yet seasoned to the cruelties of war. In fact, he'll be killed himself in a few weeks. When the last part of the bandage is lifted from the girl's face, I take a step back, fighting the urge to vomit.

I see a mass of torn flesh, bone and facial tissue. Where her left eye was is now a gaping hole. Her nose is hanging down over her mouth. She's breathing through open wounds between what was her left eye and where her nostrils should be. Her breath is an odd wheezing sound and her mouth is grotesquely misshapen. It appears that most of her little teeth are also gone. There's more missing flesh along her left and right cheek bones. From where the eye was, a portion of her brain is exposed. I wonder how she can still be alive. The medic's hands shake. Frank whispers a curse and looks up and away into a nearby coconut tree. My eyes fill with tears.

In these few seconds, I see my Kellie as this little girl. For a moment, I feel like I might lose my mind. I get flushed and I want to cry out, to curse, and to have a temper tantrum. In these few seconds, the pent up feelings of all these months of blood and guts, the insanity of this stupid war and my separation from my family comes to bear on my wounded emotions. My soul feels like a target for an assassination squad.

I look at Frank. We both know what the other is thinking and feeling. Frank is only a year older than I and his Teresa is two and one-half, and Jennifer is only one. I know in this instant how deeply Frank loves his daughters. This moment instantly bonds us even more as friends.

The rushing onslaught of feelings that bombard my senses are quickly halted because I know I can't break down here. I put aside my feelings immediately. I ask our interpreter to find out how this little girl was wounded. In the nasal and whiny exchange of information between the interpreter and the papasan, we learn that a loud explosion occurred overhead from their hooch down the trail. A part of the marking round fired at Bravo Company came flying through their thatched roof and hit the sleeping little girl flush in the face.

We decide to evacuate the little girl to the 3rd Surg in Dong Tam. The dustoff arrives in a few moments and I help load her onto a stretcher and onto the chopper. The papasan looks bewildered and frightened. I pat him on the back as we get him situated in the chopper. As the chopper lifts off, I again see Kellie on the litter and me sitting beside her. I tear up again and pretend for a few moments that my tears are from some trash blown in my eyes from the dustoff prop wash. But, they come from deep inside my wounded soul. I feel so helpless.

I do not know if she will live.

There is no time to process my feelings about the little rag doll girl. For now, there's hunting to be done; hunting the VC. We're to move by air to another location. I hate these air movements. I have never particularly liked heights and I feel so exposed in a chopper flying into and out of a rice paddy.

We move out of the hamlet along a canal that splits a huge rice paddy. A dirt road runs parallel to the canal and we divide into groups of six for pickup along the road. As I gaze over the horizon in the direction the dustoff chopper went, I wonder if the family of the little rag doll girl are

VC sympathizers. It doesn't matter now. Survival is what matters; to her and me. I still want to cry.

The choppers are in bound. We get off the road into the water for the choppers to land. Wet again! On board, we rise to 200 feet and I look to my left to the group of hooches that's been home to the little girl. As I look at it, I realize that with one eye gone and the other probably blinded, she'll never again see what I'm now seeing, even if she lives. Again, I don't allow myself the luxury of grieving for her. I know this is still VC land and we still have a war to fight.

I'm brought back to the here and now with the distant but distinct popping sound of some VC sniper down below taking pot shots at us. I look down and about a kilometer away, I very distinctly see Snoopy's Nose. That awful battle was three and one-half months ago, but as soon as I see it, I flash back as if it were just yesterday. I point to it, but the puzzled look of the soldier next to me tells me he doesn't understand. He's a relatively new guy, and I realize that the battle of Snoopy's Nose is already history.

We land and the choppers move out rapidly to extract the other half of the company as we move to secure the nearby tree line. The only sounds now are the squishing of combat boots sinking into the ever present rice paddy mud. This squishing sound reminds me of how the maimed little rag doll girl was breathing.

The second element of Alpha Company has now been inserted and we're all linked up together. We move out and soon come to a cluster of six hooches. We set a security perimeter to thoroughly search the hooches. We discover a homemade zip gun and our Kit Carson scout says this is a VC hooch and village.

Bunkers are everywhere and we begin a search of each. The only people here are a couple of old women and four kids—or so we think. I'm casually talking to a couple of the guys when not more than thirty feet to my left, a VC jumps out of some foliage and runs. He reaches a fast moving stream twenty-five meters away and dives in headfirst. As he dives in, a platoon sergeant yells, "VC! VC! Shoot the bastard!" Several men open fire at the spot where he plunged into the water. He doesn't surface. He's just disappeared as if he were some kind of magician.

We finish searching the bunkers and the decision is made to torch the hooch where the zip gun is found. As we leave the area with flames overtaking the hooch, my conscience bothers me that someone's home is being burned. I vividly remember as a child, a nearby house burned to the ground. When there was nothing left but smoke and ashes, the entire family just stood huddled and cried quietly. Yes, I know this hooch probably belongs to a VC. I can picture some VC family doing the same.

If I were a VC, I'd tell everyone I could how those mean Americans burn homes. As I reach the part of the trail that parallels the stream, I'm wondering if I should speak to the battalion commander about hooch burning. If I did, would the command see me as a rabble rouser? But, where's the morality of actions like this? Is this just part of war? Do I just minister to the soldiers, or should I have a say in events such as this? In this war, morality has a way of becoming blurred in our quest to survive.

These are not easy questions for me, nor are there easy answers. This is very different than a graduate course in ethics on some college campus.

As I walk, I'm aware that I'd be a perfect target by any sniper from the other side of the steam, a distance of only thirty meters. This threat quickly takes my mind off ethics and puts it back on survival. For now, ethical questions ceases to be an issue.

We must cross the stream to the other side, but the only way is by sampan. The lead platoon "borrows" three of the flat-bottomed boats and three Vietnamese women to ferry us across. The water is swift and each sampan can only carry four. There is only four inches between water level and the top edge of the boats. A slight pitch in any direction will capsize us.

Each trip, the sampan is washed down stream forty or so meters. The cargo load of soldiers is unloaded and each Vietnamese sampan "driver" must then paddle hard back up stream for her next load. The women are obviously frightened and confused, but they're experts in maneuvering these strange little boats. After a while, the entire company is finally on the other side of the stream.

Once across, we begin moving back downstream in the direction we just came, only on the opposite side. The tide is out now, which makes crossing some of the feeder streams difficult, as there's nothing but mud in some of the streambeds. Paul is having trouble; he keeps falling off crossing logs and getting stuck in the mud. We all sink down knee deep, sometimes thigh deep. The muddy stream is about ten meters wide. In one canal, about ten meters from where it empties into the main stream, a radio operator gets stuck. Paul tries to help him by pulling on the soldier's web gear, only to get stuck in the mud himself. I've already crossed and tell them I'll get some help. I move up about fifteen meters to the yard of the next hooch. I get some rope and just as I toss one end of the nylon line to them, VC from across the stream beginning firing at us.

For about sixty seconds, everything is happening at once. The entire company is firing across the stream into the tree line. I hit the ground behind a coconut tree. Within ten seconds, Paul dives to the ground beside me as bullets whistle all around us.

I glance around the tree and see that the radio operator is also out of the mud. Paul changes magazines in his M-16. When the first VC shot hit the mud just inches from him, he instinctively put his weapon on automatic, sprayed the area from where he was receiving fire, and then got out of the mud. He opened up on the VC with his second magazine as did all the other soldiers. Now the firing is over.

Paul is very frightened and so am I. It's a miracle that neither he nor the radio operator was killed, or me, for that matter. Bullets hit all around Paul. Thank God, he was not even hit.

We move out again and cross more feeder streams. We continue to move parallel to the river. We have made a huge circle from where we burned the hooch this morning. We stop to set up a blocking force. Outposts are established and our perimeter enables me to make my rounds and talk to most of the soldiers. Many ask about the little rag doll girl from this morning because word has circulated about how badly she was hurt. There's compassion and concern all around. The kids get to us all. They are the innocent victims in this mess.

The New Year's truce begins tomorrow at 6:00 P.M. and we're to have another thirty-six hour truce. I plan to have another round of field services like I did at Christmas. However, I must get back to Dong Tam, get my chaplain's kit, then come back to the field. Word comes that the King's chopper is inbound. He wants a quick conference with Frank before nightfall. He lands in a small opening. I ask for a ride back to Dong Tam.

During the afternoon, another male Vietnamese has been detained for evacuation back to Dong Tam for military intelligence to question. He's tied up and the interpreter tells him where he's going and that he'll be going by chopper. There's great fear on his face as he hears this. Supposedly, VC are very fearful of two things; being cut with a knife and being thrown out of a chopper at high altitude. He's terrified. The King, Paul, the detainee, with his hands tied behind him, and I walk to the chopper.

I wish I could comfort him in some way. As we lift off in the normal cloud of dust and trash, the detainee must be thinking that this chopper is the elevator to his death. He keeps looking around like a frightened animal. His pleading eyes meet mine and I attempt to gesture to him that he'll be all right. Then I point to the cross on my left collar. He doesn't completely understand what I'm saying, but he seems to relax a little more when he sees that neither Paul nor I are making any effort to toss him to the ground far below.

When we touch down at Dong Tam, the detainee looks at me with great relief. I give him a thumbs up signal and he gives me a very brief smile. I feel a tinge of warmth for him, as I've seen his terror of the past fifteen minutes. I recognize that kind of terror; I've felt it myself. So, why are we all trying to kill one another?

On the flight in to Dong Tam, I realize how very tired I am—physically and emotionally. My body aches. I can't get that poor little girl with the mangled face out of my mind. I feel my own face flush with anger that such things have to happen to children. Life is cheap in war.

I consider going by the 3rd Surg to check on the girl, but I am exhausted, body and soul. I go to my hooch instead. I'm there only five minutes when a soldier comes by and wants to talk. I don't even have time to shower as I must change from a field soldier to compassionate counselor. He tells me he wants to marry a Vietnamese girl he met when he was in another unit. He'll have to wrangle a lot of paperwork with both governments and he doesn't appear to have the patience to get that done. No doubt, being away from home town girls for six months would cause many to be attracted to any female.

It's well after dark when he leaves. I finally get a good hot shower. I stay under the water a long time. Oh, what luxury just to be under nice warm water. I wonder if I have become too wrapped up in this job. My six months are up. Maybe I should request out of the field. Somehow, it doesn't feel right, though—at least not yet.

I think of R&R in just a few days from now. I write Barbara. I hope they don't mortar us. I need a solid night's sleep.

SUNDAY, DECEMBER 31, 1967: New Year's Eve. The cease fire begins as 6:00 P.M. and is to last through 8:00 A.M. Tuesday. At mid-afternoon, I fly out to where Bravo Company is set up. It's now about 4:00 P.M. and everyone is setting their defensive positions for the next thirty-six hours of truce.

I make my rounds and talk to most of the troops. I still receive many questions about the little rag doll girl. The HQ radio operator is defensive. He says the company was not asleep, they just weren't able to receive incoming calls and didn't even know there was a problem until the marking round exploded. I assure him I believe him and understand. He seems a little relieved.

I joke about tonight's New Year's Eve party. We all hope the VC won't throw us a party of fireworks. I begin referring to the nearby canal as 42nd street in New York City, but there'll be no dropping ball at midnight.

I settle down at the command post with thoughts on last year. I attended the New Year's command reception all decked out in my dress blue uniform and watched football bowl games in the afternoon.

As I lie under the stars tonight, I long to be home.

CHAPTER FIVE

January 1, 1968–
January 19, 1968

MONDAY JANUARY 1, 1968: Happy New Year! Big deal, I think, until I realize it is 1968, the year I go home; I hope. I celebrate with an early breakfast of C-rations, wishing it were hot biscuits, gravy, fried eggs, and grits, instead of this funny looking stuff. Hot chow is scheduled for lunch. I don't have much hope for it, either. I know it won't be collard greens, cornbread, black-eyed peas and persimmon pudding.

I have a service at Bravo Company. Gun fire is heard about a mile away. I cross the canal in a Boston whale boat to Alpha Company. I make my rounds and joke about having stayed up so late for the New Year's Eve party last night.

I set up for the service in a small yard of a hooch within our perimeter. Just as most of the guys are arriving, I accidentally step off a small dike and slide down into the water. As everyone is laughing, I yell, "Happy New Year." So much for staying dry today.

As I begin the service, I again joke, telling the guys I have just baptized myself. During the first prayer of the service, the King's chopper lifts off about seventy-five meters away. I stop the service briefly because of the noise. Suddenly, a sniper opens fire. I'm the only one standing, and when the first shot whizzes by, I drop. The sniper fire is returned in a "mad minute" when everyone on the perimeter opens fire in the direction of the sniper.

We wait for five minutes after the firing stops and the service is finished with no other interruptions.

I get an ATC to ferry me the one kilometer down the stream to Charlie Company. Two other boats escort us for additional fire power should we be hit en route. This area is quite a wilderness with heavy foliage on each side of the stream. I wonder if the VC are watching us.

Troops are lazing the day away. Word is passed about the upcoming service. They have already had their hot chow. It's no five star restaurant, but hot chow from the mermite cans beats C-rations any day.

For the twenty-five minute field service, I set up a field altar using C-ration cases. Following the service, it's now about 2:15 P.M., I remove my socks to dry from this morning's mud water baptismal dunking. The warm sun feels good on my bare feet. As always, they're all withered up from being wet.

Joe Van Cycle is now the commander of Charlie Company. He and about ten troops gear up to run a patrol outside the perimeter. Their plan is to go out about 200 meters to make sure no VC are sneaking up. Van Cycle's been in Vietnam for a while longer than me. He's one of a very few field officers who hasn't been put out of commission by wounds.

"Chaplain, don't you want to go on this patrol with us?" he asks. It is Van Cycle who still swears that the VC opened fire on me with a .50 caliber machine gun back on October 5th when I was with Alpha Company in the hot landing zone.

I'm tempted to go on the patrol with them, but I finally decide I shouldn't go on such a small-sized operation, even though it'll only be for a half-hour or so. My rule is to be where the majority of troops are. Besides, with me being unarmed, a unit like Van Cycle is taking out might be pre-occupied with protecting me. I even wonder why Van Cycle, as the company commander, is taking the squad out himself. That is like the King of the Hill coming down and leading a platoon out. As they leave, I crawl into one of the dug out positions that has some overhead camouflage, just to get into the shade.

All of a sudden, gunfire erupts from everywhere. Bullets are zinging in all directions. I try to get as low on the ground as I can. Bullets are tearing through the air a few feet from Joe. His men have hit a beehive of VC just outside the perimeter. They've only been gone three minutes.

Joe calls his command post on the radio and says that they're drastically out numbered, that they're all crawling back to the perimeter and for everyone to be aware and not shoot them as intruders. He says no one has been hit. He tells the artillery forward observer to zero in the artillery, but to hold the fire until the squad is safely back within the company defensive perimeter.

In a few moments, Joe and his radio operator come crawling up to the command post. He yells for the forward observer to call in the artillery. "Hit the bastards with the eight inch stuff before they get away!"

It's only a few seconds before the first volley of shells comes whistling overhead and crashes into the foliage just outside the perimeter. Normally, we're supported by 105mm howitzers. On this operation, we have a battery of eight-inch guns firing for us. They're the largest artillery available and the explosions from the shells cause a much greater concussion than the 105s.

"Happy New Year, Charlie!" one soldier yells right after this first volley impacts just a short distance away. As frightened as everyone is, I hear many chuckles. Now, the second volley comes over and impacts. This time, almost in unison, there is a huge chorus of American GIs who are yelling, "Happy New Year, Charlie."

Fragments are falling all around us and the forward observer adjusts the artillery out a short distance. For the next fifteen minutes, the artillery pounds the jungle where the VC hit our patrol and each barrage is followed with the Happy New Year shout.

And then it's over. I'm certainly glad I didn't go out on that patrol. I move to Echo Company, which is less than another kilometer downstream. It's getting late in the afternoon and there's only one small hooch within their perimeter. I make my rounds. Everyone has heard the gunfire and they all have many questions about what happened at Charlie Company's position. I tell the story at each stop.

It's now dusk and we've been alerted that the VC might break the truce early. We've already had two major probes by the VC, this morning when the King's chopper was fired upon during my service, and this afternoon when the squad at Charlie Company was hit. Plus, last night an ARVN camp about two kilometers away was attacked.

Sure enough, right after the sun sets, we're hit by small arms fire and mortars. I dive head first behind a large pot. We've taken at least one casualty. Artillery is quickly called in and the eight inch guns begin shooting their ordinance just overhead, impacting in the area from where we're receiving fire. The incoming fire stops and the company commander orders the wounded soldier to be brought to the command post. I assure him that we'll get him evacuated ASAP.

Now, only an occasional mortar comes in, as our artillery continues to pound the VC. I lie practically on top of the wounded soldier after one round explodes quite close to us. He's frightened and feels quite vulnerable.

All VC fire now stops. It's been five minutes since the last mortar came in and artillery is discontinued. We call in a dustoff. The VC have poles about ten feet tall sticking out of the ground to discourage choppers from landing. We get the dustoff in through some of the poles and then out again with the wounded soldier.

An officer, Dan, has been here long enough to be going on R&R in a couple of days. He's exuberant and is always showing off pictures of his young blonde wife. He's been very expressive of all he's going to do when he meets her in Hawaii.

Tonight, Dan talks non-stop about his going on R&R and meeting his wife. They were married only a short time before he shipped out to Vietnam. Hearing his excitement generates my eagerness for my own R&R just a few days from now.

Soon, two listening posts hear noises just outside the perimeter. Through the starlight scopes, several VC are spotted a short distance away. The company commander calls the operations center and requests use of artillery. The VC appear to be maneuvering for another possible attack.

But we're denied artillery because we're under a truce! The company commander is angry enough to chew nails. "Our asses are at risk and they won't help us," he fumes.

The operations center calls back and says they'll allow artillery only if we're hit first. The commander says to me, "What if we're all killed? Who'll the artillery be for then?"

The VC movement continues. Then, someone comes up with a simple but ingenious plan. We can open fire on the VC with our small arms, as if we're receiving fire. The battalion command post upstream will hear the fire, though they won't know whose fire it is. Then we can get the pre-emptive artillery. That's exactly what happens. The commander orders an entire platoon on the perimeter where movement has been sighted to open fire. The commander shouts into the radio, "We're taking fire! Bring in artillery."

"Roger that, we can hear. We'll clear for artillery." This is sweet music to our ears.

During the night, the VC hit the ARVN compound again. Firing continues for a long time, and the ARVN don't need to fake a firefight to get in artillery. I guess someone forgot about the truce.

TUESDAY, JANUARY 2, 1968: The truce ends at 8:00 A.M. and we make ready to be extracted and leave for Dong Tam. I get to my hooch and learn that today is moving day. The new two-story quarters under construction have now been completed and the order is given to relocate. Paul has already begun moving our stuff.

Even though the move from my hooch isn't more than fifty meters away, the symbolism of this relocation is like going from one century into another. When I arrived here over six months ago, Dong Tam was a muddy camp with a few tropical-sided hooches with tents for tops. The engineers have modernized Dong Tam to the point that it looks more like Bear Cat and Long Binh. I don't like the change. I've grown comfortable with my hooch. It's like an old pair of comfortable shoes that I'm now being told must be thrown away. New shoes cause blisters and my soul has too many blisters as it is.

Soon I discover that my new digs are okay. I now have two rooms, one for an office and the other for my living quarters. I get a new desk, even a stateside desk chair and an extra wall locker. I also get a new bed. It only takes a couple of hours to finish moving our stuff out of the old hooch.

It's still several days until I see Barbara and the kids. I'm torn between wanting to ask for reassignment and my loyalty in needing to stay with these guys I love. Then Little Al Harris comes to see me again. He still looks younger than his eighteen years and is scared that he won't live long enough to see his kids grow up. I comfort him as best as I can.

I have to go to Saigon tomorrow to record some devotional tapes for the Armed Forces Radio Network (AFRN) so I work on preparing them. My heart is not in it, but it's a task that must be done. My soul and mind feel blocked.

WEDNESDAY, JANUARY 3, 1968: Since I'm scheduled to record my radio tapes tomorrow morning in Saigon, I catch a chopper directly there and spend most of the day visiting my seventeen soldiers. All are wounded except the muscle bound soldier with a rash. This isn't his first 'illness'. I feel a bit of contempt for him, as I see him finding ways to avoid his duty while the other sixteen heroes here have all been wounded. One soldier, for example, has lost his leg. He's taking it relatively well. But, he'll have a lifetime of being challenged all because of his willingness to do his job.

THURSDAY, JANUARY 4, 1968: The task today is to make seven short devotional tapes to be broadcast daily on AFRN for the next seven days. It's not that this isn't necessary, but I feel like I have more important things to do.

I'm scheduled to begin taping at 10:00 A.M. Not knowing how long it'll take, I want to be there on time. I never want to be late for anything, a habit of mine. In fact, my motto is, "If you cannot be on time, be early."

I enter the studio and one would have thought I was stateside. This is such a sterile place. Several soldiers who work here are dressed in khaki! I want to tell them there is a war going on out there. Khaki? Their war indeed is a very different one than what we're fighting.

This studio reminds me of an operating room. It's quiet and cool in here. Nothing indicates that the sights, sounds, and smells of the busy Saigon streets are just outside the studio, nor is there any hint of the fear and desperation that occur in an ambush or air assault.

Finally, the taping is over and I gather my manuscripts. I want out of this unreal place. The specialist who operated the equipment and I bid insincere thanks and farewells and out the door I go. I leave the specialist to fight his daily "war" and I'm ready to return to mine.

The sunshine is bright and hot. The noise and smell of Saigon is the same as it was an hour ago, but I feel as if I've been in another world.

Street side, I try to get my bearings. It's 11:15 A.M., not as sultry as I know it will be later. The smells of Saigon taint the beautiful day. The air hangs heavy with exhaust fumes from cars, motorcycles, army trucks and garbage. By mid-afternoon, I'll be long gone from Saigon. My joyful thought is that the next time I'm in Saigon, I'll be on my way to Hawaii— only five days from now! I want to shout it out.

I walk down the tree-lined street near the Presidential Palace. Shortly, I see a 9th Division Jeep and I flag it down. A sergeant and his driver stops. "Bear Cat?"

"Sure, get in Captain,"

I catch a chopper out of Bear Cat. On the way I think of Barbara and the kids. We land and I catch a ride to my new digs. I'm back "home."

I'm quite tired. Later I go to Frank Pina's room on the other side of the building and we talk. Frank's been the company commander since November.

We discuss our mutual exhaustion. The King of the Hill keeps a great deal of pressure on his company commanders, and Frank feels that pressure tonight. We both wonder about the rag doll girl, both recall we have daughters of our own.

Frank is also concerned about the reduced "paddy strength." He knows there's strength in numbers in the field and says if he could, he'd even have his clerks and first sergeant go to the field.

Two of his lieutenants come in and Frank quickly switches from his role of being a tired, fragile and vulnerable human being to that of tough company commander. His lieutenants like and respect him, but I doubt that they've ever seen the side of Frank that I've just seen.

I leave after a few minutes. I could almost see Frank as a brother under different circumstances. As I hit the sack, I recall that in July Bandito Charlie, Larry Garner, was killed soon after we had our heart to heart talk. God, I hope nothing happens to Frank. I don't know if I could take losing him; he's become such a good friend. What would happen to his two little girls? If I get killed, what would happen to my children? I can't think about this. I'm too tired.

FRIDAY, JANUARY 5, 1968: A "bird dog", which is a small, two seat observation fixed-wing airplane, has been shot down just north of the Long Dinh bridge nearby. Two companies are to go out immediately and attempt to secure the area. Reports are that the occupants are probably dead, but their bodies must be recovered before the VC can get to them.

Oh, dilemma of dilemmas! I'd planned to leave tomorrow, spend Sunday with Bert Kirby in Bear Cat, and report to Camp Alpha in Saigon

Monday to process for R&R. Do I dare go back out on this operation? I vividly remember Vic getting shot the day before he was to leave back in October. Plus, I'm scheduled to have dinner with Col. David, the brigade commander, tonight, along with his staff. I decide not to go. I don't want to risk something happening to me before I see Barbara and the kids next week. But, I feel guilty.

Two hours after they leave, a soldier with Alpha drowns, without even a struggle, while crossing a stream. Another is almost drowned. Death is so near in so many ways. I'm angry about this, although I don't exactly know why. Life is so cheap here. After tomorrow, few will ever even mention his name. He'll be replaced and in two weeks will simply be referred to as the guy who drowned near the Long Dinh Bridge. The first sergeant will have to inventory everything he owns and send it to his next of kin. What a package to receive!

I remember a few weeks ago, when a first sergeant called for me. He and the company clerk were going through the personal belongings of one of our KIAs and came across several photos of a young nude woman, posing in very suggestive positions. Army Regulations require we send everything to the next of kin. Some have even accused the unit of stealing some of the dead soldier's belongings. Therefore, not only the army regulation, but division policy is that everything be inventoried and sent, regardless.

But, these explicit photos of the woman were in question. The first sergeant's inclination was to send them. My position was that, even though the soldier was indeed married, it was possible these photos were not of his wife, because he did recently return from R&R. Do we risk creating a lifetime of additional hurt to the young, new widow? We broke the regulations and destroyed the pictures.

But the death of the soldier who has drowned is foremost in my mind. Had the incident occurred in basic training, everyone would be shaken. Here, it's just another "here today and gone tomorrow death." He's just as dead as if he'd caught a bullet.

I realize that none of what I'm feeling or thinking is logical, and it makes me understand exactly how ready I am for R&R. Had that been me who died today, word may not have reached Barbara before she left for Hawaii on Sunday. Wouldn't that be a bummer, to be notified upon arrival in Hawaii that her husband would not be coming: he had died two days ago on a mindless operation near the Long Dinh bridge!

Bert David is the brigade commander and a man of high character. I have tremendous confidence in him as a leader. As a full colonel, he naturally has hopes of making general officer. As an infantry brigade commander, he's in the right position to do so.

Tonight, I'm invited to have dinner with him, along with all his brigade staff. I'm the only officer from 3/60th invited, but that's because I'm assigned to the brigade headquarters on paper and attached to the 3/60th. Since Col. David has decided to have all officers assigned to brigade staff for dinner with him, I'm included. If it's true that it's lonely at the top, at least you eat better, as I'm about to see.

A few days ago, Harv, my brigade chaplain, tried to prepare me for tonight.

"Jim, this dinner is a really special occasion," he said seriously.

"Oh yeah? How special?"

"Special enough that all the staff will be there."

"What should I wear, dress blues and tennis shoes?" I'm joking, but Harv apparently doesn't realize that.

"Oh, no, just some clean fatigues." He looks like he wants to say more, but doesn't. He seems nervous that I might embarrass him in some way. I grin. Harv looks a little pale, but forces a smile. I can tell that he doesn't appreciate my humor. "Now, Harv, where I come from, a seven course dinner is a can of pork and beans and six soda crackers."

Reluctantly, I break out the black polish and decide to put a coat on my boots. They're no longer black, as it's somewhat of a badge of courage around camp to wear boots that have been worn in the paddies so much that all the black is worn off and it's down to bare leather. This says, "I have been there."

Then, I have second thoughts. Rather than polishing my boots, I'll just break out my seldom worn second pair of jungle boots that have been in my wall locker for the past six months. I give a quick coat, brush it down, and my second pair of boots shine like our mess sergeant's bald head.

I arrive at Harv's wardroom on the *Benewah* as arranged. He gives me a subtle once over, checking to see if I'm dressed properly. He's nervous.

"Don't worry, Harv. I know when to pick my nose and when not to." I decide to be generous, hush and allow Harv to relax.

We arrive at the dining room and I see only a few officers I know. Col. David is gracious and greets me warmly. He inquires about morale and about the drowning today. We talk briefly as other officers arrive. Finally, we're seated, and the meal is sumptuous. Even though this is to be a social occasion, there's much shop talk.

Throughout the evening, I smile and say the right things. All these officers have on pressed jungle fatigues and shined boots, just like stateside. As a captain, I'm one of the lower ranking officers present. After all,

I've only been in the army for eighteen months. Many of these officers have been in ten to twenty-five years. But, I have "been places they ain't" and that makes me feel good.

Nevertheless, they're the brains behind each combat operation. They're in operations, intelligence, supply, personnel and civil affairs and they all work closely with their navy counterparts. As the evening grows, I have more appreciation that, even though they aren't where the hammer hits the bullet, they do have important jobs. They and the foot soldiers have different wars to fight and live in different worlds. In reality, I'm a part of both worlds. That's okay because tomorrow, I leave for still another world, that of R&R.

Soon it's time to leave and someone mentions that I'm ready to go on R&R. Col. David remarks that, after all I've been through, I deserve it. I thank him and make my escape.

On the way out, I speak to Harv again. "How did I do, Harv?"

"You did good, Jim."

Indeed, I feel as if this country boy did okay tonight with the brass. I was a good boy and I showed my manners.

As I hit the sack, my last thought is, "Tomorrow, I'm outta here!"

SATURDAY, JANUARY 6, 1968: This afternoon I leave for Bear Cat and then to Camp Alpha in Saigon. Monday morning I am to process out for R&R. But, first, I have a memorial service for the soldier who drowned yesterday. I speak, the King says a few words, and then it's over.

I return to my room. Waiting for me there is Dan, the officer who was showing off pictures of this young blonde wife. I can see that something is terribly wrong; it's written all over his face. Dan has been on R&R and just returned today. He tells me that his wife met him in Hawaii, but only to tell him in person that he's no longer a part of her life, that she has found someone else; she has filed for divorce. She then proceeded to get on her plane and return to the states. So much for the blonde.

MONDAY, JANUARY 8, 1968: Even though I've made the ride to Saigon many times in the past seven months, my mind goes back to my very first trip from Bear Cat to Saigon to get my hold baggage. I vividly remember the return trip in the rain and how that was the beginning of my first major battle, with myself. That seems like so long ago. I'm so different now. Then, I was insecure, alone, and uncertain of the future. Now, the only thing I'm certain about is that tomorrow, I leave for Hawaii and my long awaited rendezvous with Barbara and the kids.

I do the necessary checking in, am assured that I'm manifested on the flight tomorrow at 5:00 P.M., get a sleeping assignment for the night, find my bunk and am told to meet tomorrow morning at 10:00 A.M. for my briefing.

Our original plan was for just Barbara to meet me. Then, we decided to include Kellie and then, what the heck, Grey too. He's now eighteen months old and Kellie is three and a half. I don't know who I want to see the most. I think of little rambunctious Kellie, then immediately think of the rag doll who was hit in the face a few days ago. I wonder if the girl is still alive and if so, what quality of life she'll have. I think of Grey, who I really don't know. I only had ten months with him before I left. Barbara says he's very quiet and reserved, unlike Kellie. I hope I can relate to him.

And, Barbara. It'll be good to lie close to her; to smell her; to tease; she gives me such security. My thoughts are not just sexual. Our relationship is much more than that. We've been together for eleven years, which is almost half of my life. She's such a vital part of me. When I go to bed tonight, it's comforting to know that the next time I go to bed, it'll be at our hotel in "our bed." I just hope this place isn't mortared tonight . . . and I'm killed. Barbara doesn't deserve that. But, then, who does?

TUESDAY, JANUARY 9, 1968: My first thought as I awake is, "Today's the day I've been waiting for." I double check my small hand carried AWOL bag to make sure I have a change of underwear, orders, cigarettes, shaving gear, and reading material. My khakis are big on me. I guess I've lost more weight than I thought. The jungle fatigues are much more comfortable, unless you wear them in the jungle in a firefight. There, nothing's comfortable.

I report to the briefing room. The sergeant giving us instructions seems bored with his job. I change my military pay certificates into real money. The customs guys check every bag for contraband. Some have actually tried to smuggle out weapons, ammunition and grenades.

Finally, we're called to turn out for our formation. We shuffle out to the busses, load up, take the short ride to the terminal, wait five minutes, unload, have our hand baggage searched again, regroup, wait some more, reload the busses and drive out onto the taxi way.

And, there it is! What a beautiful sight. The huge blue and white Pan Am 707 charter is there waiting just for me. We load and the engines begin to rev up and then we taxi. We're airborne! I really am on my way!

Shortly after, the stewardess brings us our evening meal. The contract the army must have with the charter airlines taking soldiers to R&R obviously includes a wonderful meal. I have shrimp and steak. It's delicious.

After dessert, it's dark outside as we're well out over the South China Sea. I try to get comfortable for the long flight. I concentrate on seeing Barbara and the kids. Hmmm!

Our plan was for them to get to Hawaii the afternoon before me and check into our hotel apartment. Barbara would get the kids settled, get some rest, buy some food for our little kitchen and make the hotel quarters as near home comfortable as possible. I figure with the time difference, they're in the middle of what I hope is a good night's sleep at the hotel right now. They should have arrived in Hawaii about eight hours ago. I try to imagine what the hotel will look like. I wonder if I'll be able to contain my excitement for the eight hours that it'll take to get there.

At twenty-seven, I feel old. I'm grateful to be alive and on the way to Hawaii. In the darkness of the plane, I feel warm tears welling up and I realize how lucky I am, lucky to be alive and whole, lucky to have a loving wife and two wonderful kids. So many of my heroes are now dead and many more are wounded. I think of Larry Garner. I still miss him. Wayne Merriman, the soldier who lost his legs, has probably been medically retired. I wonder how Bad Luck Tony Normand is doing. He's probably still in the hospital somewhere. I think about Vic, about that first mortar attack, about Snoopy's Nose, the hot LZ, of Paul almost being shot, of poor Dan whose wife left him for someone else. Then I force my mind back to Hawaii. This is R&R, not war.

Surprisingly, I slip into a light sleep, which is unusual for me to do on an airplane. Before I know it, the stewardess turns up the cabin lights and announces that breakfast will be served shortly and that we'll be landing in Honolulu in about two and one-half hours. With those words, I'm wide awake. I figure that Barbara and the kids are up now. Even though we agreed that she wouldn't meet me at the airport, it would be just like her to surprise me there. We'll be landing just before noon. After breakfast, I try to read for a while, but I'm too excited to concentrate. I look at my watch a thousand times.

I feel the unmistakable tilt of the plane's nose as the pilot changes the attitude of the plane for our slow descent. I know now it's not long until I'll see them—maybe even within thirty minutes, if they decide to go to the airport.

As we continue to descend, I keep glancing out the window almost as if I could see them on the ground. At first all I see is the Pacific Ocean, but then, abruptly I spot land. I picture Barbara telling the kids it'll only be a few more minutes before Daddy gets here.

"Buckle up," we're told. All is quiet now on the plane as the vast majority of us are meeting wives and family and we're all probably thinking and feeling the same. I can now make out trees, houses, cars and even road signs as we near touchdown.

There's the familiar slight forward lurch and squeal of tires as the wheels touch the asphalt runway. I'm now probably only two or three miles from where they are, regardless of where they're planning to meet me.

The 707 stops, and it takes several agonizing minutes to unload. As I walk into the receiving area of the airport, many Hawaiians are greeting us with Leis. It's not that I don't appreciate their efforts, but I came to Hawaii for more important things. My attention is diverted to a boisterous group of excited wives, sweethearts, and children cordoned off across an open area of the terminal.

Everything is a blur. I don't even know if I thanked the Hawaiian girl for the Lei. I'm straining to see if I can spot my beautiful Barbara. As each serviceman spots or is spotted by his wife or family member, there are spontaneous squeals and shouts of joy. I'm not really disappointed that Barbara isn't here. After all, she's following the "rules" we set up and that's a part of her I love.

We quickly load onto buses that are to transport us to the R&R center. The guys who've had a brief reunion with their wives are all smiles. One lieutenant even jokes that he has already had sex with his wife in the crowd. Everyone is in a jovial and joking mood.

For once, we don't have to wait as the buses quickly begin pulling out of the parking area heading for the R&R center a short drive away. As we arrive at the center, the crowd waiting is at least twice the size of the crowd at the airport. Even before I disembark, my eyes quickly scan the large crowd of young families, hoping to get a glimpse of Barbara.

We unload and are told to go directly into a small auditorium for our in-processing. As we disembark, more and more of the guys are stampeded by their wives. I slow my pace, hoping that by doing so, Barbara will be able to spot me.

It's midday and the sunshine is bright, but I have not yet spotted my sunshine. As promised, the briefing is very short. "Do not leave the Islands during R&R," we're told. "Write down R&R emergency numbers . . . what to do in event of illness or accident . . . etc, etc." I barely hear what is said, as I search eagerly for my wife. I'm now getting more than a little worried.

We're released. Still no Barbara. My elation is turning to panic. One of the R&R personnel obviously senses my predicament and asks if he can help. I quickly tell him my situation and he takes me to a phone where he calls our hotel.

"She hasn't checked in yet," we're told. NOT CHECKED IN? She was to arrive yesterday afternoon! I panic. My helper then takes me to a nearby bulletin board to check for any messages that might be left for me. None.

In a flash, I decide that if they're in North Carolina sick, I'm going to board a plane and fly home, rules or no rules. I must first go to the hotel, since my bags will be delivered there. I'll then call the airline to see if she has arrived and, if not, I'll call home and track her down. Then, I'll simply take the next flight to the US mainland. After all, I have seven more days. I won't spend R&R alone!

Why wouldn't she at least have called the R&R Center and/or the hotel? This is so unlike her. Maybe she was in an accident! My mind is going 100 MPH and I work to calm myself. If I get to the hotel, then I can find answers to my questions.

I thank my helper and tell him I'll take a cab to the hotel and work out from there how to find her. The crowd at curbside is still hectic. Excitement abounds as everyone seems to be hailing taxies. Their excitement is in marked contrast to the hurt and fear I feel. After seven months of planning, how could this be happening? I feel so alone and isolated in this crowd.

Just as I hail my cab, I hear a loud voice calling, "Is there a Captain James Johnson here?"

"Right here," I yell.

A friendly major tells me, "I have a message for you."

"Is it from my wife?"

"No, it's from Delta Airlines. They just called. You wife's flight from the States was delayed by weather and she's missed her connection to Hawaii. She's on another flight and it should be arriving at the airport just about now." He hands me a piece of paper with the flight number.

I thank him profusely. Thank God, she's here or soon will be. My mood soars once again. I decide to go to the hotel and wait, since she's likely to go straight there from the airport, realizing that I've already arrived.

I turn to my hailed cab, which is still at curbside, and suddenly someone flings her arms around me like a professional wrestler. But the perfume tells me it is not a wrestler, it is Barbara! My mind staggers! She's supposed to be just now landing. I can't think because she's squealing so loudly. We're both crying as I lift her off the ground. Our tears are mixing in the bright sunshine.

In the next two seconds, I feel a strong clamp on my left leg just above my knee. Through my tear blurred eyes, I see a little blond head thigh high and hear her screaming, "Daddy, Daddy!" I loosen one arm from Barbara and pick Kellie up. She has bolted from somewhere in the crowd, run just behind Barbara and is not going to be left out of this hysterical reunion.

"Where's Grey?" I shout over the commotion. Before she can answer, out of the corner of my eye, I spot him in the arms of a middle aged Hawaiian man at the edge of the curb. How did he get there and who is that man? I later learn that he was Barbara's cab driver from the airport. When they arrived, Barbara spotted me about to get into my cab and yelled to the driver to hold onto the kids, fearing that I'd get away before she could get to me. Kellie was too fast for the driver and broke away.

Grey looks bewildered by the crowd but not anxious. We take the few steps to him and the four of us now are in each other's arms hugging and crying. Grey isn't sure what to make of the whole thing. Surrounding us are those who apparently became aware of my plight and are now clapping and hollering for us like cheerleaders at a ball game.

"We're here. We're here," I shout. "Let's get to the hotel." We pile into the taxi and as we pull away from the curb, I think, if heaven is any better than this, I can't stand it!

TUESDAY, JANUARY 9 THROUGH MONDAY, JANUARY 15, 1968: As we're in the cab for the short ride to the hotel, we're all in the back seat, as close to each other as we can get.

Then, Kellie, who is sitting next to me, says, "Sock, Sock, Sock," and grins at me. She remembers! We had a little game last year. When I dressed her, as I put on her socks, I'd lightly tickle her feet while saying, "Sock, Sock, Sock." The fact that she remembers fills me with excitement.

So begins this, the biggest and most important operation of my war. On the ride to the hotel, Barbara recounts what happened on her trip.

"I knew the weather was bad in the Midwest," she says. "I was to fly from Charlotte to Dallas, change planes to San Francisco, and change again for Hawaii. When I sat down on the plane in Charlotte, I'd no sooner strapped the kids into their seats than one of the pilots came back and told me that my flight out of Dallas had been canceled, which meant I would miss my connection out of San Francisco to Hawaii. I burst into tears and then the kids, seeing me cry, began to cry too. The poor pilot didn't know what to do. He said that Delta would get me to Hawaii, but it would be a later flight and for me not to worry. He asked if I wanted to fly on to Dallas or stay in Charlotte for a later flight. 'I'm not getting off this plane,' I announced through my tears! 'That's okay, that's okay,' he said."

"I only had to wait a short while in Dallas before we flew on to San Francisco. But of course I *did* miss my flight to Hawaii and they said I'd have to stay overnight. They gave us a free hotel room and food. Instead of leaving early afternoon on Monday, it was this morning before we left.

They even volunteered to get the message to you about my delay. The flight actually arrived about twenty minutes ahead of schedule."

We arrive at the hotel. It's exactly what we need with a bedroom, a pull-out bed for Kellie in the living room, a crib for Grey and a small kitchen. Tonight, the kids want to sleep with us and do until they both go to sleep. Then, we put them in their own beds so that we can have the privacy we've both been looking forward to.

The entire week is heavenly. We hire an older woman to baby-sit the kids one night in the hotel and we take a taxi to a nice seafood restaurant for dinner by candle light. Our taxi is a Cadillac, fitting for the week. We visit the zoo, walk in parks and on Wakiki beach, rent a car one day to drive around the island, take naps, cook in and generally do what we want to do when we want to. The week is a wonderful respite from mud, mosquitoes and bullets. I decide not to visit Pearl Harbor. I don't want to see anything that reminds me of war.

I speak little about Vietnam and each time I find myself thinking about it, I consciously direct my thoughts to something else. This week belongs to us, not the Viet Cong. Barbara is loving and lovable. The kids are won-derful. We frolic on the floor and act like there's no tomorrow, no time when this will have to end.

But, of course, it will. Each tomorrow brings us closer to the end of R&R. Like all good things, when good things are happening, the future has a way of quickly becoming the past. Though it's odd, I don't exactly dread returning to Vietnam. I know that I only have five months until I rotate to the states. Plus, I can get a reassignment out of the field when I return if I wish, since I'm well past my six months of combat operations.

So, even though this R&R is heaven with my family, I know that my tour is much closer to the end now and that feels good. The last morning brings a few tears but Barbara and I are both resolved that the sooner R&R is over, the sooner I can return and the sooner my tour will be over.

MONDAY, JANUARY 15, 1968: We decide to say our good-byes at the R&R center instead of having Barbara and the kids go to the airport. We arrive at the center a little ahead of my reporting time and check in. I have the final few moments with them, but it's somewhat unreal, as many other families are also ending their week in heaven.

We say a hundred times in these last fifteen minutes, "It won't be long until the tour is over." The kids are a little restless and I'm nervous.

Finally, a sergeant calls out. In three minutes we are to form a line to load the busses. A last round of hugs, kisses and good-byes are exchanged between 175 GIs and families. Barbara's eyes tear up but she doesn't cry.

The kids seem somewhat in awe of what is happening. I give a final good-bye peck on Barbara's lips and a quick hug to the kids before boarding the bus. I give one last wave and glance over my shoulder, then I'm gone. It's almost a relief now to be leaving.

A wave of sadness comes over me as the bus pulls out for the short ride to the airport. Now we're airborne. I reflect on what a wonderful week this has been. I almost feel whole again. For the previous seven months, I have felt like an outsider to my family.

Halfway back to Vietnam, I realize that Barbara and the kids must now be airborne. It's an unhappy and disconcerting feeling to know I'm flying 500 MPH west and they're flying 500 MPH east.

TUESDAY, JANUARY 16, 1968: We make our final approach to Tan Son Nhut Air Base. After I reclaim my bags, I get a bunk in the officer's quarters, eat, and settle in for the night. I wonder what has happened in the 3/60th since I left.

WEDNESDAY, JANUARY 17, 1968: I change into my jungle fatigues and find a two and one-half ton truck from the 9th Division going to Bear Cat with division soldiers returning from R&R. I like the feel of my jungle fatigues better than I do khakis. Women would call jungle fatigues an 'outfit.' A better term is 'death suits'—without neckties. I always thought neck ties caused anxiety and nervousness. I was wrong. Firefights cause this and there are no neckties within 1000 miles of this place. Truth is, I hate ties and I hate this war.

The truck driver tells me that rumor has it that the Mobile Riverine Force had nineteen KIAs and many wounded a few days ago. He doesn't know from which unit. My heart sinks and my stomach knots. I pray it was not 3/60th.

I'm dropped off at 3/60th rear and I then learn the ugly and shocking truth: it was 3/60th! I learn that Alpha Company had most of the nineteen KIAs. My God! Alpha Company was next in line for me to have gone out with had I not gone on R&R. I wonder about Frank, Little Al, and David Hershberger.

I catch a chopper to Dong Tam. I'm feeling guilty that I wasn't where I was "supposed to be." But how can I feel guilty for being alive? Should I get out of the field now instead of waiting a few more weeks? I'm torn and the sound of the Huey blades seems to be beating at my emotions. Is a career worth the daily risks? Combat is where I get my wings for a future career, or at least that's what I think. I've already received a Bronze Star for valor, been put in for another as well as an Army Commendation

Medal with "V" for valor. I'll probably get an Air Medal too. I'm now seven months in the field. When is enough enough?

I do want to live to return to heaven on earth. Is that wrong? Being pulled in these directions makes me depressed. I realize that just yesterday this time, I was still on a high as I was flying back from R&R. Now, I'm getting down. My coach has turned back into a pumpkin!

We land and I quickly go to my new digs. Depression hangs over the unit like a heavy fog. Paul tells me he has already written the letters to the next of kin, that Harv has signed them and even held the memorial services. When I hear that, I become angry. That's my job!

At 4:00 P.M., I go talk with Frank Pina. He's stoic, which is unusual for him. The fight was terrible, he says. They were hit on two sides and most of the company was trapped in cross fire. Many of the wounded were stranded in the rice paddy for the entire night and no one could get there to help.

I go back to the office and Paul gives me the rundown on the KIAs and wounded. Little Al Harris was shot in the stomach. He yelled throughout the night and no one could get to him to help. He was apparently in a continual state of panic. Now he's finally out of the field. What a way to go home, shot in the stomach.

The radio operator for the artillery forward observer died, but it was apparently from fright. Not a mark was found on his body. He must have been literally scared to death.

Chuck, the self proclaimed Jehovah's Witness who was the unit reporter, refused to move, adding more confusion to a confused night.

David Hershberger was one of the KIAs. I want to hit a wall, or something, or someone. I feel the pain his parents and girlfriend must be having.

I go see the King of the Hill. He's remorseful about the losses but essentially non-communicative. He just wants to forget it and move on. That's typical of the King. He welcomes me back and seems genuinely glad I'm here. He and I have developed a special relationship.

This is certainly not the welcome back I'd envisioned. Hawaii seems like years instead of days ago.

Supper is tasteless. It's dark and I walk the 200 meters to the turning basin. I've only been back to Dong Tam for five hours and here I'm heading out to the field. It'll be an all night boat ride to the area of operations and I'll decide tomorrow with which company to link up.

THURSDAY, JANUARY 18, 1968: The troops beach shortly after first light and I remain on the aid boat. Later in the afternoon, I decide it's time to get off the USS *Scarecrow* and link up with one of the companies. I learn that the King of the Hill will be coming to the aid boat while his chopper refuels. He lands, embarks and says he is going to Charlie Company for the night and, yes, I can ride there with him when the chopper returns. Suddenly, I really want to get with a company. This is where I belong.

I don't like riding in such a small chopper because of my size. I vividly remember the evening after my first firefight last August when I caught a ride on a bubble top. I'm too big for this. I feel like an NFL tackle riding a tricycle.

At 700 feet, we suddenly see three VC on a rice paddy dike. The King motions for the pilot to go after them. We go into a steep dive, heading straight to the frightened VC now running at top speed on the dike. The King has his M-16 ready and hands me his .45 pistol. I hope he doesn't expect me to shoot—I have no intention of doing so. Surely the King remembers I'm a non-combatant?

Two of the VC dive into bunkers beside the dike and we bank hard to line up the third one who jumps head first into a small three foot wide canal adjacent to the rice paddy. The King empties a magazine of ammunition into the water and quickly places another full magazine and empties that one as well. Then he grabs his .45 from me and empties it.

We're circling tight, about fifty feet off the ground. I'm wondering if the other two VC will decide to shoot at us. But, they stay hunkered down in their bunkers.

Then the King motions the pilot to bank over the bunkers. As the chopper circles in a slow, tight loop, I'm exposed and hanging out the right side. If they fire at us, it will be like shooting a cow in a stall. He empties two more magazines of M-16 ammunition into the bunker openings.

The King motions the pilot to set the aircraft down, saying "We need to check out the bunkers." I'm scared beyond reason. This is crazy. It would be just the King and I and I'm not ready to be part of a two-man search party for three dead, or maybe not dead, VC. What if we set down and they have other buddies in the tree line? Fortunately, the pilot refuses to land. He yells, "The dike is too small. We can't balance the chopper on the dike without risking toppling into the water."

Thank you, thank you, Mr. pilot, I think. You may have just saved all our lives. I almost wet my pants I'm so scared.

Then, the King motions us to leave and I'm so very glad. Two days ago I was in my own personal heaven. Just now, I thought I might go to the real heaven!

We finally get to Charlie Company, which is co-located tonight with Echo Company. I make my rounds and everyone is surprised to see me. It's been almost two weeks since I've seen most of these guys.

I go to Echo Company and Joe Jenkins has his command post set up around a hooch. Word has rapidly passed around about our escapade. Everyone wants to know if I shot any VC.

The King calls a meeting of the officers and platoon sergeants of both companies. We gather outside the hooch. He talks about body counts and then says, "Chaplain, what do you think our body count is today?"

"At least one, probably two and maybe three." I do believe he killed the one who jumped into the water. I don't see how he could have lived with as many bullets as the King shot into the shallow water where the VC had jumped. The King is proud and seems even prouder that I am verifying his body count.

Proud of killing? This isn't rabbit hunting. It seems almost as trivial as that. Higher command continuously makes body counts important. I don't feel good that some human beings were killed today before my eyes, even though they would've surely killed us without blinking.

I guess it's okay emotionally not to see the VC as people because to do so might drive us crazy. In later years, it does drive some crazy. It's easier to see this as a game with points scored, not people killed.

FRIDAY, JANUARY 19, 1968: At 2:00 A.M., I'm awakened by excited voices. "Why didn't you kill the SOB?" someone is shouting on a radio. Joe Jenkins is angry. He throws his steel helmet hard on the ground. A soldier out on an observation post (OP) encountered a VC walking nonchalantly up to his position. The OP chose not to fire. Then the VC apparently spotted the OP and ran. Joe is livid. Now the OP will have to be changed to another location because the VC now know where it is. Joe yells back on the radio, "You'd have gotten credit for another body count."

I'm sick of hearing about body counts.

We move out. An old man is brought to us who has been shot through his mid section. He has a huge fist sized exit wound over his left kidney. Yet, he's upright and walking, which I find amazing. A medic bandages him up. The man is in good spirits and even smiles some as if his wound is nothing more than a bloody nose.

The only other people around are a few women and children and another old man of perhaps fifty. He's detained but appears harmless. We're ordered to group in the nearby paddies for extraction to another landing zone. As we move out, the old man stops at a homemade bird trap and extracts a good sized bird. He grins at us through decaying teeth. He's obviously proud of his catch. He keeps the bird with him all day, treating it lovingly, almost as if the bird is his grandchild. Strangely, even though the old man is being detained and he's not certain where we're going, he doesn't appear to be frightened or intimidated by us.

We are to move by air, and Charlie Company will be the first extracted. As we begin to form for pick up, we hear a report from a pilot of receiving ground fire.

The choppers come back quickly over the tree line and we jump on board. As I run to jump on, I instinctively look at the skin of the chopper for bullet holes. I see none. Someone yells to the door gunner over the noise of the engines and asks if they received fire. He shrugs as if he doesn't know anything about it. I relax a little. Surely, if they had actually received fire, they'd know it. On our approach, I look down at our LZ and I see the guys from Charlie Company standing leisurely in the nearby tree line. They look like they're just hanging around the barracks waiting for a week-end pass, but they obviously aren't under fire. I'm relieved.

We touch down, exit and make the customary run from the choppers. A local family is in the typical Vietnamese squat, eyeing us as if we're aliens. I spot the bird man, who's still with us. I wonder what he thinks about his first helicopter ride.

It's getting hot. We move along a tree line with VC bunkers and down a canal with no water because the tide is out, which means tough going again in knee deep mud. I tire quickly. I learn that the earlier report of fire was an error and came from a new pilot who was overly nervous.

The call comes for extraction, but we have a problem. The ATCs can't get up the little 100 foot wide stream to pick us up and we can't get to the larger stream about half a kilometer away before dark. The tide is out and the water is too shallow for the ATCs.

A decision is made to use an assault support patrol boat (ASPB) as a shuttle ferry. It has a much more shallow draft than the ATCs. But this is extremely dangerous. Thirty soldiers at a time are loaded onto the small bow and rear deck of the boat. There's absolutely no protection should the VC hit us. This is like riding a New York subway train with no top or sides at 5:30 p.m. during rush hour. One B-40 rocket could get twenty or more of us, and a sniper can easily get half of us before we could possibly react.

I remove my flak vest. No one in his right mind would consider this crazy ride in any environment, especially in a combat zone. We're less than forty feet from the heavy foliage on both sides of the stream. I wonder where the VC are. We're ducks on a pond. Fortunately, we make it out safely and rendezvous with and load onto the ATCs. The VC have missed their chance.

11:15 P.M.
Friday, January 19, 1968
Hello Sweets,
I've certainly been busy since I got back from R&R. I guess it was good that I got so busy when I got back. I hope you made it back okay. I just can't say enough about being with you and the kids. The best thing about the end of R&R is that now the end is in sight. I love you, Sug, so much that it hurts.

The Mekong Delta, its streams and numerous waterways.

Bear Cat "international" airstrip

Dong Tam, My Tho branch of the Mekong River, turning basin, sand dredges

Dong Tam "waterfront development"

Chaplain James Johnson stands in front of his "hooch" the Office of the Chaplain, 3/60th Infantry

The children at the My Tho Orphanage

Armored Troop Carriers (ATC's) and Monitors attached to USS
Colleton

Memorial service for Lt. Larry Gardner, August, 1967

Typical crossing of a stream. Photo by Charlie Taylor

Crossing a jungle stream with the aid of a rope

Chaplain Johnson—Rung
Sat—note no weapon,
September, 1967

Staying dry in the jungle was impossible. Photo by Charlie Taylor

"Bubble Top" chopper on aid boat

Chopper landing on deck of *USS Scarecrow* aid boat

Crossing the treacherous
bamboo foot bridges
where they were exposed
to sniper fire

Fire—photo by Charlie Taylor

Blown up track

A proud day for Chaplain Johnson and his first Bronze Star with "V" device for valor

Chaplain Johnson shares a
moment with Captain Joe
Jenkins, commander of
Echo Company

Thanksgiving of 1967 was shared with Pastor Ha and his family.
This photo later played a major part in a miracle

Chaplain Johnson baptizes Lt. Butch Hartson in the turning basin at Dong Tam

Local Vietnamese, mainly women and children, gather for treatment at one of the MEDCAPs

Christmas of 1967 the children line up for goodies at Pastor Ha's orphanage and school

Christmas Eve 1967 communion service for Bravo Company

Christmas field service for
Echo Company

Crossing a stream on one of the sampan boats

Dustoffs from the aid
boat

Pastor Ha's recently remodeled church showing the damage. The VC had used it as their
headquarters for the eighteen hour battle

Memorial service for dead heroes

Captured VC weapons

John Iannacci and Jim Johnson in a Mekong Delta rice paddy, 1996

Young Buddhist monks with Jim, Denny, John, and guide and interpreter

Pastor Ha's thirty-three year old "baby" daughter, holding the twenty-eight year old miracle photo made Thanksgiving of 1967. John Iannucci, Dennis Schoville and Johnson have since raised enough money for her to build a new home which she moved into in October of 1999

A happy reunion: guide, Johnson, Ming (recently arrived from Holland) Barbara Johnson, Mrs. Ha.

Dong Tam, 1996 View from Route 66 new bridge; former turning basin to the right

CHAPTER SIX

January 20–February 5, 1968

SATURDAY, JANUARY 20, 1968: Tomorrow we move back aboard the ships. My new home will be the "Apple," or more correctly, the APL. It's not nearly as comfortable as the *Colleton*.

SUNDAY, JANUARY 21, 1968: Today is moving day! What a mess! No one knows where anyone is supposed to be. I finally find the area where the officers berths are located and decide to just pick a bunk. I take a top one. I have much less room than I did on the *Colleton*. I have no desk, not to mention an office and I only have a tiny locker. I can't even find a private place to make a tape to Barbara. Everyone is complaining. Joe Jenkins, bunked just below me, compares our situation to that of sardines in a can.

All in all, morale is beginning to sag. No one is happy about the move. Some of the soldiers are already beginning to complain about a few of the shipboard navy trying to "boss" them around. I decide I'd better keep tabs on this because some sailors just might get "abused" if they don't cool their arrogance.

It's time for bed and I realize that my bunk selection might have been a bit hasty. Directly over my head, about eighteen inches away is a blasted fluorescent light. It illuminates the entire compartment and glares right in my eyes! How can I sleep with it glaring in my face?

MONDAY, JANUARY 22, 1968: I fly to the hospitals in Saigon and Long Binh. On the way back, I stop to see Bert Kirby at Bear Cat.

TUESDAY, JANUARY 23, 1968: Today we have an area chaplains' meeting at Bear Cat. One of the 'brass' chaplains from Long Binh is to lead the gathering. He smokes a pipe, and I don't like that. It's almost as bad as cigars!

After the meeting, Charlie Clanton, who's been reassigned from one of the cavalry units to the division support command (DISCOM), asks if I'm going to ask for reassignment. He says there'll be an opening in DISCOM soon and that I need to ask if I want out of the field. I decide to talk to Big Bob Wood, the division chaplain, about this the next time I'm in Bear Cat.

WEDNESDAY, JANUARY 24, 1968: Back at the ships, we have three soldiers who've refused to go to the field, and they're being held temporally in the brig on the *Benewah*. The King wants me to visit and interview them.

I've never been to the ship's brig before. In fact, after getting directions, I still have difficulty finding it because it's so small. Once there, I ask the guard to let me in to visit the troops.

"They can't have visitors until after lunch," he says arrogantly.

"Who says?"

"Policy."

Big deal, this jerk must believe he has "the brass" behind him. I feel myself flush with anger. "Well, my policy is that since I'm these soldiers' chaplain, I can see them anytime I want. So, let me in!"

"Sir, I can't. I'll get in trouble." He verifies he was assigned here from brigade headquarters.

"Soldier, if you don't let me in, you'll be in more trouble than you ever dreamed of. Now, I didn't sleep well last night and I'm in a bad mood. Unlock this door. That's an order." I've never used rank like this before, and I'm not happy to have done it now. This is not like me. But I'm irritated that this punk thinks he can throw his weight around. Right now he represents all that's bad about how this war has gone and how some of my heroes have been treated.

"Yes sir," he says. "But will you take responsibility for violating policy?"

"I'd be delighted to. Here's my name. I want you to make sure you give it to your superior and tell him I made you break policy." By now, I'm talking rather loud. He unlocks the door. The soldiers are grinning because they have heard our discussion.

"Chaplain, that guard's been acting like God's second in command all day. I'm glad you didn't take any crap from him," one of the soldiers says.

Grinning, I sit on a bunk and ask them what's going on. For the next thirty minutes, all three men talk about why they don't want to go back to the field. What can I do, encourage them to change their minds so they can get shot or killed? I tell them they'll be court-martialed if they continue to refuse to go to the field. We have a matter-of-fact conversation about their options. Their rationale is that going to LBJ is better than getting killed.

I return to the APL. After a memorial service, I walk up to the outside top deck, thinking that if this memorialized soldier had refused to go to the field, he'd probably still be alive.

THURSDAY, JANUARY 25, 1968: Today's operation is in Mo Cai. I leave with Charlie Company at 3:00 A.M. During my junior year at Wake Forest,

I took a job delivering newspapers in the dorms for some extra money. I had to get up at 5:00 A.M. and I thought that was bad. But, at least I didn't risk being ambushed while delivering papers.

We beach on an island and load onto choppers. We rise quickly and make a huge circle to the left over the river, complete a 360 degree turn and head up river. We land about two miles across the river from the fire support base. The 105s have softened up the area and the results are numerous craters from the exploded shells.

Our search and destroy mission is uneventful. At 12:30 P.M. we stop in a small village of four or five hooches and set up a blocking force. It's a lazy couple of hours. At 2:30 P.M., someone wonders aloud what might be in some of the bunkers in the hooches. Out of curiosity, one of the guys crawls into one. He exits quickly, looking like he's just seen the one-eyed, one-horned flying purple people eater.

"Some gooks are in there!"

"Throw a grenade in and kill the SOBs," someone yells.

"Hold it," Frank Pina says. "Don't throw any grenades. Tell them to come out with their hands behind their heads," he tells our interpreter.

Slowly, two women, a small child and an old man emerge from the bunker. They look like they're halfway up the gallows' steps. Apparently, when they saw us coming a few hours ago, they huddled in their bunker, thinking we'd just pass on through the area. It must have been very difficult to keep the small child quiet for such a long time in the cramped space of the bunker. They don't know how close they have come to being killed.

We get the order to move to an area to be extracted at the river. I pick some bananas on the way because I'm out of C-rations and the ride in will be a long one. I decide to ride aboard an ASPB because the King is aboard and this will give me a chance to spend some time with him. We're the only two passengers aboard. The King and I have a long conversation while we are en route. He's quite concerned about morale and troop welfare. Yet, few of the troops ever see this compassionate and caring side of him. So goes the life of a commander.

After dark, I decide to eat the bananas. They taste horrible.

FRIDAY, JANUARY 26, 1968: Half of the night the fluorescent light just over my head is on. I finally put a towel over my head. I go to sleep but then I get too hot.

SATURDAY, JANUARY 27, 1968: Another truce will occur for Tet. That means we'll set up and have a few days of down time in the field. None of us are sure what Tet is; something about a lunar new year celebration. I don't really care. I just want to continue to mark off my 365.

SUNDAY, JANUARY 28, 1968: After service, it's another lazy day. Morale is relatively good. I hear some grumbling from some of the soldiers who claim the navy crew of the APL is harassing them. I decide to look into this when we return from the Tet truce.

MONDAY, JANUARY 29, 1968: I leave with Echo Company for the pre Tet operation. We embark in the middle of the night for the long ride.

We're to set up for the Tet truce, which begins at 6:00 P.M. today. We beach and sweep for about 1000 meters where we come to a canal cross-roads. The plan is for Echo Company to set up on a corner, Alpha Company on another corner and Bravo Company on another with a company of 3/47th on the 4th corner. Charlie Company is pulling fire support base security. We'll be set for the duration of the truce so it's necessary to dig in.

The best of my understanding is that Tet is to the Vietnamese somewhat like a combination of the 4th of July, Labor Day, Thanksgiving, and Christmas. The annual celebration is a big deal. Many of the ARVN soldiers will return to their homes for the Tet celebration. This does not make me feel secure. What if the VC decide to hit some of the ARVN units while they're half fit?

We're located near the Cambodian border at another no name point on the map. A brief staff meeting indicates that intelligence is saying the enemy will intentionally violate the truce tonight or early tomorrow. Previous reports were for a post Tet offensive, but now, it may be during Tet. South Vietnamese leaders are apparently ignoring the reports. My stomach tightens.

At 9:00 P.M., I hear a significant amount of radio chatter. Our fire support base located two miles down stream is under mortar attack! We go on 100 percent alert. But the fire support base attack is over shortly. We suffer no casualties.

Soon after 9:30 P.M., our real attack occurs; not from the VC but from the mosquitoes. They're absolutely terrible. I have covered myself with repellent but that does no good. Everyone is grumbling and cursing these insects.

TUESDAY, JANUARY 30, 1968: At 4:00 A.M. the radio operator (RTO) awakens me and says, "Alpha-6 wants to talk to you on the radio."

I can't imagine what Captain Pina wants at this time of morning. I pick up the radio and Frank says, "We need you at our position at first light. Can you get here ASAP? I'll brief you as soon as you arrive. Over."

"I'll be there ASAP. Out."

Frank's voice sounds different. Something's up. The radio operator says he heard a single shot in Alpha Company's position about ten minutes before but nothing was said on the radio about receiving fire. Snipers seldom fire just one shot. I suddenly feel anxious. Frank has called for my help many times in the past, but never during the night like this. I can't go back to sleep wondering what's up.

At first light, I walk the few meters to waters' edge, wake a Boston whale boat operator and ask to be taken the thirty meters to the other side of the small stream to Alpha Company's position. Once there, I quickly find Frank.

"What's going on, Frank?"

"Jim, I'm glad you came over. We have a problem. One of our new men killed another. It was apparently an accident." Frank's face is drawn.

"What happened?"

"The idiot dropped his M-16 in the dark and his new buddy was asleep a few feet away. The M-16 went off and blew the man's brains out. He never knew what hit him."

"Who was he?"

"I don't know." Frank asks the three or four others in the command post, but no one knows. "His body is over here. Maybe you knew him."

We walk a few paces and the unmistakable form of a still body is under a poncho. I remove the cover to look at the soldier as everyone else turns and looks away. I recognize the smell of blood and death, but I do not know the man. The exit wound of the M-16 bullet has left a fist-sized hole and taken a major portion of the soldier's brain. I cover him again and say a silent prayer. I want to cry. I hardly know the sound of my own voice as I tell Frank I do not recognize the dead man.

"We have to get his body out of here on the resupply chopper," Frank tells me. "Is there anything you need to do with him, Chaplain?" Baptists don't do last rites. Even though Frank is Nazarene, he wants things to be done properly. That's the military part of him.

"No. I just need to spend some time with the guy who shot him."

I am directed to another new man, am told his name is Sam.

The sun is up now as I make my way to the defensive position shared by the five man fire team. Everything looks normal. No one, though, is looking at anyone else.

"Hello, Sam. I heard what happened." There's a pause.

"Yeah, it was bad, Chaplain." He won't make eye contact.

"How did it happen?"

After an awkward pause he says, "I just dropped my M-16, I guess. I thought the safety was on. The gun went off and it scared the daylights out of me. My platoon sergeant started cursing at me. That was before either of us knew that anyone had been hit. It was dark and we couldn't see. He didn't make any sound at all."

"How did you know he'd been hit?"

"The sergeant wanted us all to hunker down since the shot may have given our position away. He called out one by one to all the squad members. He didn't answer. The sergeant cursed at him and said to 'wake up.' He came over with his red flashlight and saw he'd been hit. There was nothing we could do." Sam is speaking in a monotone.

"Is there anything I can do for you?" I ask.

"I don't think so."

"I'll keep you in my prayers. If you want to talk, let me know. I'll be around. I know you didn't mean to do this." He tears up slightly, but quickly forces his emotions back down. I feel so inadequate.

I walk the fifty meters back to the command post with a heavy heart. I wish there were more I could do or say. I feel so badly for both Sam and for the family of the KIA. I resolve to spend more time with Sam. Here's a nineteen-year-old draftee who's killed, not a VC, but a friend. I can't begin to imagine what impact this will have on him in future years, assuming he makes it through this hell alive.

"The chopper is inbound to pick him up," Frank tells me.

We load the body and the crew chief only gives a brief glance at the body wrapped in the poncho, as though if you don't look at it, it isn't real. Dead bodies remind us of how mortal we are and as young guys, none of us want that reminder. This war has a way of interfering greatly with life. God, I want out of the field—and this danger.

The chopper flies away over the horizon. If this accident had occurred in the civilian world, there'd be a wake, a funeral, condolences, and the soldier who killed his buddy would have much support, counseling and understanding in helping him deal with his shock, grief and guilt. Here none of these rituals are possible. This in itself is tragedy on top of tragedy.

Frank decides he will send Sam out on a short recon patrol. I concede that it will probably be better for him. All he'd do here is remain in his defensive position only a few feet from where the accident occurred. I suggest that when he gets back, maybe Frank could change Sam to another fire team. Frank agrees.

I spend the next several hours making my rounds to the other Alpha Company's positions. They all have questions about what happened. I emphasize that it was an accident and that we all must be very careful. There's no joking and bantering this morning. Grief is as heavy as morning dew.

Tet is supposed to be a happy time. It's not starting out to be happy for any of us.

WEDNESDAY, JANUARY 31, 1968: At midmorning, a soldier says to me, "Chaplain, something big is happening. I just heard on my transistor radio that several cities up north are being hit by the VC." He has his transistor radio on AFRN. We soon learn that USARV has, as of 10:00 A.M., terminated the Tet truce. Obviously, something really big is up. Our orders are to stay close to the waterways in the event we need to make a rapid move toward the population centers.

Even though the news is still sparse, the word is that the VC have mounted attacks on a number of cities from the DMZ to the Delta. Supposedly the Delta cities of My Tho, Ben Tre, Cai Lai, Cai Be, Vinh Long and Can Tho are under attack or will be soon.

"Fifteen minutes until we'll be picked up," is the command from Frank. The entire battalion is to relocate to another fire support base. The boats come and we're gone. We arrive at the new fire support base at 4:00 P.M. and unload. Anxiety is rising. Intelligence says many other cities are expecting imminent attacks, including Saigon.

At 10:00 P.M. we load up quickly. No one knows where we're going. The darkness and rapidity of our departure mean that we'll inadvertently leave some gear behind. Tomorrow the artillery will police up what we've left in the dark.

We're told that a battalion-sized VC ambush is waiting for us between here and the main river, which is about two kilometers away. I wonder if this will be another Snoopy's Nose. The boat captains have orders to fire with every weapon if we're hit but to keep moving through the kill zone. All infantry are combat ready with weapons loaded and ready to fire over the sides of our boats. I'm terrified. The night is pitch black. I can barely see the tree line on the banks of the small 150 foot stream. "Please let us get to the big river quickly," I pray. To preserve our concealment, we use no flares from the artillery as we travel down the stream.

The only sound is the steady hum of the boat engines. We have radio silence and are told to keep it that way until we reach the river unless we're hit.

The first VC rocket hits a boat up ahead. In half a second, every gun on every boat has opened up. Red tracer rounds are flying into each stream bank and green VC tracers are coming back at us. Several boats are hit but none are incapacitated. Reports of wounds are called in. The navy commander reinforces the order that no boat is to slow.

My ATC rear-ends the boat just ahead in the dark. I'm already hunkered down on my knees but the collision throws me on my back. After three or four minutes, I see no more green tracers, but we continue to fire as we move on down stream.

Then, it's over. A cease fire is called and we've arrived at the river. The second boat in the convoy, which is an ASPB, reports one navy KIA and several wounded. Apparently, the first rocket did the damage. All our fire power has quickly suppressed the VC fire.

Ah, the safety of the huge Mekong River. No more playing bumper cars while people shoot at us! We took only one KIA and only a few wounded, all navy crewmen. The VC intent was to delay us from moving to the scenes of the major battles in the cities, but that didn't work.

On the long ride back to the Mobile Riverine Force base, the guys are talking about the ambush. Almost all are relatively new. None were at Snoopy's Nose, but they've heard of it and know I was there and keep asking me to compare the two. Of course, this ambush was over in minutes whereas Snoopy's Nose lasted all day and into the night. But, I don't tell them that. I just say, "An ambush is an ambush. I'm glad we got out of this one."

THURSDAY, FEBRUARY 1, 1968: After a long hypnotic boat ride, we finally arrive at the flotilla. It's 2:20 A.M. and we're told hot chow will be served in the mess hall and that we'll embark again after first light. No one knows where.

As I get to my bunk, I talk to Will Davis, who's now the battalion adjutant. "Will, what's going on?"

"Chaplain, the world isn't coming to an end but the VC are trying to make us think it is." Will goes on to tell me that this appears to be an all out offensive by the VC and North Vietnamese Army. Almost all of the major military complexes and cities are under attack, even My Tho, Vinh Long, Ben Tre and Can Tho. Even the USARV HQ compound at Long Binh is being attacked."

"That means those brass hats will finally get a taste of what we've been getting all along." I tell him.

"You got that right, Chaplain." Will laughs. "But, this is a tough way for them to learn about the real war."

I eat, shower, and hit the sack. First light will be here shortly and I'll need as much rest as possible. I'm troubled about what Will said about My Tho. I wonder about Pastor Ha and the kids at the orphanage. I say a prayer for their safety.

Four hours of rest is wonderful but not near enough. It seems that no sooner am I asleep than the call comes to prepare to load. Still, no mention is made of where we're going. The ships are anchored near Vinh Long.

Back on board the ATCs we're told we're heading to My Tho. The 261st and 514th VC battalions are there. They've taken control of the northwest section of the city, and much of the city is on fire. The northwestern section! That's where the orphanage and Pastor Ha's church is located. My gut tightens.

We're told to prepare for street fighting. We stop en route at the Dong Tam turning basin to pick up shotguns. This is in addition to, not in place of, M-79s and M-16s.

I've made the trip to My Tho many times over the little potholed road from Dong Tam, out the gate through "Dog Patch", and on to My Tho. The eight kilometers ride has never been easy because one never knows if a sniper might be lurking in the nearby trees. But once arriving in the city, I've always felt relatively safe. Today, as we leave Dong Tam on the boats, I don't feel safe at all.

As we get out into the My Tho river between Dong Tam and "VC Island," I can already see the plumes of dark smoke arising from My Tho, even though we're still eight kilometers away. The reality of how ferocious things must be in My Tho is revealed in the smoke.

We now know where we're going, and it doesn't look good.

Fighter jets are making strafing runs on My Tho. If the VC are so entrenched that we have to bomb the city, it must really be bad. The boats stay in the middle of the river as we get closer to My Tho. In most of our combat operations, we never know for sure if we'll have contact with the VC. On this mission, we know the VC are here and en masse.

On cue, the boats turn for the riverbank full speed for us to beach. Thankfully, we're unopposed on landing as we go in from the east side of the city. It's 3:30 P.M. Almost immediately, I see a sight that will remain with me forever. Hundreds and hundreds of panicked Vietnamese civilians are streaming away from where the action is. These are women, old men and children, all carrying what they can but in a hurry to get away. The mass is so large that sometimes it is hard for us to maneuver against the exiting horde.

We cut through a number of side streets and alleys heading west and soon begin receiving small arms, automatic and rocket fire. The going is slow as each pocket of resistance must be driven away or eliminated.

As night nears, the intensity of the fighting increases and we continue to receive small arms fire, some rocket propelled grenades and B-40 rockets. We've taken some casualties but no KIAs. The street fighting and door to door clearing of the VC pockets of resistance is methodical and progressive. We have now turned slightly north. At 5:40 P.M., more air strikes are called in.

Knowing how difficult it will be to maneuver in the dark streets, we're ordered to secure a battalion perimeter around a Catholic monastery and some nearby buildings and prepare to assault again at first light. This must be like it was in WW II street fighting.

By 9:00 P.M., most of the firing has ceased. Our command post is on the porch of a large building. I'm not sure where in the city we're now located. I remember that there's a Catholic compound not too far from the orphanage but I don't know if this is the one. Right now, I don't care. I'm just glad the shooting has stopped.

Flares hang lazily over the city. The dim light provides us just enough illumination to keep perspective of where we are. Several of us explore the upstairs of this building and locate a few cots with mattresses. We arrange some of them so that anyone who sleeps can at least have a more comfortable place than on the hard floor or ground.

I decide at 10:00 P.M. to rest on one of the cots in what looks like a monk's cubicle. I find some irony that here I am, a Protestant, resting in a Catholic monk's bed in the midst of a battle. At least I have a comfortable bed, and no need for a sleeping pill tonight! Thank God for small favors.

During the night, we receive periodic sniper fire and on occasion incoming RPGs, but little sustained fighting.

FRIDAY, FEBRUARY 2, 1968: We know the city must be slowly and systematically cleared of VC. If they stand and fight, we also know that wherever they are located, that area will likely be destroyed. Yesterday, our fighter jets were bombing the city bus station. I'll learn later today that the VC used the bus station basement to store weapons for use in this offensive.

At 6:30 A.M. we move carefully to the north through back streets which are no more than dirt paths. No Vietnamese civilians are seen anywhere. They all evacuated yesterday. It's like a ghost town with all the hooches and small buildings but no people. As we move cautiously, we begin receiving some light incoming fire.

Within about two blocks we come to the edge of yesterday's destruction. Explosive devices have damaged and destroyed many structures. We stop our forward movement because a huge shell is half embedded unexploded in the front yard of a hooch. We're afraid to pass near it for fear it will explode. We're told to go around the area.

While we're waiting, I have a talk with a young lieutenant named Dennis McDougall who has only been in country for three weeks. He reminisces about his wife and is homesick for her. He shows me her picture. He carefully places the picture back in the front pocket of his fatigue shirt and we move out.

We break out into a small open area and I realize this is the back side of the orphanage. I don't even recognize the area at first because we're approaching the small compound from the rear, something I've never done before. We've always driven in from the main street about 100 yards away down through a small alley and then into the compound.

Then I see that the little building that houses the small administrative and office area and the sleeping quarters for the orphans has been blown up! I can't believe it! I don't want to believe it! The VC have blown up "our" orphanage. The open air classroom building containing the three classrooms is also severely damaged.

I run the few steps to the destroyed building and peek inside hoping not to see any dead children. I don't. What I do see is rubble from the caved in roof that has smashed their little beds. Many of the artillery ammunition boxes that we gave the orphanage a few months ago for storage of their personal belongings are now in disarray. I'm intensely angry with the VC for creating this chaos and wreckage and for victimizing the orphans once again. I just hope they are alive and safe.

It's now 9:15 A.M. We maneuver toward the alley that leads to the street. This is the alley that I normally would use when visiting the orphanage. Heavy fire has been received near the street for several minutes and now the firing becomes intense. We establish a skirmish line in the row of small hooches in front of the orphanage compound, where the alley comes from the street.

Dennis McDougall, whom I talked with a few moments ago, and one of his M-79 grenade launcher gunners, snake their way up the edge of the alley. Dennis takes the M-79 and begins firing grenades at the nearby VC. Each time he loads, he then swings his body out quickly, fires the grenade and ducks back for cover. After he's done this several times, a VC apparently times his move and just as he swings out to fire, the VC slams an AK-47 round into him. Dennis crumples in the alley. I'm crouched down about thirty meters to his rear along with several other soldiers in our skirmish line.

Realizing they're both very exposed to the VC, the soldier with Dennis hits the ground and low crawls back to us.

"The lieutenant is hit. I think he's dying," he says. I can see Dennis lying in the alley with blood coming out of his mouth and nose.

"Where's he hit?" I ask.

"I don't know. But he looks like he's bleeding all over."

I ask a medic, "Will you go with me and help drag him back here?"

"You lead, Chaplain, and I'll follow. But we'll have to move quickly." I tell the company commander what we're going to do.

"Be careful, Chaplain. Those bastards may still have him in their sights."

We dash to Dennis. Each of us grabs an arm and I pick up his M-16 and we drag him back. It only takes two to three minutes total but it seems like a lifetime. My adrenaline is flowing. All the while, small arms fire is coming at us from several directions.

We place Dennis beside the sparse foliage next to the first hooch in the skirmish line. He's unconscious. The bullet has hit him in the chest. There is a massive amount blood coming from his mouth, nose and ears. We quickly cut away his fatigue shirt and see the hole in his chest.

A stringy mucus like material flows from his mouth and nose. There is so much blood, and the mucus looks like body tissue. We attempt to keep his mouth clear.

I begin talking softly in his ear as the medic places bandages over his wounds. "You're going to be okay. We're going to get you medevaced in just a few minutes." He tries to respond but only gurgles and coughs. I remember the picture of his wife in his front fatigue pocket and take it out. It is saturated with his blood. The only thing left in his pocket is a New Testament. I remove it, too.

"I'm putting the picture of your wife in your front pants pocket so it doesn't get lost." He opens his eyes and nods. "You'll be OK. Just hang in there with us." Deep down, though, I really believe he's dying. I tell him I'll pray for him and I do, holding my mouth very close to his ear.

"Chaplain, we're calling in artillery on those bastards on the street. Tell the lieutenant that we're going to pay them back for what they did to him," the company commander tells me.

"Did you hear that?" I ask. He nods weakly. I'm not convinced he understands anything at the moment.

"On the way," the artillery forward observer screams. I'm holding Dennis's hand. There is a huge explosion.

"That's close," I shout to the medic next to me.

"What was that?" A medic yells as smoke and dust erupt from the hooch next to where we're hunkered down two feet away.

"Help, I'm hit," someone screams. Others yell for help. I jump up and dash the ten feet around the corner to the rear entrance of the hooch. Inside, it seems as if everyone has been hit.

"Everyone stay down," someone shouts. We all assume that we've been hit by a VC rocket propelled grenade and that others will follow. We're still receiving small arms fire. I crawl through the rubble and quickly learn that no one is dead but ten are wounded. Lieutenant Phil Page is still standing and looks dazed. He must have a hundred fragment wounds, most very small, varying in size from a pencil lead to a pencil eraser. Blood is oozing but not gushing. Others have varying degrees of wounds.

"Call for another dustoff. We'll need at least one more chopper," I yell to the company commander's radio operator.

"Chaplain, I have no feeling below my knee," one soldier says. This is the same soldier with whom Joe Jenkins had the run in a few months ago over his KKK markings. He's lying on his side and looks to me for assurance.

"Let me see." His boot is mangled and blood soaked. I unlace what's left of his boot and inside is nothing but torn flesh and bone fragments.

"You'll be OK," I lie. "I'm going to relace your boot and we'll get you out of here in a few minutes." Thank goodness he can't see his foot, or what's left of it. My purpose in lacing his boot is to keep his foot from falling off. I also hope it'll serve as a makeshift tourniquet. The surgeons will have little trouble finishing the amputation. There's little left to cut.

We're all working frantically with the wounded, when I hear someone yelling, "No, no, add 400 meters! Do you read me? Add 400 meters!" This is the artillery forward observer who's calling in the artillery. What came in on top of us was our own artillery round. The direction of one of the guns at Dong Tam, eight kilometers away, was aimed slightly off, causing the round to impact 400 meters from where it was intended.

Corrected, artillery is now beginning to impact closer and closer. Volley after volley whistles in where the VC have held reign for the past thirty-six hours. Tactical air strikes with napalm have also been called in on the VC positions up the street.

"Chaplain, we've got to get that dustoff in here," the medic tells me. "The lieutenant is going to die if we don't. Some of these other guys may also bleed to death if we don't get them out. What are they saying about the dustoff?" There's panic in his voice.

"I don't know but I'll crawl to the command post and find out." Small arms fire is still coming from several directions as our artillery continues to pound the VC positions.

"We've got to get these wounded out of here. Two are in bad shape," I tell Chip.

"OK, Chaplain. We're going to lift the artillery as both dustoffs are close."

The medic and I slide a poncho under Dennis because he'll have to be carried fifty meters to the opening next to the orphanage, which is the only place the dustoff can land. One of the on board medics gets us a stretcher, we quickly place Dennis on it and heave it back onto the chopper. As I turn away to help load the other wounded now being brought by other soldiers, I take a last glimpse of Dennis. He has his left hand in his left pants pocket.

This dustoff lifts and the second one lands and the rest of the wounded are quickly loaded. Then it, too, is airborne back to the 3rd Surg at Dong Tam. Almost as soon as they're over the tree line, the artillery begins its mission again.

As I sprint back to our skirmish line, I'm praying that Dennis makes it. But with the AK 47 bullet that has slammed into his chest, I have my doubts. As I'm lying low while the artillery is doing its job, I'm aware of tears running down my cheek. It's not the orphanage, or the kids, it's Dennis's hand on his wife's picture. I can't help thinking of Barbara.

We're now moving up the alley toward the main street. As I turn the corner, I take one glance back toward the orphanage. I do not want to face the fact that I will probably never learn what has happened to the kids, Pastor Ha and his family.

The artillery is now lifted and I only hear sporadic gunfire that sounds like it's a couple of blocks away. As we reach the main street, my senses are assaulted from all directions. Death and destruction are everywhere. Scores of dead bodies litter the street. Buildings and vehicles are blown up, and many are in flames. There are bodies without heads or limbs; there are bodies of old men and women. I can't tell if they're VC, civilian or ARVN. Cars, Lambrettos, and bicycles are scattered as if King Kong has rampaged down the street and smashed everything in sight.

Two destroyed civilian ambulances are about thirty meters apart. I wonder if they were both on rescue runs and barreled into the VC stronghold. One has the front wheels and front end extensively damaged by an explosion. The dead driver is crumpled down on what was the passenger side. The second ambulance has also been hit and is sitting cross- ways on one lane. A second B-40 rocket round has hit on the driver's side and its unexploded warhead is wedged between the door and the chrome strip just above the door. Its driver isn't in sight. Both ambulances have many bullet holes.

The VC have vacated this area of the city within the past few minutes. We're still only a couple blocks from the orphanage compound. Weapons litter the street. Not far from the ambulances is a pile of B-40 rockets about the size of three bushel baskets. The VC left these in their haste to escape from our artillery. Numerous AK-47s and Chi-Com carbines and some small automatic weapons are scattered over a wide area up and down the street.

We're still moving cautiously down each side of the street. A US advisor to the ARVN meets us and thanks us for our help to the 7th ARVN Division. He looks as emotionally emaciated as we feel. He tells me they

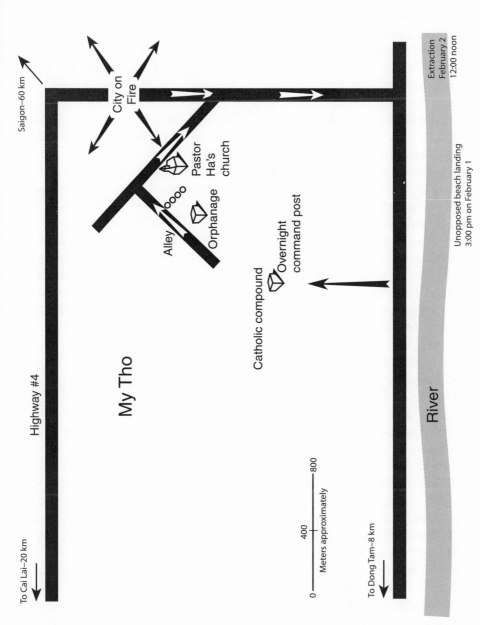

To Cai Lai–20 km

Saigon–60 km

Highway #4

My Tho

City on Fire

Pastor Ha's church

Alley

Orphanage

Catholic compound

Overnight command post

0   400   800
Meters approximately

To Dong Tam–8 km

River

Extraction
February 2
12:00 noon

Unopposed beach landing
3:00 pm on February 1

My Tho February 1–2

had known for some time that the VC were storing weapons throughout the city but they didn't know where. They had found some before the offensive began but with My Tho being a large city, they couldn't know for sure where their weapons were nor how many. He says the air strikes on the bus station yesterday killed many VC who were holing up in and around there.

We continue moving down the street and then we come to Pastor Ha's church. Its recently renovated and redecorated pink structure is an absolute mess. The outside walls have hundreds and hundreds of bullet pockmarks on all surfaces. I quickly glance inside. It, too, is in shambles. Although the structure is still standing, it appears that several explosive devices have detonated inside. The advisor tells me that the VC used the church as their command post for the past eighteen hours. As they were driven out of this area less than half an hour ago, there was obviously an intense shootout here with the approaching ARVN from one side, our artillery from another side, and us coming from a third side.

Pastor Ha had taken such delight in his little church as a beacon of truth and hope in a city besieged by war. I wonder if Pastor Ha also is a victim.

As we continue to move down the street, the horrible scenes continue. Nearby in a small canal are several bodies. A baby is floating face down.

Fifty feet further down the street, a young mother is dead, lying on her back with her head grotesquely twisted and her neck obviously broken. A whimpering infant lies on her body, attempting to nurse.

A little further down the street, a bicycle lies crumpled atop a prone young father whose fatal wounds are still bleeding. Two hysterical children, a boy and a girl of perhaps three and five years old, are each tugging hard on the hands of their dead father pleading with him to get up. Both children have cuts from shell fragments. I want so badly to pick up the children and comfort them. But, I can't. I feel for the pulse of their father and there is none. I call out to a nearby ARVN soldier and ask him to get some help for the children. He, like several of us, has tears in his eyes.

I've been through this sector of My Tho many times going to and from the orphanage. I barely recognize it now. The area has countless craters from explosions. Store front businesses are blown up like match boxes stomped by a schoolyard bully.

By now it's 11:00 A.M. It seems like a long time ago since we evacuated those wounded soldiers at the orphanage. We're now about a half mile from the orphanage compound. Nowhere in the city do I hear any gunfire. Apparently, the VC have all left.

We get word that we'll be picked up by boat at midday for another operation elsewhere. A National Policeman offers us some confiscated Cokes and peanuts. We're all hungry by now. When we left yesterday and headed for My Tho, everyone was told to take as little food as possible and take extra ammunition instead. I had some C-ration peaches this morning. The Cokes are warm but they taste good with the peanuts.

As we make our way the half mile back toward the river, we're a somber group. Everyone is physically tired and our only therapy is the order to "move out."

The boats come, and at 12:00 noon we load and head back up the river toward Dong Tam. I can't get my mind off the two little kids tugging at their dead father's arms screaming for him to get up. I think of my own Kellie and Grey and try not to remember the carnage of the day.

We have moved near Cai Lai, about fifteen miles south southwest of My Tho. We're expecting the VC to retreat to and regroup in this area and are hoping to get in place and engage them again. We sweep in small circles as we did last night. A few of the local ARVN outposts have been overrun and we receive some sniper fire. Mostly, we stay near the boats and wait on the VC.

Intelligence informs us that as the VC were spotted leaving My Tho, they were attacked by our artillery with white phosphorus shells. Many more were killed or wounded.

SUNDAY, FEBRUARY 4, 1968: The night is uneventful. We stay in place in a blocking force. The soldiers in Bravo Company pulled artillery security and weren't at My Tho. They are quite inquisitive about what happened. When I tell Joe Jenkins about the soldier with the mangled foot, his response is, "Damn, I hate him for being a KKK, but I wouldn't want anyone to loose a foot." This reflects Joe's compassion.

Word comes in that we're to fly to Vinh Long. Jim McDonald, the commander of Bravo Company, and Frank Pina, the commander of Alpha Company, both ask me to fly in with their companies. They look worried. I decide to go in with Alpha Company, but later switch to Bravo Company.

Alpha, Bravo, and Echo Companies are all to be airlifted near the Vinh Long airfield. The ARVN units in Vinh Long are under heavy pressure from hundreds of VC. The 3/60th along with the 3/47th are to form a cordon around the west and south sides of the city to keep the VC from escaping. The Song Co Chiem finger of the Mekong River is to be blocked by the boats.

We line up to be picked up for the ride to Vinh Long. Today, as it was in My Tho, we know the VC are at Vinh Long.

We fly low over the Vinh Long airfield which, even from the air, we can tell has been hit hard. It's 5:00 P.M. when we land and we're unopposed. We move into a large rice paddy, which straddles a huge Y shaped tree line. Alpha and Bravo Companies are now maneuvering together and Echo Company is to maneuver a few hundred meters to our right. The 3/47th is coming by boat and is to beach nearby.

We begin moving up a narrow dirt road when we are ambushed. The VC are in a large cemetery on our left near a Buddhist pagoda! The fighting is ferocious. Our guys give them a heavy layer of fire, but the VC are entrenched behind the numerous tombstones. M-79s are used as indirect fire and after a while, most of the VC fire is suppressed. Both Alpha and Bravo Companies are engaged. George Guthy of Alpha Company is the point man and as he's crossing a small bridge, a rear guard VC pops up and fires a RPG. George, a short kid from New York, fires his M-16 and hits the VC, but the grenade explodes and blows George off the bridge. He refuses to be evacuated. Like so many of our guys, he is willing to "play hurt" as we used to say in football when an injured player stayed on the field.

We've taken several casualties by nightfall. We must get the wounded out, especially one soldier who has been shot in the chest. Our perimeter is quickly established with Alpha and Bravo Companies having a joint defense. VC sporadically fire RPGs into our positions. Each time one explodes, I am unnerved. Echo Company is some distance away and they, too, are engaged.

Most of the wounded are from Alpha Company but several soldiers from Bravo Company are also injured. We decide to get a dustoff in beside the pagoda. There's only a very small space for a chopper to descend into among the trees. It'll be very dangerous but, we're in a hornet's nest of VC and we aren't sure how many more of us will be stung tonight.

A medic is attempting to put an IV of plasma into a man shot in the chest. I keep talking to the wounded soldier trying to keep him from going into shock. As always, I keep assuring him that we're going to get him out in a little while and that he'll be fine. He has no exit wound so we don't know what internal injuries he might have. The medic has trouble getting the line into a vein. I try to hold a red flash light for him to see. I'm not sure he ever gets the line hooked up properly. This soldier must get to the hospital.

The dustoff is on the way. We use strobe lights to guide the chopper in. We're still periodically receiving small arms fire and the opening between the pagoda and nearby trees is so limiting. The pilot is forced to turn on his landing lights to see where to put down his aircraft and that makes him an inviting target.

The medic, the wounded guys, and I are almost directly under the Huey as the pilot painstakingly and gradually lowers the craft. At the sound of the main rotor blades striking the tree limbs we all hit the ground, thinking it is enemy fire. If the chopper crashes on top of us, it will explode and we know we'll be crispy critters! Needless to say, are were relieved.

We quickly load our wounded aboard and I yell into the open window of the pilot's cockpit, "God bless you. You're a brave man." From the illumination of his landing lights, I see that he's grinning. He gives me a thumbs up and yells back, "No, you guys are the real heroes."

He now cautiously elevates his craft above us, rotor blades still clipping the vegetation. As the chopper rises, loose twigs and dust are flying everywhere. At seventy-five feet, he lowers his nose, cuts his lights and quickly picks up air speed. Thank God, they're out safely. Like so many of our wounded, I know I'll never learn if the wounded soldier survives or not.

No one sleeps during the night. Periodic small arms fire is exchanged, and RPGs and an occasional B-40 rocket come into us throughout the night. But Alpha and Bravo Companies take no additional casualties. Frank tells me that just across the nearby stream, his men using their starlight scopes can see perhaps thirty dead VC.

Echo Company, which is about one kilometer away, was not so fortunate as Alpha and Bravo Companies. At 8:30 P.M., not long after our dustoff chopper departed, Echo Company was attacked head on. We could only hear the sounds of their battle; we couldn't help. The VC attacked them full force in a frontal assault. Artillery was heavy and for two hours, I could only imagine what was happening just over the tree line.

MONDAY, FEBRUARY 5, 1968: After first light, as I'm making my rounds at Bravo Company's positions, I see that much of this area has been damaged and destroyed. The VC wreaked havoc here on their way into nearby Vinh Long.

John Iannucci is a nineteen year old draftee from Staten Island. He's been here for about three and one-half months and has yet to receive his pay, little as it is. He's fighting for his country pro bono, but his father is sending him money so he can buy cigarettes and toiletries. John and his buddies look old and tired, and his squad has spent the night in a pig pen for protection. It is days and nights like these that age young kids in a hurry.

As I'm talking with John, some Vietnamese civilians drift back into the little hamlet to survey the damage done by the VC. A couple who look to be in their late fifties stop two hooches away from us begin wailing.

I sprint the few paces over to them, pointing to the cross on my left collar. They continue to cry, pointing at two oblong piles of ashes on the floor of their burned out hooch. I had seen the ashes earlier in the morning but paid no particular attention, not knowing what they were. Then, I make out the partially burned image of two bodies. The VC have apparently torched them. The couple points to the bodies, then makes the gesture of someone shooting and then striking a match. The mamasan tells me in broken English that the bodies are those of her aged parents.

The elderly couple's hearts are broken and so is mine. They hang on to me and sob for several minutes. How I wish I could speak words of comfort to them in their own language. But holding them will have to suffice. The man stops crying and begins to shout. He points to a leg bone of one of the bodies. He finally stops yelling and takes two pieces of twisted tin from the blown up hooch next door and, gently, almost lovingly places them over the ashes.

It's time for us to move out, and I don't want to leave this couple. But, there's a war and I must go. I place my hands in a prayer gesture under my chin and bow to them. I glance back after a few paces. They have the most hopeless, hurt and forlorn looks I've ever seen.

As I walk away from the murder scene, I find myself feeling an inner rage unlike any I have felt before. It's as if a reservoir is full after a huge rain and the pressure on the dam is building. I'd like to find a VC, any VC, and beat him senseless.

As I move down the dirt trail I begin seeing the results of yesterday afternoon's battle. I cross over a foot bridge about thirty feet in length, and a soldier in the column ahead yells, "There's a dead VC in the water." I see the man, face down in water about eighteen inches deep, still clutching his rifle. Ten paces beyond are four more dead VC, one with his leg blown off. The other three are already beginning to bloat. Insects are swarming around their faces and wounds.

I'm surprised that the VC have left these bodies behind. They normally operate in three man cells. If one gets wounded or killed, it's the responsibility of the other two to carry their wounded or dead out of the battle area. If more than one is hit, other three man cells are to pick up the slack.

We see blood trails where wounded and dead have obviously been dragged out under cover of darkness. We're moving toward Echo Company's location, which is about 500 meters away. Along the way, I see at least thirty more dead VC. Weapons and documents are also scattered. We must have indeed surprised the VC. In their effort to escape our artillery, gun ships, bombs and small arms, they left many prizes behind.

I admit I'm glad to see these dead VC but as a Christian, I'm not proud of my feelings. These guys all have mothers and wives and girlfriends, but after what they did to the civilians I don't have positive feelings for any of them.

Some of the soldiers are now almost gleeful. Strewn over several hundred meters are bodies, weapons, and documents. After what we have been through the past several days, it's hard to see these dead VC as human beings; we see them as good riddance. I'm stunned and sorry about the feeling.

I'm eager to get to Echo Company's position because during the night they had a KIA and it was an officer. I want to know who he is. When I arrive at their command post, everyone looks like they're in a daze. Last night's frontal VC assault is still vividly reflected in their haunting eyes and dirty faces. Chip, the company commander, tells me it was Lt. Ron Wood who was killed. Ron had been slightly wounded by some fragments in November. His mother had written to me several times. Even though I have never met Ron's family, I feel close to his parents because their letters reflect a deep love for their only son. I also know that he was engaged.

I learn that in their frontal attack of Echo Company's perimeter last night, several VC charged across a shallow pond and came straight at Ron's position. He and his men were behind an earthen dam about four feet high, which was perfect protection. But for some reason, instead of throwing a hand grenade from his crouched position, he stood up to throw it. His grenade killed three of the charging VC, but Ron never knew that because just as he released the grenade, a bullet caught him in the head.

The three VC Ron killed are still in the shallow water about forty feet from where he tossed his grenade. I have a sudden urge to throw rocks at their bodies. I can now better understand why in history, conquering warriors dragged bodies of their dead enemies through the streets.

By now it's 10:00 A.M. We've been out for eight days straight and most of us are very weary. Then, we get good news. We're told to prepare to be airlifted out; we're going in.

As we move out into the open rice paddy to prepare for pick up, we see even more bodies. A lieutenant says he has counted sixty-four dead VC and comments, "The only good VC is a dead VC."

I've not had a shower for eight days; have eaten nothing but C-rations, seen so many dead bodies, and been so scared so many times that I'm numb. I'm so tired. When I get to the APL, I sign the notification of next kin letters for our KIAs that Paul has typed for me and get a wonderful shower. I haven't shaved or brushed my teeth, for days. I go to the officer's dining room for dinner. What a contrast. The navy observes its formality as the senior navy officer aboard sits at the head of the long dining table and everyone else sits along the sides. Since the APL isn't actually a ship, just a barracks barge, the highest ranking navy officer aboard is an ensign, which is the same as a second lieutenant in the army. He can't be more than twenty-three. Tonight, this strikes me as funny. Here's the King of the Hill who's a lieutenant colonel and most of his staff and commanders are captains and majors. Yet, a lowly ensign sits at the head of the table. It's not that the shavetail ensign is gloating over his position because he obviously feels quite ill at ease.

I'm in bed early. I need time to myself and bed is the only place for this. I spend a few moments preparing for the service tomorrow under the ever present fluorescent light. My preaching professor in seminary would be appalled at how little study time I'm putting into my sermons of late.

I wonder what Barbara and the kids are doing. The division chaplain has scheduled a meeting in a few days at Bear Cat. I've decided that I'll try to arrive early and ask for an assignment out of the field. The decision feels good.

I learn that I've been recommended for a very high valor award for getting Dennis McDougall out of the alley in My Tho. I'm so tired, it doesn't seem to matter. It feels great to simply lie on a nice mattress, in air conditioned climate, and sleep.

CHAPTER SEVEN

February 6–March 6, 1968

TUESDAY, FEBRUARY 6, 1968: Bravo Company moves out again this morning. Intelligence says that many VC have moved out of Vinh Long southwest and Bravo Company's job is to attempt to interdict them. The other companies are to stand by to assist should they contact the VC.

Then the call comes. Bravo Company and the boats have just been ambushed! The rest of the battalion is to move out immediately. I'm still on the pontoon. I run upstairs and get my field gear.

We had hoped for at least three days rest.

Chip, the twenty year old commander of Echo Company, seems particularly vulnerable since their battle two nights ago when Ron was killed. Chip's a nice kid. But, that's exactly what he is, a kid. A captain this young is almost unheard of. He enlisted, went to officer candidate school, was commissioned and has been promoted to captain. He's still wet behind the ears, yet, he's responsible for the lives of 100 soldiers in combat.

Morale is low. I decide to go out with Echo Company. Most of these guys have been in country only a few weeks. Yet, they've already seen significant combat, more than enough to last a lifetime.

I have a feeling that if I keep rolling the dice, my number will come up. As we leave the main river and go into a smaller stream, I feel the anxiety mounting among the troops. I joke with them and say, "I'm tired of taking orders every day. When I get back to the world, I intend to create my own army, then I'll take only my own orders."

Then it happens again! A B-40 rocket is launched into the ATC two boats ahead. Instead of running through the ambush, we beach and take the VC head on. Small arms fire is coming from several directions as we run off the ramps into the tree line.

The boat hit by the rocket has numerous soldiers wounded and we must get them out. A rice paddy is just past the tree line about 100 meters away and we decide to move the wounded off the ATC and attempt a dustoff from there, if we can secure the area.

It's now a little past 2:30 P.M. I work feverishly with the injured. Of the ten wounded, three are in bad shape. I talk to them while we apply field bandages. As usual, I pray with several of them.

It's physically hard work carrying these guys to the edge of the tree line. Just walking through water and mud is difficult. Several times we receive small arms fire and must cease moving the wounded and take cover. I and a newly arrived lieutenant named Greyson Raulston find ourselves taking cover in the same location several times.

Then I see them. An NBC camera crew is filming what we're doing. I can't imagine how they got to the APL and on this operation. As we begin moving the wounded to the edge of the tree line, I want to tell the camera crew to put their blasted equipment down and help. It takes four to move each litter the 100 meters through the calf deep mud. My concern is getting the guys out.

Finally the dustoff comes. We quickly load the litter patients aboard and the chopper lifts off. A second dustoff lands and we finish the process. The NBC crew continues to film as we move the wounded out.

At 3:15 P.M., the VC have withdrawn and we are ordered to reload onto the ATCs again for another short move.

We move a few hundred meters to where Bravo Company is and disembark. Several wounded from Bravo are being brought to the aid boat. All three companies are in contact now with the VC. I join Bravo Company and once more spend some time crouched behind a fallen log with Lieutenant Greyson Raulston. Alpha Company is pushing toward us about 600 meters away. Echo Company is to our right. Most boats are now beached along a gradual curve in the stream.

Fighting is heavy and the artillery, gun ships and jets alternate putting heavy ordinance on the VC positions. This is reminiscent of Snoopy's Nose, though with less intensity. We're still taking casualties as the VC continue to fight back. I get a call requesting that I move back to the aid boat if possible because a Bravo Company soldier is being brought there who has thrown himself on a grenade and is badly wounded.

As I low crawl back to the nearby aid boat, I spot three soldiers dragging a wounded man on a poncho. We get a litter from the aid boat and place the young man on it and move him to a dry spot just in front of the aid boat. Then I see how badly he's wounded and recognize Tom Kinsman. They tell me his squad was hunkered down when suddenly, a grenade tossed by a nearby VC comes in. Instantly, this hero threw his body on top of the grenade just as it exploded. His flak vest kept him from being killed immediately, but his wounds are numerous and serious.

He's still conscious but dazed. He can only mumble although I get the impression that he's aware of what's going on around him. I tell him we'll get him to the hospital in just a few minutes. I hope he doesn't go into shock. His wounds look very bad and I wonder if he'll make it to the hospital. Surely he'll be put in for the medal of honor for this action.

I'm concerned about the dustoff landing on the aid boat, as it will be fully exposed to the nearby VC, but it comes anyway. Two medics, a river rat on the aid boat, and I lift the litter over our heads and onto the deck. Then we climb the few feet to the landing deck and get the litter aboard the chopper. Three other wounded also get aboard and then the chopper is gone.

Fighting continues until shortly after dark. We evacuate several other wounded, some with bad injuries. Then it's dark and a lull in the fighting occurs. I decide to stay on the aid boat for the night as the three companies have their perimeter established together and most of the ATCs are beached and serve as part of that perimeter.

At 9:30 P.M. I step onto the bank of the stream at the front of the beached aid boat. All hell breaks loose two boats away. Enemy green tracers are hitting the boat and bouncing off. The aid boat and several others return fire. I jump down into the aid boat well deck thinking that a huge battle is taking place, then, it's over. Just like that, the shooting stops.

WEDNESDAY, FEBRUARY 7, 1968: The rest of the night is uneventful. By morning the VC are gone. Each of our companies sweeps their area. Thirty five VC weapons are found which include carbines, BARs, machine guns and B-40 rocket launchers. We learn that this area was to have been the temporary base camp for the VC to regroup after leaving Vinh Long. We sure messed up their new home.

At midday we get orders to prepare for extraction back to the Mobile Riverine Force base. On the way in, I wonder about Tom Kinsman. What makes a man throw himself on a grenade? I feel honored just to have been able to help this young hero.

At 4:00 P.M., we're sent back to the APL. I shower and prepare for supper.

"Chap, did you hear the news?" Joe Jenkins asks, and I can tell by his tone that it is not good news.

He tells me Colonel Hill has relieved Chip, the captain in command of Echo Company. I am shocked at this news. I like Chip. Yes, he's immature, but he made captain at twenty. Joe explains that the King felt Chip overreacted Saturday night in Vinh Long when they were hit. After Ron was killed, Chip called in automatic artillery and two tubes of artillery were burned out in the process. The King felt the battle conditions weren't severe enough to warrant this overreaction, so he has decided to relieve him of command.

I go into the officer's mess and it's obvious that everyone has heard the news. There is a subdued atmosphere, but no one mentions why. Neither the King nor Chip have arrived in the dining room yet, and no one knows what to say. Instead, several of the staff officers question me about the soldier who threw himself on the grenade.

Then the King of the Hill comes in. He glances around the room uncomfortably but looks at no one directly as he takes his seat. As he reaches for the bread, he hesitates and then says, "In case you don't know already, I've relieved the Echo Company commander of command for reasons between the two of us." It's as if he can't even say Chip's name.

There's an uncomfortable silence until the adjutant breaks it by saying, "Where will he work now?"

"I'm not sure. Probably in division somewhere." Then, as an afterthought, the King adds, "Lt. John Christy will take temporary command of Echo Company until we can get a permanent replacement."

Someone mentions the weapons we captured and then the room is filled with chatter about the last operation. Everyone is glad that the subject of Chip's removal is over. He doesn't come to dinner. I feel anger at the King, yet I don't know the details nor the rationale behind it. I also feel a bit sorry for the King, too.

I leave dinner and go onto the outside deck to look for Chip. I discover him back on the fan tail, alone, looking out into the growing darkness.

I tell him I heard what happened, that I'm sorry, and ask if he is okay.

"I'll be okay." He pauses, then adds, "If I'm such a bad commander, why did he give me the command in the first place?" Even though it's getting dark, I can see his eyes are wet. "That son of a bitch has no idea what it was like out there Saturday night. He was back at the TOC somewhere safe and sound. I did what was necessary to save my men. Ron was already dead and the gooks were everywhere. Hell, Chaplain, he'd have relieved me for not being aggressive enough, if we'd been overrun. You can't win with that bastard."

"Chip, I don't know what to say except I'm sorry."

"Yeah, thanks Chaplain. That means a lot. No one else has said a word to me".

"I guess no one knows what to say," I tell him. He opens up then and I hear the frustration in his words.

"I guess so. Shit, when you get right down to it, the bastard probably is saving my life. At least now I can get a staff job like those other SOBs and not have to be shot at. I wanted to be a career officer. Went to OCS at nineteen after just one year of college. I was the youngest officer candidate in my class. I figured I'd go back to the world, go to boot strap and make the army a career. But now that's down the drain. Shit, I'd rather pump gas for a living than go through this anymore. A bad officer's efficiency report will kill my career, but, I don't care. At least, I don't have to worry about getting out. That decision's already been made for me. Screw 'em all."

We talk a little more. It's now full dark and I tell Chip I must go back inside.

The 3/60th has taken a lot of casualties in the past few days. In fact, we had three killed and nearly forty wounded in the past thirty-six hours. We had five KIAs and almost 100 wounded in the past ten days. Now Chip is a casualty of a different kind. A Purple Heart won't honor his emotional scars, a Bronze Star will not reward his personal bravery. He is hurt. He knows the shame of what others may think of him and perhaps even fear that he'll have to lie to his kids when they ask what he did in the war. What will he say, "I was relieved of command."?

Chip did a good job, in spite of his inexperience and immaturity.

THURSDAY, FEBRUARY 8, 1968: I conduct two memorial services today, one for Ron with Echo Company and the other for the four KIAs from Alpha Company. I hate these memorial services more each time. I can tell I'm getting sick, my body is beginning to ache.

After the memorial service the King suggests we stop having these for a while. He fears they are hurting morale. I tell him that not having them could send the wrong message, that we didn't care for the dead. Besides, death is what affects morale, not memorial services.

We have the first real staff meeting in a long time, and I am able to put much of the past two weeks in perspective. Intelligence gives a detailed briefing of what has happened during the Tet offensive. The VC have taken massive losses. This is the first time they've stood en masse and fought in a very long while. They've done much damage but they've also taken very heavy casualties. "We kicked the shit out of them," reports the S-2. They may eventually replace their lost and destroyed weapons, but it'll be a long while before they can replace their lost man power.

The S-2 gives many statistics about how many KIAs the VC have had, how many weapons have been captured, etc. This kind of "them and us" comparison is okay for staff meetings, but would this information help the family members of our casualties? The reality behind these reports is still trauma for family members and I fear it will last for years to come.

The person who ever thinks, "No gory, no glory" misses the point entirely. I'm feeling bitterness well up in me like bile. I must soon get out of this insane mess. Eight months is entirely too long and it's getting more and more difficult for me to keep things in perspective.

I don't feel well physically, emotionally or spiritually. I may go on sick call tomorrow. I'll take care of my emotional and spiritual ills later.

FRIDAY, FEBRUARY 9, 1968: I go on sick call with a fever of 101 degrees. The Doc orders bed rest for a few days and I don't argue. But I must conduct a religious service first. When I finish, Doc reminds me of his order and gets a bit angry with me.

"Jim, I thought I ordered bed rest for you."

"You did. And I'm going to bed now that my service is finished."

"Do so pronto. If you don't, I'll put you in the hospital."

SATURDAY, FEBRUARY 10, 1968: I'm still sick. I sleep most of the day in spite of the ever present glare from the fluorescent light. Doc checks on me several times during the day.

SUNDAY, FEBRUARY 11, 1968: I feel better. I conduct Sunday services and counsel several men. I always seem to have more work than I can do. I'm feeling guilty that I haven't made my hospital rounds.

MONDAY, FEBRUARY 12, 1968: Reports come in that the VC have been mortaring Dong Tam almost daily for the past several days. One of the headquarters clerks comes to me and says, "Chaplain, the gooks hit your hooch."

"What do you mean?"

"Your hooch got a direct mortar hit and so did the out house in front."

I think he means some fragments have hit my new digs, and I tell him I'll check it out today when I go to the 3rd Surg.

Paul and I catch a chopper to Dong Tam. I send him to survey the damage, telling him I'll be there shortly. I stop at the hospital first.

When I get to the hooch, chills run up and down my spine as I walk into the battalion area. The first thing I see is the new two seater outhouse that sits about fifty feet in front of my hooch. It's in shambles.

Then I see my hooch. A round has hit just inside the door. My bunk is gone, in fact little is left of anything. Paul stands just shaking his head. "If you'd been here, you'd be dead." He's right. My mattress and the wall above the bed is splattered with fragments. My stateside fatigues, those awful symbols of a newly arrived troop that I wore the first days at Bear

Cat last summer, are all filled with holes. I stand there shaking at the thought of what my body would look like if the round had hit me.

I guess the VC didn't like my new digs.

TUESDAY, FEBRUARY 13, 1968: Today we're to move further south toward Can Tho. The VC are regrouping in that area and our upcoming operations are to be there. Tomorrow, I'm going to Bear Cat and it's then I plan to ask Big Bob Wood about reassigning me. I'm excited, scared and guilty about this, but I must do it.

WEDNESDAY, FEBRUARY 14, 1968: I catch a chopper off the *Benewah* to Bear Cat.

THURSDAY, FEBRUARY 15, 1968: Today's the day I'll ask to be reassigned out of the 3/60th. My anxiety is high. I feel like I'm about to become disloyal to the King, Joe, Will, Frank and all the new replacements who're arriving daily.

I must go to the hospitals in Long Binh, but first I get my driver to take me by the division chaplain's office. I ask Denny, the assistant division chaplain, if Chaplain Wood is in today. He tells me he will be back later and wants to know if there is anything he can do for me. I ask him to tell Chaplain Wood I need to see him, that it is very important. Denny wants to know more and I am offended that he is so nosy. This guy keeps his head shaved and we all refer to him a Mr. Clean. I tell him it is personal and off I go to the hospitals.

Returning to Bear Cat, the closer I get, the more anxious I become. I fear that Big Bob will turn me down, or at least not have a place for me.

Now, I'm back at Big Bob's office. Bob is a Roman Catholic priest. We call him Big Bob because of his position as division chaplain and the deep authoritative way in which he speaks. Today, Bob is like God. He holds my destiny in his hands.

I walk right in and Bob looks at me over his reading glasses from behind his stateside desk.

"Hello, Johnny, have a seat."

I've only had two or three prior conversations with him and they've all been casual conversations always in the presence of others.

"You want a beer?" he says. I'm not sure if he's kidding or serious. I wonder if he thinks my first name is John, or if he is using 'Johnny' as short for Johnson.

"No thank you, sir."

"How are things in the Delta? I hear 3/60th has done a fantastic job against the Cong."

"Yes sir." Pride boils up. "It's been quite an experience during the past few weeks."

"Harv tells me you're always out with the troops. That's what I like, a chaplain who's not afraid to get his feet wet. He says your commander thinks you hung the moon. You going to stay in the army, Jimmy? We need good chaplains like you who aren't afraid to get out with the troops. Some of these Long Binh and Bear Cat chaplains are chickens' asses. They'd hibernate in a bunker for their entire tour if they could."

I realize he does know my first name. I want to get off this subject and get to why I'm here, but, I don't know how.

"Jimmy, I heard you're in for the a big time valor award for what you did in My Tho. We'll have to make a big deal about that to Frank the next time he gets here."

He is referring to Frank Sampson, the two star Chief of Chaplains, also a Catholic priest. I'm surprised to hear Bob refer to the chief by his first name.

"What can I do for you Jimmy?" he says finally.

"Well, Chaplain Wood, . . . I . . . um . . . I want to ask about the possibility of getting reassigned out of the field," There. I've said it. The floor doesn't collapse nor does the roof cave in.

Big Bob looks at me with no particular expression. "How long you been in the 3/60th?"

"Since I arrived in country, sir."

"And how long is that?"

"A little over eight months, sir." I tell him.

"How many times have you been in firefights?"

"I'm not sure, sir. Probably about twenty, not counting mortar attacks and snipers."

"My God, Jimmy, you've been through it."

"Yes, sir." I do not hesitate to agree.

"Hey, Denny, come in here." When Mr. Clean arrives, Big Bob asks him who they have leaving Bear Cat so they can put me in his place.

I exhale, relieved, and aware for the first time that I have been holding my breath. Bob asks me if I want to stay in the division or go to one of the support units. My answer is to stay in the division if at all possible. Denny explains that the only opening might be the division support command. Charlie Clanton is there now but will be leaving the fifth of April.

Bob says, "Let's cut orders and let Jimmy replace Clanton. We can get him up here the first week of April."

My heart sinks. That's still one and a half months away. "That'd only give me a little over two months in DISCOM." I surprise myself with this statement.

"When's your DEROS?" Bob wants to know.

I tell him my Date Eligible to Return from Overseas is about the twenty-fifth of June.

"Hell, Denny, let's get Jimmy a replacement and get him on up here sooner to replace Clanton. So what if there's an overlap? Maybe Clanton can get an early out or something and get back to wherever he's going." Big Bob's tone of voice makes him sound like he's miffed at something.

"Okay, I'll see what I can do," says Mr. Clean.

"Jimmy, we'll get you up here as soon as we can. We'll let you know."

I suddenly feel exhausted as I walk out into the late afternoon sun.

MONDAY, FEBRUARY 19, 1968: Only one company is going out today and that'll be early afternoon. I conduct a service on the *Benewah* and return to the APL for another service. More troops are present at this service than usual. Some of the guys don't look too happy. At the conclusion of the service, about ten guys stay behind. "Chaplain, can we have a word with you?" one of them asks.

"Sure. What's on your minds?" I want to know, and they are happy to explain. Every morning three or four of the navy guys have been rousting them out of their bunks to clean the place up.

"It doesn't matter how exhausted we are or if we just got back from an operation at 4:00. A.M. They wake us up, get us out of bed and make us start mopping and being the maid. It's not that we don't want to clean up. It's just the timing and their stinking attitude. They won't let us get any rest! It's worse than basic training!"

I offer to see what I can do. I find the navy chief who's been identified as the main perpetrator. Calmly, I state the problem. He reacts as if he's highly offended that anyone could possibly question his precious rules. I explain the necessity of these soldiers getting good rest.

"This place has to be kept clean," he tells me. "If we didn't make them clean it up, it'd be a pig pen." He says all this while chewing on a toothpick.

"There's no problem about cleaning it up, Chief. The problem is the timing. These guys need their rest. Can an adjustment be made about the time, especially when they've just come in from an operation?"

"Hell, Chaplain, rules is rules. All bunking areas are to be cleaned before breakfast, not afterward."

"Can't you be flexible, especially the mornings after we return from an operation?" I ask.

"Like how?" His toothpick dances between his lips from side to side.

"Like midday or even afternoon on the day after we end an operation." By his expression you'd have thought I had asked him to walk naked in front of Lady Bird Johnson.

"Chaplain, if you give these guys an inch, they'll take a mile. Rules is rules," he repeats.

"We'll see about that, son." I decide to take this directly to the King of the Hill. "You haven't heard the last of this." I walk away.

I hightail it to the King of the Hill and as I tell him our complaint, his face flushes bright red. I don't think I've ever seen him so angry. When I finish, he says, "You tell those guys I'll get that damned rule changed right away. Christ, they at least have a right to some decent sleep. Stay on top of this, Chaplain. I'll see the ensign right now and get this fixed. If you hear anything else about it, let me know."

"Yes, Sir. Thank you."

I find three of the guys playing cards on one of the bunks and tell them what the King said.

"Did he really mean it, sir?" They're astonished. Many troops are under the impression that all the King of the Hill cares about is a high enemy body count. I know that isn't so, and they're beginning to see that, too.

"You bet your sweet bippy he did. Let me know if this problem doesn't go away."

By mid afternoon, word obviously has spread around that everyone will get to sleep in on the days after an operation ends. Everywhere I go, guys are thanking me.

Over the remaining time of my stay here, Chief Toothpick never again even looks at me, much less speaks to me. Several guys say they heard that the navy ensign chewed him out for being so rigid. Regardless, now, the troops can get their deserved rest.

Just when I think I'll take a mid afternoon nap, word comes that the battalion must move out immediately. An estimated three battalions of VC have been spotted below Can Tho. We're to boat ashore about two kilometers away and then be air lifted into the VC area. We're to leave in fifteen minutes.

I'll go with Echo Company. I don't like the feel of this quickly called operation. We're going again where the VC have already been spotted. Every time we do this, there's a high cost in wounded and dead. This feels like My Tho, Vinh Long and the second ride through Snoopy's Nose.

Charlie Company will go in first and Echo Company next. The choppers come and Charlie Company is gone. The anxiety is sky-high. Within five minutes, Charlie Company has landed. We listen to the radios to determine what's happening. They're taking some fire but no solid contact yet. I feel a little better. If three VC battalions are there, they aren't fighting yet.

The choppers return, we load and leave. We fly in low over the tree line into a huge rice paddy area. We descend and jump into the wet and the choppers are gone. I hear no shots. Charlie Company is to our left about 200 meters away. Our plan is to link up with them and move into the tree line. Doug Almond, the Charlie Company commander, radios us that the fire they received was from the V shaped tree line directly in front of us but they were probably just snipers and are more than likely now gone.

We're approaching a small pineapple and banana field that juts out into the paddy from the tree line about 100 meters away.

"Sir, I see movement in the tree line behind the pineapple field," says one of the soldiers.

"That's probably a forward element of Charlie Company," says the commander.

"No sir, that's not Charlie Company. They're further to our left."

John Christy, the acting company commander, calls the platoon leader located at our front right. "Do you see any movement in the tree line?"

"Roger that, Echo-6. It looks like the tree line is filled with gooks."

"Are you sure? Why aren't they firing on us?"

"I don't know. But there's heavy movement everywhere I look. We need to fire on them before they hit us."

The rice is taller than in most paddies, about up to our knees. I have an eerie feeling. Now I, too, see movement in the tree line. The VC could have left the area when Charlie Company landed. They must be waiting for us to get closer. I don't like this. Why aren't they shooting at us? We're in the open! You can't miss chopper formations bringing two companies of infantrymen heading your way through an open rice paddy.

Then, like so many battles before, everything breaks loose. The VC open up on us with all they have. I hit the ground with the first shot and hear the terrifying sounds of VC bullets cutting through the tall rice. Talk about traumatic! This appears to be a full force unit. I'm petrified. I continue to hug the mud, wishing I could get lower.

Those on the front edge of our formation are returning fire but with the tall rice, it's hard to see where to fire. Since Ron was killed, everyone has been warned about standing up in the midst of a firefight.

"Get the gun ships to fire on those SOBs in the tree line," someone yells.

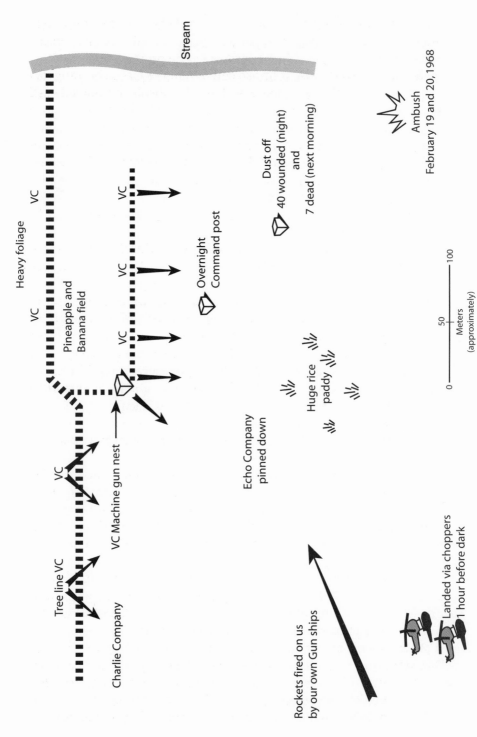

Stream

Heavy foliage

VC

VC

VC

Pineapple and Banana field

VC

VC

VC

Overnight Command post

Dust off
40 wounded (night) and
7 dead (next morning)

Ambush
February 19 and 20, 1968

VC Machine gun nest

Tree line VC

VC

Charlie Company

Echo Company pinned down

Huge rice paddy

0   50   100
Meters (approximately)

Rockets fired on us by our own Gun ships

Landed via choppers 1 hour before dark

Ambush February 19–20

"We've got them coming in now," one of the radio operators yells back.

To my rear, I hear the first of two gun ships. Great! I roll over on my back and see the first gun ship clear the tree line on the rear side of our rice paddy. I see two streaks of smoke come from the Cobra heading directly toward us. I'm thinking how glad I am that they're on our side as I follow the path of the fired rockets anticipating that they'll sail over our heads and onto the VC in the tree line. Relief turns to terror as I see the rockets coming directly at us! In an instant, two loud explosions occur no more than fifty meters to my rear! They must think we're the VC! Another rocket exits and hits a new medic square in the stomach, killing him instantly, even though the rocket didn't explode.

"Call them off, call them off! They're firing on us. Call them off," I yell.

The pilots obviously don't realize it's us in the paddy. "S-3 air, call those gun ships off. They'll kill us all. Call them off," John Christy yells into his radio.

The gun ships have now banked to the right and are circling to make another run. "Please God, don't let them fire on us again," I pray. Receiving fire from the VC is bad enough but to be caught in a cross-fire with them and our own gun ships is sheer terror. I'm still on my back looking at the two gun ships on the darkening horizon. As they're approaching for another firing sortie, I feel like I'm looking straight into the gun barrel of a madman on a shooting rampage.

They must have gotten the word, because at the last second they sharply bank and fly off to our left. Thank God! Now all we have to worry about are the VC.

The gun ships return in attack formation, one trailing the other by about 500 meters. I see two more rockets exit the pods. This time they shriek over us by not more than fifty feet. Thankfully they impact on targets seventy-five meters to our front, which is exactly where the VC are firing on us. The first gun ship banks hard to the right as the second fires two more rockets at the same area.

They make several more runs with miniguns blazing. Artillery is now called in. During the volleys, smaller explosions are occurring all around us. The VC are now hitting us with their 82 mm mortars and RPGs. We have nowhere to go to protect ourselves from their fire.

Calls are coming in that we're taking a lot of casualties. Men are shouting that someone nearby is hit. This same panicked message is yelled out from many different positions. The screams are coming from my right, front, left and rear. There's no way we can get any of the wounded evacuated now. The fire is too intense to do anything but continue to hug the ground.

It's now almost dark. I low crawl toward the command post about twenty meters to my right front. One of the radio operators tells me two guys from first platoon are sneaking up to try to take the VC machine gunners out. Just at the corner of the pineapple field, a VC machine gun has been firing on us almost continuously. They are about fifty meters to our front.

I hear the unmistakable sound of two hand grenades just ahead of us. "We got em. We got em," I hear someone yell. The two brave soldiers who crawled to within ten meters of the VC machine gun position without the VC even knowing it, took them out with grenades.

Soon, all the firing slows. We survey the wounded; many have been hit. We call in dustoffs. It's now completely dark and safe enough to stand up without fear of the VC spotting us.

For the next hour we have several dustoffs come in for our wounded. I help move several wounded to the make shift triage area. There's no real triaging in the dark as we're still in the open and can't use anything but red flashlights to locate wounds and place bandages. Medic John Ryan is crawling from wounded to wounded covering their wounds the best that he can. Everyone is covered with mud and many of the wounds are oozing blood, mixing with the mud.

By 9:30 P.M., we have half of the forty wounded evacuated. The others will be taken care of in the morning. Unfortunately, we also have several dead. We'll not evacuate the bodies until morning.

This all makes me sick. I feel intense anger building up inside of me. Certainly, it's toward the VC, but, I also harbor anger toward the politicians who keep this war going! God, this is hell on earth! We have six KIAs including one Vietnamese Kit Carson scout.

What a miserable place to die.

We haven't taken any fire in over an hour. It seems that maybe the VC have moved out of the area. A staff sergeant and a PFC volunteer to move into the nearby tree line and conduct a reconnaissance to make sure it's secure. I wouldn't volunteer for this task for a million dollars. These two heroes are very brave. The PFC is relatively new. We're still in the open paddy and flares have been overhead for the last forty-five minutes. The faint light is just enough to keep bearings of where we are in relation to the tree line.

The two-man team leaves our narrow perimeter. I see them walk carefully by the VC machine gun nest. The sergeant makes a gesture to us in the faint light by holding up two fingers and then an open hand to his throat to indicate both VC machine gunners are dead. Ten minutes pass.

Then I hear the sound of AK 47s, M 16s and hand grenades. We can't fire because we don't know exactly where the recon team is. I fear all hell will break loose again. But then, silence.

We wait five minutes. All is still quiet. Then, we hear him before we see him. The staff sergeant emerges from the banana trees doing a low crawl. He's alone. Once out in the opening, he comes to his feet and trudges to our position.

"What happened?" asks the company commander.

"My partner's dead."

"You sure?"

"Yes. One round caught him in the head. He was dead before he hit the ground."

The company commander wants to know how many VC there were.

"Four or five. When they shot him, I dropped, pulled the pin on a grenade, threw it, then emptied a magazine from my M-16. Then I threw another grenade and fired another magazine."

"What happened to the VC?"

"I think I got them all with the first grenade. I didn't see any movement. I saw three or four on the ground. I threw the second grenade just to make sure."

"And you're positive your man is dead?" the commander asked.

"Yes. I crawled back the few feet to where he was lying. I got no pulse. He never knew what hit him."

I'm amazed at how calm this sergeant is. When he lights a cigarette his hands quiver only slightly.

Another squad member wants to know if we should we try to recover his body.

"We can't risk any more casualties. We'll get him at first light," John says.

We settle in for the night, all of us covered in slimy mud. We're still only about 200 meters forward of where we jumped off the choppers. This last KIA now makes a total of seven.

I don't sleep. I think only of Barbara and the kids. I hear in my mind over and over the dreadful sounds of those AK 47 bullets tearing through the rice and whistling just over my head. No sound is like this. None! I hear the sounds of the grenades that killed the VC machine gunners. I see those gun ship rockets that could have killed me.

In the quiet, I have an almost overwhelming feeling of fear that I won't get out of this war. What I do know is that I hate this fear and hurt! I hate it! I hate it! I hate it! Won't it ever end?

TUESDAY, FEBRUARY 20, 1968: Finally, light begins to brighten the eastern sky. Two squads are assigned to recon the tree line with the primary objective to recover the body of the dead PFC hero of last night. They bring his body back as well as several VC weapons, including the VC machine gun, a B-40 rocket launcher, several RPG rounds, steel helmets, and some ChiCom rifles.

We get all the bodies in one spot for evacuation. Of the seven dead, one is a Chieu Hoi, which means he was a former VC who came over onto the government side. The resupply chopper arrives. I help load the dead bodies onto the chopper. It is the least I can do. Each body is covered with slick, slimy mud. I can only recognize them by their dog tags. I only know two or three, which means most of them are new replacements. I suppress the urge to cry.

The smell of death is prominent. The medic, a radio operator, the chopper crew chief, and I load the seven bodies aboard the aircraft that is now their hearse. We have to stack them aboard like logs. It just doesn't seem right, but we have no choice.

There's no time to grieve. We must prepare to move out. We're to move two kilometers to the river and be extracted.

First, though, we're to move back through the VC positions of last night. Our formation goes by the VC machine gun position. The two dead VC are sprawled on their backs. Each dead VC must have at least twenty holes in his face and other exposed parts of their bodies. Someone in the column takes his white plastic spoon from his C-rations and sticks the handle into a wound made by the fragments. The next soldier in line does likewise. By the time I pass the position, each dead VC has a dozen or more plastic spoons protruding from his body.

There's no shouting or cheering as we pass the bodies. The defiant symbolism of "sticking it to them" may be desecration of the dead, but this is a way of emotionally coping with what's happening each day of this god-awful war.

As we move on, someone says many more VC bodies are off the trail a few feet away. I've seen enough dead bodies for now, Americans, Vietnamese and Viet Cong. I'm just glad to move out, which we do rapidly. John Christy, the acting commander of Echo Company, is walking barefoot. I ask why and he says he lost his boots. I don't ask how. It doesn't seem to matter.

WEDNESDAY, FEBRUARY 21, 1968: I have a combined memorial service on the pontoon for Charlie and Echo Companies, and HQ. Practically the entire battalion attends. Even some of the navy crew of the APL are present. In the afternoon, most of the battalion goes to a nearby river bank that's almost like a beach and for the first time in weeks, we have a party. I stay for a while, then return to the APL after a couple hours. I need some time by myself.

THURSDAY, FEBRUARY 22, 1968: For several weeks Earl Strickland, from Durham, North Carolina has mentioned wanting to be baptized. Today is the first time we've had an opportunity to do so. He, Paul and a couple of Earl's friends catch a boat to the nearby shore. Here I conduct a baptism by immersion in the muddy Mekong River.

SUNDAY, FEBRUARY 25, 1968: Today, a call comes from Denny. He tells me they are cutting my orders to be reassigned to the Division Support Command. My reporting date will be the sixth of March.

I'm ecstatic! I'm finally getting out of the field! Then, just like switching off a light, I'm overcome with a very different sensation. My mood tailspins. I must now see the King of the Hill and tell him. Will he think I'm bailing out? Or worse still, will he see me as a traitor?

I am in a turmoil. I love the 3/60th, I love the guys. I'll be leaving some very good friends.

The King is at a meeting at brigade HQ on the *Benewah*. I wait. The longer I wait for him to return, the more anxious I get. I go outside onto the pontoon to watch for him to return on the shuttle boat. Finally, he arrives. I feel almost like I am delivering a death message. I meet him as he comes into the mess area.

"Sir, can I talk to you for a moment?"

"Sure, Chaplain. What's up?"

"Well, sir, they're going to move me to division HQ."

He looks stunned. "What do you mean?"

"The division chaplain is having orders cut to move me."

"Well, I can get that straightened out! I'm not going to let them do that to us!" He has suddenly become angry—not the reaction I expected. It's worsened by the fact that I've misstated the truth. The way I put it, I've given him the impression that 'they' are moving me; not that I have asked to move.

"Sir, I really do need to move."

The King pauses. "Why, Chaplain? Is something wrong?"

"No sir. It's just that . . . well . . . I guess I'm just about burned out." I hate the phrase "burn out" because it is used in the drug culture, but it's the only thing that seems to fit how I feel.

"How long have you been here now?" He looks concerned.

"Eight and a half months, sir. I've been in country since the end of June. It's just time to move on, not that I'm scared or anything." I wonder if he knows I am lying through my teeth?

The King now has a look of compassion and understanding, for which I'm very grateful. "That's longer than I thought. I guess you've been out there much longer than any of the other officers. You're such a tremendous asset to me. Okay, I'll let you go so long as they send a replacement *before* you leave. By damn, I don't want to be without a chaplain. And a good one! I won't have one who won't go to the field!"

"Sir, I'm sure they'll send a good man here to take my place."

"That's the only condition that I'll consent to let you go."

We talk a little more about dates and then the conversation switches to tomorrow's operation. He expresses appreciation again for all the operations I go on and my relationship with the troops.

"You've been a very valuable set of eyes and ears for me to the soldiers. I don't know what I'd do without that." The King shakes my hand. "I'll miss you, Chaplain. But, I understand and wish you the best."

A heavy load has been lifted off my shoulders. Word passes among the officers quickly that I'll be leaving. Jim McDonald, the Bravo Company commander, tells me he'd like for me to go out on one more operation with them before I leave. I agree.

"So you're leaving me, huh? I'm not going to let you do that," Frank teases.

"I may have to go AWOL, then, to get out. What's the worst they can do if I do that, send me to Vietnam?"

"No, we'll make you join the girl scouts," pipes in Joe.

Their good natured ribbing makes me feel better. Naturally, I enjoy being liked. I decide not to go with Bravo Company tomorrow but rather with the aid boat and then link up with one of the companies after we've been inserted.

I go to sleep relieved. Now, if I can just stay alive for the next eight or nine days, I should be home free.

MONDAY, FEBRUARY 26, 1968: "Jim, are you going with us?" asks Jim McDonald on the pontoon.

"I'll join you guys later today. I'm going out on the aid boat," I tell him.

"You're going to miss all the fun of an air assault."

I make a joke about having waited too long to buy my ticket.

"Come on, go with us. This may be the last chance you'll have with your leaving."

I consider going. It's almost like Jim is pleading with me. I decide to stay with my original plan to embark on the aid boat and then switch to Bravo Company. As we're moving in convoy downstream, I think back to the many miles I've ridden on these boats since last summer. I'm grateful that it won't be for many more. Bravo Company is airborne now. I have an uneasy feeling in my gut, and I don't know why. Then, I hear it! Bravo

Company has gone into a hot landing zone. My mind flashes to last October when I went with Alpha Company into my first hot landing zone and how scared I was then. Many of the soldiers in Bravo Company are new, and I feel for what they must be experiencing right now. Panicked voices are on the radios. Bravo Company is being hit hard. Of the twelve choppers ferrying in the troops, eleven are damaged by ground fire. As they leave the rice paddy, one is shot down. Although the others fly out on their own power, eight are damaged to the extent that they fly back to the Can Tho airfield for repairs.

Bravo Company is pinned down and reports numerous casualties. The aid boat is not able to reach the wounded. We're circling in the river. Alpha and Echo Companies are on the boats with plans for another chopper to airlift them in near the area of operations to help relieve the VC pressure on Bravo Company. My first intent is to figure some way to get to either Alpha or Echo Company.

A medic on the aid boat tells me they are going to fly all the wounded to the *Colleton*. When I ask why they are not sending them to the 3rd Surg, he explains.

"It's too far. It'd be like a thirty minute flight one way and Bravo Company is taking too many casualties. They're gathering all the navy doctors at the *Colleton* for triage. They're also flying in two surgeons from 3rd Surg for any surgery that can't wait until we get them to Dong Tam."

The *Colleton* has a small medical area just below the landing deck. Even though it doesn't have the components of a 3rd Surg, this plan makes sense, as the flotilla is relatively near the area of operations. My plan is now in place. I'll return to the *Colleton* and minister to what sounds like numerous wounded as they come in.

I'm dropped off at the fire support base at 3:00 P.M. Alpha and Echo Companies are now beached and attempting to move toward Bravo Company, but both have encountered heavy fire and they, too, are taking casualties. I see one of the assistant division commanders. He doesn't know me, but I know he has a chopper. Boldly, I decide to request use of his chopper to take me to the *Colleton*. He agrees.

The chopper only takes a few minutes to land on the *Colleton*, which is anchored in the middle of the Mekong River just northwest of Can Tho.

I walk the few steps from the small landing pad on the *Colleton* down to the medical facility. No wounded have arrived yet. Several doctors, nurses, and medics are marking time, waiting for the wounded to arrive. A navy doctor I've gotten to know well over the past few months tells me he has heard we'll have a lot of wounded and KIAs.

"How many KIAs?" I want to know.

"Not sure. But several have been reported. Bravo Company has really been hit hard."

I remember that Jim McDonald wanted me to go in with them. I realize now that I may have unknowingly saved my own life by declining the invitation to go in with Bravo Company.

For the next several hours, the dustoffs make steady runs bringing soldiers whose flesh is torn and mutilated by bullets and fragments. I talk to each wounded soldier brought in. With some I pray. Those who are stable want to talk about how terrible this battle was. The hot LZ has traumatized all those from Bravo Company. Some near the command group were almost overrun by the VC who fought to within just a few feet of the command post. Jim McDonald had to become a rifleman for a while, just to survive. VC and American wounded and dead were everywhere. The VC stood and fought ferociously until after dark. Jim has been shot in the knee.

As I work into the night, I'm constantly reminded that I came very near being with Bravo Company on this operation. I'm grateful I was not there today, yet I still feel some guilt that I wasn't. I keep working.

One soldier especially makes a mark on my memory. My navy physician friend catches my eye from across the room that's now filled with twelve to fifteen wounded soldiers. Doc motions me over. I notice an injured man has a bandage on the back part of his head. The medics have placed him on his stomach.

"I can't see," he repeats several times to no one in particular. He's not panicked and doesn't seem to be in much pain. I'm thinking it's because he's lying face down on the litter. I get on my knees so I can talk to him.

"I'm Chaplain Johnson."

He says calmly, "Chaplain, I can't see."

"Do you want me to turn your head a little?"

"It won't do any good, Chaplain. I've tried that and I still can't."

Doc motions me over toward him.

"I'll be back in a few minutes," I say, as I rise and walk away from his stretcher.

Doc tells me the man is blind. He explains that the bullet has hit the back part of his skull and neatly blown away some of his brain tissue. Tragically, it is the part of the brain that enables him to see. "It's been shot away, Doc says. He'll live but he'll never see again." I reel with the thought that this nineteen-year-old kid will never again see a friend smile, pick out a beautiful flower for his girlfriend, or even look up a phone number.

After what Doc has just told me, I suddenly have a violent urge to let out a primal scream.

"Put another clean bandage on his head and get him ready to go to the 3rd Surg," Doc tells a nearby nurse. "You'll be alright, soldier," he lies.

"They're going to send you to the 3rd Surg in Dong Tam," I tell him.

"Where am I now?"

"We're on the *Colleton* but you'll be on your way to the 3rd Surg shortly."

God, I feel so inadequate. But what can I tell him? That they'll fit him with strong glasses so he'll be able to see? Things will be better when he get to the states, that he'll be taken care of? Nothing I can say will bring the part of his brain back that's out there in the mud somewhere.

"I'll see you in a day or so at the 3rd Surg," I finally manage. I want to bite off my tongue when I realize what I've just said, the 'I'll see you' part.

"Thanks, Chaplain. Am I going to make it?"

"You bet. You're in good hands."

Several times during the night as I keep working with the newly arrived wounded, I want to stop and cry. But I can't. Numerous dustoff flights have landed just above us on the ship's helopad but I've been too busy to keep count. I just know that we've received many, many injured. After being triaged, other choppers then begin flying the wounded to Dong Tam.

Many of the men talk about how horrible the past few hours have been. Keith May has been shot in the stomach. He was in the mud for nine hours before any of his buddies could get to him and get him dusted off. Several times, even though severely wounded, Keith demanded his buddies be dusted off before him. Medic John Ryan is one of the few who was not hit. He saved the lives of several of the more severely wounded.

Sometime very late at night, I finally take a break and walk outside in the inky darkness on the ship's small external passageway. This is the first time I've been out of the treatment area all night. The narrow cat walk is not more than three or four feet wide. I grip the guard rail as I look out into the night. I light a cigarette, and standing in the cool breeze I look out over the horizon and see the flares lazily hanging over the battlefield three or four kilometers away where our heroes who haven't been hit are no doubt hunkered down. I can't imagine how many wounded have been brought in. Maybe thirty-five, perhaps fifty or more. I look at the bright glow of my lighted cigarette in the black night and realize the blinded soldier will never again see what I am seeing. I momentarily feel nauseated.

I take about three aimless steps down the small walkway from the door of the medical triage room and stumble onto something that almost causes me to fall. I'm suddenly angered that someone has been so thoughtless as to leave anything in the small passageway that could cause an accident. "Thoughtless, mindless idiots," I mutter, as I instinctively reach down to move what has almost tripped me.

My hands touch a rubberized surface and for an instant I try to imagine what is underneath. Then, it comes to me like I am shot! It's a body bag! I almost tripped over a corpse! As my eyes are slowly adjusting to the darkness, I see numerous body bags lining the passageway next to the ship's bulkhead. Some of the bodies of our KIAs have also been brought in on the choppers, and someone has stored the bodies out of sight.

I can't begin to count them. Hot tears run down my cheeks. I don't sob, but I just continue to softly cry. I don't attempt to stifle what I'm feeling. I spoke with some of these guys on the pontoon this morning. I cry for them and also for myself. Any of these lifeless forms in these body bags could have been me.

"Don't miss out on the fun," is what Jim McDonald had told me. Some fun, getting shot. More fun for their wives, girlfriends, parents, friends and children when they learn of the grim reaper's visit.

I cry for ten minutes, maybe twenty, I don't know. It's as if eight and one-half months of feelings are suddenly breaking loose. My mother used to encourage me not to bottle up my feelings as was my father's habit. I don't feel anger, I just feel very profound sadness and hurt, and a little guilty. As I stand there, I grant myself permission just to feel what I feel, and know that's okay. I want to pray but I can't. The tears continue.

These guys had no one to hold them as they drew their last breath. I now do the next best thing that comes to mind. I bend over each body bag and touch their heads, one by one, saying nothing. I don't know if they are from Alpha, Bravo, or Echo Company, if they are white, black, Hispanic, big or small, officer or enlisted men, and none of this matters now. They're all dead. I love them so very much.

After a while I compose myself and smoke another cigarette. I hear the artillery still firing in the distance. It's funny, I don't even wish the VC are being killed for this. I only wish that all the killing will stop, and that my hurt will go away. The tears have stopped, and I indulge a few more minutes in the cool late night breeze, realizing I now am able to pray, and I do.

TUESDAY, FEBRUARY 27, 1968: Last night has melted into another day. In the wee hours of morning, after the wounded had all been flown out to 3rd Surg, some of us curled up in the corner of the small medical facility and dozed. No one left as we were not sure that all the wounded had been evacuated.

At the area of operations, shortly after first light, the remnants of the VC force attack again. This fight is short lived, but we take a few more casualties.

Then, the operation is ended. The troops are ferried back to the flotilla and are in by early afternoon. As the troops unload onto the pontoon, trauma shows on all their faces. Those who have been here for a while, but are fortunate not to have been hit, look like zombies. The new guys just look terrified. A soldier doesn't have to be an Einstein to see how high the chance of being wounded or killed.

We have a total of sixty-five wounded and nineteen killed in yesterday's fight. A detailed report is given about the estimated number of VC killed and how much weaponry has been captured. I tune out when they start talking about VC casualties and how hard we hit them. My soul is too worn to care.

Only twenty-six soldiers from Bravo Company walked out. The rest were killed or wounded. One brave and loyal hero took fragment wounds in the morning portion of the fight and refused to be evacuated only to be hit again later during the night and killed. Another, who was in John Iannucci's squad, was shot in the stomach early in the encounter and lay in the muddy rice paddy all day until he was evacuated late that night.

I keep having images of the blinded soldier last night and the body bags. I just feel void. I'm lethargic. I feel like my insides have been cut out! I don't ever recall feeling as empty and confused as I do now.

Morale is as low as I've ever seen it. If being overworked and underpaid can drop morale, what can being shot at continually and seeing buddies shot and killed do?

WEDNESDAY, FEBRUARY 28, 1968: Next week, I'll be reassigned and I'm ready. I have the memorial service for Bravo Company. This has never been an easy thing to do and today, it's especially difficult. It occurs to me that only months ago many of these men must have fantasized about where they would be next Christmas. Their deaths are no fantasy. Soldiers stand in formation, many on crutches, many with arms in slings.

THURSDAY, FEBRUARY 29, 1968: This is a leap year. This fact extends my tour of 365 by one day. Today is a repeat of yesterday's memorial service, though today's service is for Echo Company. Again, the pontoon is full and many other soldiers and sailors are a part of the service. Some stand on the upper level decks of the craft and look down on the pontoon.

FRIDAY, MARCH 1, 1968: I'm filled with both excitement and anxiety. I'm excited because this will be my last combat operation and I'm ready for some relief. I'm anxious because it seems all operations in the past couple of months have been like playing Russian roulette and we keep getting the chamber with the bullet. Maybe all the chambers have bullets.

Frank Pina and I have become really good friends. Other than Joe Jenkins, I'm probably as close to Frank as I am to anyone. His exterior is one of hardness but he has to be tough in order to survive this war as a company commander. Inside, Frank is a very sensitive man. But one must know him well to see that side of him.

Today Frank says, "Jim, it's our turn for you to go out with us, isn't it?"

"I'll try to link up with you tomorrow," I tell him. "I need to go with Bravo Company since they have been cut to ribbons in the past few days." We both know that with Jim McDonald having been shot, they have a stand in commander for this operation.

My habit has been to rotate going on operations with the various companies. However, if a company is having morale problems or if they've had significant combat engagements, then that's the company I go with on the next operation.

We're flying into the area of operations, the same area where Bravo Company was hit so hard on Monday. I look around at the troops and almost all of them are newly arrived since the Tet offensive began one month ago. For many, this is their very first operation. I make a special effort during my rounds to speak to as many of the new guys as possible. They look so fresh in their new sharp green jungle fatigues. I fear that for many these will become their death suits.

We're down and on the ground, and as we move out I hope the VC are not here, not on my last combat operation.

Throughout the morning, both Alpha and Bravo Companies have sporadic contact with the VC. Only a few rounds fired on us; we return fire, call in a few volleys of artillery, and move out again. This situation is repeated several times.

Near noon, a soldier in front of me says, "My God, this is the same rice paddy where we were ambushed the other day!" Apparently it wasn't recognizable to him at first because we're approaching the area from a different direction.

We spot the Huey chopper that was shot down as it was leaving. It's nothing but a burned and melted mass of metal now. The two pilots and two crewmen were rescued and the gun ships then used the downed chopper as rocket target practice to destroy it so the VC could use no parts. The resulting fire melted the remains, which is a solitaire reminder of the hell of Monday. We stop for lunch with Alpha and Bravo Companies co-located. I eat quickly and make my rounds to both companies. I chat with Frank Pina and his small command group.

"You going to stay with us, Jim?" Frank asks.

"No, I'll join you later. I need to stay with Bravo Company for now. Some of the new guys seem to be rather shaky."

Frank says, "We need you, too." He is smiling, but I detect a hint of seriousness that speaks of anxiety, which is a little unusual for Frank.

I pull him aside. "You seem a little edgy, Frank."

"Maybe. I just don't know if I can trust some of these new guys to react when the going gets tough. So many are new it's scary. It's almost like having a company in basic training."

"They'll be okay," I tell him. "They have good leadership."

"I hope so, Jim. Keep your head down."

I assure him I will and tell him I'll see him later.

I return to Bravo Company and we move out again with both companies abreast. After about 500 meters, the terrifying sounds of a fire fight begin. Explosions of incoming mortars and rocket propelled grenades are going off all around me. Bullets tear through the foliage. The force of a nearby explosion knocks me into a canal next to the trail. The tide is out and I have landed in mud, but there is agonizing pain. I'm not sure if I've been shot, all I know is that my right shoulder is killing me. I feel around for warm blood but find none. Then, I realize my shoulder must be dislocated.

Several years ago, I played college football at Wake Forest. During my freshman season, my left shoulder was dislocated in a tackling drill. The pain was so great at that time that I nearly passed out. A trainer skillfully maneuvered it back into socket by using a balled up fist and slow movement of my upper arm. I spent Christmas vacation that year at Baptist Hospital in Winston Salem, having reconstructive surgery.

Pain immobilizes me, but I can't just lie here. If the order is given to get up and move, I know there's no way I can comply. My fingers are beginning to go numb.

I know I need someone to get this shoulder back in place. RPGs and mortars continue to come in on us and I feel very exposed to the VC indirect fire. I realize that I've got to put my shoulder back in place myself. How can I possibly do it? The pain is so great it feels like fire inside my joint.

The soldier just behind me in the canal is now aware that something is wrong. "Chaplain, are you hit?"

"No, I'll be okay," I grunt.

"What's wrong?"

"Nothing. I'll be okay."

"Hold on Chaplain. I'll crawl up to where you are." He sounds like he's about ten meters behind me.

"Stay where you are." It takes all my energy just to talk loud enough over the firing and continuing explosions for him to hear me. For some reason, I don't want anyone to know how badly I'm hurt, or that I'm hurt at all.

I'm on my stomach in the mud. It's difficult getting my left arm under my body and underneath my flak jacket to even feel my right shoulder socket. I must somehow turn on my left side or maybe even my back if I'm going to get this done. Turning on my left side is torment. I press the left side of my head into the mud and try to bow my body upward. Then, I realize that the upper part of my flak vest is covering the lower part of my right shoulder socket, which has sunk toward my rib cage. I must unlace the front of my flak vest and run my left hand underneath it in order to place any pressure on the shoulder socket. By the grace of God I'm able to do this, slowly and painstakingly.

I can now feel under my arm and determine the direction I think my shoulder socket has been displaced. I must exert pressure using my left fist to push the misplaced shoulder back into place. I take a deep breath, grit my teeth, close my eyes tightly and push. Nothing happens except for more pain. I rest for a moment, while the battle continues to rage all around me. I must try it again. "God, help me to do this right," I pray. I push, and for one brief moment, I think I'll pass out from the pain. Suddenly, it feels as if it slips into place. In a few seconds, the pain has significantly subsided. I know I have to move my shoulder to see if I was successful. I dread attempting this. But, I do, very slowly. No additional pain. "Thank you, God!" I move some more. I did it!

"Chaplain, where are you hurt?" The soldier is no longer behind me; he has slithered up beside me in the mud.

"I'm okay now. I just dislocated my shoulder. I put it back in place, though."

"I'll call for a medic."

"No, I'm fine now."

"I'll get John Ryan over here. He's just over to our left. Or at least he was until the VC hit us."

"No. Maybe I'll see him after this fight is over. Just take care of business."

"Okay, Chaplain. Keep your head down," he says, and crawls back to his position in the mud.

I remain still for a few moments, exhausted.

Our gunships and artillery are coming down hard on the VC positions. Bravo Company is to be extracted by air immediately because the VC have sunk an ASPB in a nearby stream. A security cordon is needed around it while salvage efforts are brought in to attempt to recover the boat from the bottom of the stream. We move out to the open rice paddy for pick up. The melted hulk of the nearby crashed chopper is a solitary reminder that we can be next.

I hear that Alpha Company has ten wounded and some KIAs. I consider whether I should try to get to them, but I realize this is impractical. I feel my presence is still needed more with Bravo Company. Besides, Echo Company is coming to augment Alpha Company.

Choppers are brought in and we're flown about one kilometer away and land beside a stream. We hump another 300 meters to where two boats are making a slow circle around an anchored flag that indicates where the boat has been sunk. The infantry security cordon is quickly established.

As we set our perimeter, one of the radio operators says excitedly, "Hey, Captain Pina's been hit."

"It can't be!" I say. "I was talking to him just before that firefight broke out." I don't want to believe Frank's been hit!

"It's true. I'm monitoring his radio now. He is trying to get Patron 6 on the horn now. Listen up."

"Patron 6, Patron 6, this is Patron Alpha-6 . . . over." It's Frank, attempting to raise the King of the Hill.

"Patron Alpha-6, this is Patron 6 . . . Over."

"Patron 6, this is Patron Alpha-6. I've been hit and am turning command over to Patron Alpha-1-6 . . . Over."

"Patron Alpha-6, this is Patron 6. Can you continue? . . . Over."

"Patron 6, this is Patron Alpha-6. No. I'm coming in on the next dustoff . . . Over."

"Patron Alpha-6, this is Patron 6. Roger that. See you soon. Good job. Out."

From the sound of Frank's voice, he sounds strong. Probably just a fragment.

"He sounds okay to me, Chaplain," says the Bravo Company commander.

"Me too. But if he's not hurt badly, I'm surprised he's going in."

"Yeah, me too. Probably just a precaution. Alpha Company is going in before dark anyhow. Frank probably figures he'll just evacuate to go get patched up and be ready for the next operation."

"That makes sense." I see the dustoff chopper in the distance circle, land at Alpha Company's position and leave again. I feel good that Frank is aboard and will be taken care of back at the *Colleton*.

A boat arrives with a small crane atop and just before dark, they raise the ASPB. The crew is 150 feet away from our command post and a monitor and ATC are positioned in the opposite direction of the salvage crews to suppress any VC fire should they sneak up and attack from the opposite bank of the stream.

Alpha Company has now been extracted and we're the only company left in the field. The navy decides to suspend recovery operations until first light tomorrow. I'm a little disappointed. I want to go in tonight and end my field career.

Shortly after dark, I move to several different positions. At 9:00 P.M., I'm in a position with five guys, all new. One soldier is really impressed that a chaplain is here. This is his first operation and we discuss extensively where he's from, his religious faith, and his fears of being here. He and his new buddies have a million questions and we talk for an hour or more.

When I tell them that this is my last operation, they grow quiet and seem somewhat letdown. One soldier asks me to have a prayer with them and I gladly do. They seem so young and vulnerable. I feel so old, but also vulnerable.

As I lie under the stars, I reflect on all that's happened to me today. My shoulder is sore and I wonder if I'll eventually have to have surgery on it like I did when I was in college. I know that tomorrow I will go in for the last time. I miss Barbara and the kids. I feel guilty about leaving these new guys in the field.

Then, I think of Frank. I picture him patched up and already in the dining room telling the staff officers about how he has been hit. Sleep finally comes in spite of the local mosquitoes and their attempts for me to do otherwise.

SATURDAY, MARCH 2, 1968: After first light, the river rats are again hard at work attempting to salvage the ASPB. Throughout the day they work diligently pumping water from below and attempting to patch the holes that apparently are allowing water to re-enter almost as rapidly as it is pumped out.

At 11:00 A.M., two river rats descend through the hatch into the water inside the boat. Within thirty seconds, one surfaces from the hatch. After another thirty seconds, panic erupts. Several rats begin yelling. The second man must be trapped inside! Another two minutes go by while the panicked sailors decide how to attempt to rescue the sailor missing inside the water-filled hull. One rat quickly crawls back inside and another follows.

These two brave sailors are down inside for perhaps another forty-five seconds. Then, one surfaces and yells, "We've got him, we've got him. Pull him up." The sailors topside quickly pull all three out. The one sailor has been under water for nearly five minutes. He's limp and unconscious, perhaps dead. They quickly begin giving him CPR.

Finally, I see the near-drowned sailor beginning to move his legs. Soon, one of the sailors flashes us a thumbs up signal that he's breathing and we clap and a few soldiers hoot and holler. The grim reaper has been cheated this time.

The river rat is brought by boat to shore and we call in a dustoff for him. He's fully conscious now and resistant to being dusted off, but we send him into the hospital as a safety precaution.

Finally, the boat is repaired and no longer taking on water. The navy decides to tow it back to the repair ship and they leave. The ATCs are on the way to pick us up and take us in. This has been a long day—and my last one on combat operations. Hip, hip, hurrah!

It is almost dark before the ATCs arrive to extract us. We load up and leave. Wouldn't you know it, on the way down stream, we receive VC fire. It's not a full fledged ambush, but we take small arms fire and a few RPGs, which explode on the sides of a monitor and one ATC with no casualties. The boats return fire and the attack is over in minutes. Still, this fight in the dark is unnerving. "Please, Charlie, I'm going in from my last operation. Let me go in peace." I can do without the VC giving me a going away party like this, thank you.

Soon, we're in the open water of the Mekong River. Then I hear more bad news. An ASPB, which is the same type of patrol boat we've been guarding, is sunk, not by VC fire—it has simply gone down from the wake created by another boat. The accident occurs down the river a couple of kilometers from us. Unfortunately, two river rats are drowned as the ASPB sinks. I'm sick to my stomach at all the needless death in this stinking war.

It's almost 11:00 P.M. when I finally get to the APL. I'm tremendously relieved. I've finally completed my last operation. It's now downhill on my 365. I'm tired and ready for a long hot shower.

First, I open my wall locker. Paul always puts my mail and any incoming or outgoing correspondence on the top shelf. There's some mail from Barbara and a disposition form about some chaplains' meeting. But on top are four notification letters for our KIAs from Alpha Company yesterday. Of the first three, two are new guys. I recognize the third name.

"Dear Mrs. Pina . . ." begins the last letter. My God, there's only one Pina—Frank! How can Paul make such a gross error as this? Frank isn't dead. I heard him on the radio yesterday afternoon. I ball up my fist and hit the next wall locker as hard as I can, hurting my knuckles, and feeling the pain once more in my sore shoulder. But my soul hurts the most.

Joe Jenkins and two other officers come in to see what the ruckus is all about. He sees me with the letters. "What's this about Frank, Joe?" I'm almost shouting.

He pauses before he speaks. "He was dead by the time the dustoff got here, Chap." Another pause.

"It can't be. I heard him on the horn. How could he have died?" I'm nearly hysterical now. Time all but stands still. I want to scream out, hit something again, or do anything. "Joe, how can he be dead?" I say. Joe looks helpless.

"He was shot in the chest. The medic and Frank thought he would be okay. But, he apparently had internal bleeding." He goes on to tell me the S-5, the civil affairs officer, was with him on the chopper. Frank stopped breathing about two minutes before landing. The S-5 jumped off the chopper on the *Colleton* when it was still ten to fifteen feet from touch down to alert the medics. But it was too late. Frank was dead.

"Shit, shit, shit!!!" That's all I can say. I immediately head for the shower. I just want to get under the hot water and cry. I stand there and I sob. I beat the walls of the shower with my fists. I just keep saying, "Shit, shit, shit." This is the only word that fits my feelings at the moment.

I keep thinking, Frank can't be dead. It's been over twenty-four hours now and I wonder if the army has notified his wife. Will his little daughters even remember him? How will their growing up be affected by Frank's death? I stay in the shower for fifteen minutes, then get out and get ready for sleep. I refuse to sign the notification letters tonight. It's as if I delay it, I can delay Frank's death. Tomorrow will be soon enough.

12:10 A.M.
Sunday, March 3, 1968
Hello Sweetheart,
This'll be short because it's so late Saturday night and I'm tired. I just got in from my last operation. My replacement is on the Colleton now. This operation was another bad one (4 KIAs and 10 or 12 WIAs). One of the KIAs was another very close friend. I'm glad I'm getting out of the field.

I keep remembering Frank's conversation on the radio with the King as he was taking himself out of the field. He was so calm and matter of fact. It couldn't have been more than five minutes after I heard this conversation that Frank died. As I wait for sleep to come, Will Davis begins to talk about the same thing I have on my mind. Will says that he spent most of a day with Frank less than a week ago. One of Frank's radio operators had been killed last Monday. He had a major portion of his face shot away by a bullet. Wills tells me that Frank commented on how terrible the injury. He had then said, "Will, when I saw his face blown away, I saw my own death. My time is coming soon, I can feel it." Davis says he was at Bear

Cat picking up some new replacement troops yesterday when he got the call that Frank had been killed.

"Chaplain, I cried like a baby. This is the first time I've cried since I got to Vietnam."

Later, Henry Roland, a squad leader from Echo Company, tells me that his squad arrived at Frank's position after the firefight. Frank insisted Henry help the men first. Frank even lied about being hit himself. "Get my men out." Frank had said.

I think about the last thing Frank said to me, "Keep your head down, Jim."

SUNDAY, MARCH 3, 1968: The flotilla leaves Can Tho to travel back to Dong Tam at 4:00 A.M. We arrive in late afternoon.

> *7:00 P.M.*
> *Sunday, March 3, 68*
> *Hello Sweetheart,*
> *I can almost get excited when I think that it's only about three and a half months. It's 115 days now. Big difference in 365 days! Sure feels good to be out of the field.*

MONDAY, MARCH 4, 1968: This morning, I conduct two memorial services, one for Charlie Company and one for Alpha Company. The second one is the most difficult because Frank Pina is included. He has stood with me in front of these troops before, and should be with me now, not his boots, steel pot and rifle.

We're anchored in the middle of the My Tho river near Dong Tam and are scheduled to have two or three days down. The S-1 tells me before I leave the APL for Dong Tam that my replacement has arrived. Before I go to a scheduled unit party, I stop at my "new digs" and learn he stayed here last night. I'm glad he's here, but I instantly find myself slightly resenting anyone taking my place here. This is my turf. I am surprised at myself.

I meet my replacement and he's on crutches! He explains that he twisted his knee at Bear Cat playing volley ball. He's embarrassed about his injury. I'm afraid the King isn't going to like getting someone on crutches.

When I return to the APL, the King finds me and he is quite upset.

"What's this about your replacement being injured?" he barks.

I explain he has a twisted knee and the King wants to know how long it will be before he can go to the field.

"I'm not sure, Sir. He says the doctor has him on crutches for a week."

"Hell, this won't do. They send a replacement who can't even walk." The King's face is red.

"Sir, he'll be OK. I hear he's a good man."

"He'd better be." He asks me when I am leaving. I tell him the day after tomorrow. I wonder if he's thinking of trying to keep me here until my replacement's leg is better.

"Okay, but if he doesn't work out, they'd better send me someone immediately. We've been ignored long enough down here in the field. Bear Cat does what they want and we get what's left over."

"Sir, I'm sure everything will work out."

TUESDAY, MARCH 5, 1968: Tomorrow I am to leave for Bear Cat. The VC are apparently angry at not being invited to our second stand down party so they crash it by dropping fifteen mortar rounds onto us at 5:00 P.M. This ends the party.

WEDNESDAY, MARCH 6, 1968: I enjoy my last breakfast along with some good natured toasting and roasting by some of the officers. Then, I'm off for the fifteen minute shuttle boat ride to Dong Tam. Paul is with me and borrows a jeep to haul my stuff to the landing strip to await the chopper that will fly me to Bear Cat. Then, it's a brief goodbye and handshake with Paul and he leaves. "Keep your head down, Paul," I tell him. And then he's gone.

The chopper comes, I load my gear aboard and we lift off. As we circle to the left out over the turning basin and the river, I glance to the right and down to the five ships of the flotilla and mentally wave goodbye. I glance to my left at Dong Tam. It's now almost three times the size it was when I first arrived last summer.

I use this flight for reflection. I have tremendous pride for having spent the past three-quarters of a year with the 3/60th. I have loved and been loved by hundreds of heroes, many of whom are now dead and most of whom have been wounded. I find while I greatly feared the VC, I do not hate them. I do hate war. Even though war may sometimes be a political, social or economic necessity, it's a terrible price for any one soldier to have to pay with limbs, eyes, or life.

I also know I've served under two wonderful leaders, Monk Doty and John Hill. Their styles and personalities were drastically different, yet they have both taught me so very much. I've made it this far and even though a part of me has perhaps died inside, I'm still alive.

The chopper is descending and I know I'll have to make a transition to an entirely different war than the one I just left.

CHAPTER EIGHT

March 7–June 25, 1968

THURSDAY, MARCH 7, 1968: Division HQ is only a forty-five minute chopper ride from Dong Tam, yet the contrast between the two is like the difference between caviar and peanut butter. The Bear Cat war is not fought with bullets, booby traps, rockets and mortars. This war consists of reports and inspections. Except for location, Bear Cat is like stateside duty.

I'm assigned to HHC and Band of the Division Support Command. I'll have special duty at the "Reliable Academy," a training center for newly arrived troops. I quickly learn that staff meetings aren't about the war I just left but are about things like guard duty at the NCO Club and life guards at the service club pool. DISCOM has troops involved in diverse jobs and locations with supply, signal, maintenance, transportation, aviation and medical.

I have a nice office in the chapel, located about fifty meters from my hooch, the HQ and the mess hall. After a week, my transition is complete.

Shortly after I arrive at Bear Cat, I become a "two digit midget." This means I have less than 100 days until DEROS. It feels good.

I quickly become bored but constantly remind myself how lucky I am not to be getting shot at.

FRIDAY, MARCH 8, 1968: I pray at my first Academy graduation exercise, knowing there will be many more.

SUNDAY, MARCH 10, 1968: Busy day. Graduation, service at the Academy, fly to Ben Luc where I will conduct two more worship services and then back to Bear Cat.

WEDNESDAY, MARCH 13, 1968: Another memorial service. This is not for a KIA but for a soldier who died when he wrecked his Jeep. Some say he was joy riding. That doesn't matter now because he's just as dead as if an AK 47 round had plowed through him. His family will be just as sad.

SUNDAY, MARCH 17, 1968: Four worship services today. I've done tons of counseling this week.

SATURDAY, MARCH 23, 1968: Today I hear a excuse I've not come across before. A new soldier heading to the 3/60th says he can't go to the field because he can't swallow pills.

FRIDAY, MARCH 29, 1968: A warrant officer pilot wants to talk. He's had the horrifying experience of being shot down. He wasn't hurt but is having frequent and unpleasant flashbacks.

1:10 P.M.
Sunday, March 30, 1968
Hello Sug,
Well, another month down the drain after today. It's eighty-seven days and a wake up to DEROS. In six or seven weeks, I'll go over four years for pay purposes and my base pay should go from $556 to $611 per month. I love you.

After such an intense eight and one-half months of being in life and death situations almost daily, my routine here is less than challenging. Yet, this is what I asked for. I may be alive because of this.

My work is similar to my reception station job at Ft. Knox. I pray at the almost daily graduations at the Reliable Academy, conduct the hated character guidance classes for E-5s and below, do much counseling and attend to staff work that I've never had to do before. At least weekly, I go to Long Binh to visit our soldiers who are sick at the hospitals. I also grudgingly visit LBJ, as we usually have several incarcerated soldiers.

I usually have two or three services on Sundays as well as flying down to Ben Luc south of Saigon for a service.

I fantasize daily about my return to the world. I can't wait.

MONDAY, APRIL 1, 1968: The two most colorful officers in DISCOM are majors named Milt and 'Rope.' Milt is the S-1 (Personal officer) and Rope is the S-3 (Operations Officer). They're good friends but have opposite personalities. Milt sees humor in most everything and carries out practical jokes with a straight face. He's usually loose as a goose. Rope, on the other hand, is uptight about everything. His anxiety is always high!

Even though they're great friends, Milt loves to play jokes on Rope and often enlists other officers in the fun. Once, in the officers mess for supper, Milt suggested that as Rope comes in and is seated, when any of us speak to him, we pick a spot about twelve inches above his eyes and focus on that spot as we talk instead of having direct eye contact. We gleefully agree. It's immediately obvious that no eye contact makes Rope nervous. After six or seven brief but confusing interchanges with several officers, his anger rises. He slams his fist onto the table, rattling dishes, and curses, "Why don't any of you look at me?" Everyone practically rolls on the floor in laughter. Only then does Rope realize he's been set up.

Another time, Milt suggests that when Rope comes in for supper, we make eye contact with him and then immediately dart our eyes away from him without speaking. Rope gets very nervous again. As predicted, he explodes, "What's going on here?" which gives us all more belly laughs.

The most memorable practical joke occurred today. Rope is pending orders and he's very eager to learn of his next assignment, since his DEROS is in early June. Everyday at the evening meal, the conversation has gone like this:

"Milt, did my orders come in today?"

"No."

"When will they come?"

"When they get here," as Milt rolls his eyes upward.

With anger rising, "Department of the Army is trying to screw me," Rope says, his anger rising. "They always do. Milt, can't you get my orders?"

"Just be patient."

This conversation is repeated almost verbatim during the last two weeks of March. Today, Milt learns that Rope's alert order has come to the S-1 office. Rope has received the assignment he's requested to Alabama. Seeing the opportunity to have some fun at Rope's expense, Milt decides to cut a fake set of orders assigning him to Korea! Plus, he's only authorized fourteen days leave between Vietnam and Korea instead of the normal thirty. Orders are never issued from one hardship tour directly to another. The only thing on these fake orders to indicate they're not valid is that in the place of the date, the orders read "April Fool." Milt also cuts his real orders, but hides them in his desk drawer.

The fake orders to Korea are placed in Rope's distribution box. Milt alerts four or five of us and we quickly gather in the S-1 office. Milt then calls Rope on the field phone.

"Rope, I think your orders are in."

"Hot dog! I'll be right there."

Rope's office is just behind the S-1 office. He charges through the door in less than ten seconds. Nothing distracts him.

Rope grabs the stack of orders and his eyes dart over the page to find his next assignment. He's silent for a few seconds, then shakes his head. He curses quietly. Five seconds more of silence pass as his eyes dart over the orders again. "Damn, they can't do this!" He begins to quiver slightly. "Those idiots can't do this!" He's now yelling.

We're all peering over file cabinets at him trying to hold back our laughter. He's still unaware of our presence.

"Milt, what are those SOBs trying to do to me?" he screams.

"What do you mean, Rope?" Milt is calm and cool.

"Those bird brains are sending me to Korea! They can't do this to me." His face is beet red. "Plus, I'm only getting fourteen days leave!"

Rope grabs Milt's arm and shakes him. "They can't do this to me, can they?" He sounds like he might cry. He's now shaking all over.

"Rope, look at the date of the orders."

"What does the date have to do with anything? They're sending me to Korea. I'll go AWOL before I let those pig heads send me to Korea."

"Look at the date."

"Screw the date!" Rope slam dunks the entire stack of orders on the floor, knocking over the trash can and sending loose papers flying. By now, fifteen or so other officers and enlisted men have heard the commotion and have entered the S-1 office to see what's going on.

"Rope, look at the date." Milt is now practically yelling himself. "The date, Rope, the date," Milt screams.

Rope finds the date. Five seconds pass. "April Fool? What does this mean? April Fool!" He's still loud but a little calmer now.

"Today is April Fools' Day. Here's another set of orders." Milt reaches into his desk for the real orders. "Read these."

Another ten seconds pass. "Hot dog! I got my assignment. Milt, you egg sucking dog, I'm going to kill you," Rope says, grinning. He grabs Milt around the neck as if to choke him.

"You evil rat, you're always trying to screw with my mind. I'm going to kill you right now. You're dead meat."

"Then, your orders will be for LBJ," I yell.

"I don't care, Chaplain." He's laughing and shaking Milt at the same time. "This egg sucking dog deserves to die!"

TUESDAY, APRIL 2, 1968: From day one at DISCOM, I have had a steady stream of soldiers wanting to counsel. About half of this is done in my chapel office and the other half is with newly arrived soldiers at the Reliable Academy. Typical problems include spiritual needs, Dear John letters, pregnant girlfriends, no mail, and conscientious objectors to war. There are those who can't adjust, who feel the army has screwed them, want to go home to get married, go back on R&R and marry the girl, etc.

TUESDAY, APRIL 2, 1968: Today a soldier wants emergency leave. His wife lives with his parents and they have beaten her.

WEDNESDAY, APRIL 3, 1968: A soldier wants one thousand dollars from the chaplain's fund to give to his girl friend. We all want to win the lottery! Started to rain today for the first time. Monsoons are fast approaching. This is first rain in five and one-half months.

8:00 P.M.
Wednesday, April 3, 1968
Hello Sweetheart,
It's just eighty-four days now. They're clicking off. I've gotten most of my backlogged mail now except for the fudge. Be sweet and all that stuff.

2:10 P.M.
Thursday, April 5, 1968
Hello Sweets,
Just one more chaplain in the division will leave before I do. I'll be next.

MONDAY, APRIL 8, 1968: Dennis McDougall, the lieutenant shot in My Tho, is back in Bear Cat. He has written me a couple of times from Japan. I was glad he stopped in to see me today. Made me feel good because he says I saved his life by pulling him back when he was hit. He's quite a miracle. On February 2, I never thought I'd see him alive again.

FRIDAY, APRIL 12, 1968: A soldier not only receives a Dear John letter, but his girl friend encloses in the letter her engagement ring as well. He tells me he can't stand the pain.

SUNDAY, APRIL 14, 1968: Alert at 1:00 A.M. Nothing happens. Yet, the command "thinks" we may have received two or three incoming rockets. I "think" they don't know their rear ends from a hole in the ground.

Farce. Inequality. Unfairness. I use these condemning words and more to describe my feelings about awards in Vietnam. Two cases in point. Questions have arisen about the new M-16 rifle, its accuracy, its tendency to jam, etc. A Department of the Army (DA) team is in Vietnam to investigate the M-16. A young E-6 is in charge of DISCOM's arms room. In preparation for the team, he works hard and obviously does a good job. The DA team does an inspection on the arms room and makes favorable comments to the command about it. The E-6 is given a Bronze Star for achievement.

The second case: One night, and only one night while I'm at Bear Cat, we go on alert when supposedly a few rockets are fired into the base camp.

As the siren warning sounds, naturally everyone runs for bunkers. In one unit elsewhere on Bear Cat, four or five soldiers are awarded Purple Hearts for skinned and bruised knees and elbows received while scampering into the bunkers. An officer from that unit told me this was done to "build morale."

Literally hundreds of the 3/60th soldiers deserve awards but don't receive them. Since it takes time to appropriately write award recommendations, and since we were out almost constantly on combat operations, often there simply is no one who can write up the recommendation. Or, more often than not, the paperwork is lost at division headquarters. By the time it's discovered, either the proposed recipient or the one who has recommended the award, has been wounded or killed and no one is able to follow up.

Worse still, division HQ has a tendency to down grade awards. One division officer, when confronted with why so many awards were down graded or turned down, simply stated, "It's the infantry's job to fight. An award is for doing something above what a normal soldier's job is." Who does he think he is?

It's not that I feel that any of those who get awards don't deserve them. However, those who *do* deserve them often receive no accolade. Countless soldiers in the infantry are caught in a system that rewards some who are less deserving than others.

9:00 P.M.
Monday, April 15, 1968
Hello Sweets,
Grey sure can say a lot of words now. I can tell from the tapes there is a big difference since January. I'll be glad to get home to some good eggs, grits and sausage. I won't mind seeing you either!

MONDAY, APRIL 30, 1968: When a soldier is killed, word is rapidly sent to the states through command channels so that notification of next of kin is accomplished as soon as possible. An officer, who is often accompanied by a chaplain, makes this notification. This is usually done within a few hours of the death. At Ft. Knox, I had that unpleasant task several times during last year's assignment. The only thing worse than telling a wife or parent that their husband or son has been killed is to actually be present when he is killed. Both are horrible aspects of this war.

When a soldier is killed, the body is taken to the graves registration unit at Saigon for proper identification, which is coordinated with the soldier's unit. The body is then embalmed and prepped to be flown to the US. It usually takes no longer than two or three days. Upon arrival in the United States, an escort of equal or higher rank than the deceased accompanies the body to the final destination.

This process was begun for Capone who was one of the soldiers killed that horrible night on February 20th. Notification was made to the Capone family of his death. They were told his body would soon arrive with escort. Then, the family waited. No one called. The Capones made inquiries about when their son would arrive. They were told that the body was on the way. But still no body arrived.

Their grief turned to anger and bitterness and something much worse, a little hope. They had been told that their son was dead, yet, no body had been received. After several long and agonizing days, thoughts began to turn to the possibility that maybe he wasn't killed after all. Maybe it was a mistake, perhaps he became separated from his unit and was wandering about lost in the jungle somewhere.

Back in Vietnam, low level flights were ordered over the flight path thought to have been made by the chopper evacuating Capone's body. If the body had fallen out of the aircraft, the likelihood that it would be seen at this late date is very low. The conclusion is made that the body has been lost. Officials don't know if it was left in the field, fell from the chopper going to Dong Tam, fell from the chopper taking it from Dong Tam to Saigon, or perhaps was even sent to the wrong family in the states. The army is tremendously embarrassed; the family is naturally angry and bitter.

During the natural process of grief, an initial denial is followed by the questions, "Are you sure?" or "How do you know it was my son?" Then, there's anger, depression, and the outpouring of emotions. Eventually, the process circles back to reality and one accepts the death. This paves the way for the gradual return to a routine, albeit newly created. The presence of the dead body enables the grief process to proceed naturally. But here's the Capone family with no body. Their grief process is severely hindered.

As a result of this embarrassing episode, the Department of the Army mandates an investigation team to attempt to determine what actually happened to the body. The team is to interview persons who were present the night of Capone's death, those who may have handled the body at Dong Tam and Saigon, and others who may have knowledge of what actually happened.

I am interviewed twice, first on April 30 and then again on May 2. I know one of the officers on the team, a lieutenant colonel, because he's a transportation officer in DISCOM. The other two officers are both colonels and look stern and businesslike. I notice from their shoulder patches, that they are US Army, Vietnam Headquarters. The team chief, a supply officer, begins the interview.

"Do you solemnly swear to tell the truth, the whole truth and nothing but the truth, so help you God?" He asks me.

"I do." My response is as honest as my marriage vows.

"State your full name, rank and current position," which I do.

He then explains the purpose of the "interrogation" (he actually uses that word, not interview) is to find out what happened to Capone's body and who was responsible for losing it. As he talks, his initial demeanor is condescending and patronizing. I immediately don't like him.

"Did you know Capone?"

"No sir, I did not."

"Did you know of him prior to the night of 20 February?"

"I knew of him because of his name and my familiarity with his unit. I spent considerable time with his company on combat operations." I say.

"What do you mean, 'because of his name'?"

"Capone, sir. That's a recognizable name, especially because he was from Chicago. You know, as in Al Capone." From his look, I am not certain he makes the association.

"I see. I don't quite understand something. What were you doing on combat operations? You're a chaplain."

"It was my job." I explain.

"How's that, Chaplain?" He peers curiously over his glasses at me.

"It's my job, Sir, to be with my troops wherever they go. I went out on all combat operations."

"Really?" His attitude seems to shift a bit. "So you were there when Capone supposedly was killed."

"There is no "supposing" about it, Sir. He was killed. And yes, I was there." I remember the day well and tell him what I saw. "I helped load the seven bodies onto the chopper for evacuation. We looked at all the name tags and dog tags."

"A name tag doesn't mean it was him, does it?" he asks.

"I suppose not. But who'd go around switching fatigue shirts? There'd be no point in his doing that."

The man shifted a bit in his chair. "Did anyone else know him?"

"Yes sir. His squad members. They're the ones who brought his body for evacuation."

"How far was that?"

"About 50 meters." I tell him.

He scribbles on a pad and after a slight pause looks up at me again. "How many bodies were loaded onto the chopper?"

"Seven. Six were Americans and one was a Chieu Hoi."

He seems a little embarrassed that he doesn't know what a Chieu Hoi is, but he only hesitates and then asks me to explain. I do, all the while thinking he must be really new in country.

"Tell us about loading the bodies into the chopper."

"The medic, a radio operator, the chopper crew chief and I loaded all seven bodies into the chopper. We laid them side by side on the floor with two or three of the bodies stacked on top of the bottom ones."

The team chief then asks me what the bodies looked like. I want those memories to go away, not be prolonged because some clown needs a detailed description, but I go on, hoping this will somehow help the Capones. "They were all covered with mud."

"What do you mean, 'covered with mud'?"

"Just that. They were covered with mud, head to toe. Sir, if you are in a firefight in rice paddies and you are wallowing in mud and trying to stay alive, you get muddy. It's simple. You get muddy." I repeat myself and realize my irritation with this dumb brass hat is beginning to show.

"Why were the bodies not cleaned up?"

"Sir, there was no way to clean the bodies up." My voice rises slightly. "The Vietnamese rice farmers don't have drive through car washes at the edge of their rice paddies."

The transportation officer, who knows me, steps in and takes over the questioning, perhaps sensing my irritation at the team leader's ignorance. "Chaplain, is there any possibility Capone's body was accidentally left in the field?"

"Absolutely not. He was loaded onto the chopper."

"Do you have any doubt?"

"None whatsoever." I tell them, certain of this point.

"What do you think happened to the body?" asks the first colonel.

I feel like telling them I am not here to do their job for them. "I don't know. Perhaps it slid out of the chopper while it was making an airborne turn. Or, maybe the graves registration people lost it, or sent it to the wrong destination."

"Were the chopper doors closed when it left?"

"Probably not, though I don't remember specifically. Most re-supply choppers fly with open doors. If they were open, and as muddy and slick as the seven bodies were, it's possible that Capone's body just slid out."

"Wouldn't the crew chief have noticed if a body slid out?"

"Probably not," I repeat, "especially if he was focused on looking for VC on the ground." Several more questions follow and the interview is ended.

The next interview a couple of days later is similar but shorter. I don't know if I'll ever learn what the eventual conclusion is about the lost body.

The anguish that the Capone family experiences from never receiving the body only adds to their tragedy. As a father, I cannot begin to imagine what it must be like to lose a son, not to mention never having the body to bury and a gravesite to visit. I feel so very sorry for the Capone family.

MONDAY, MAY 6, 1968: I'm having trouble with one of the chaplain assistants. He's lazy, undependable, won't bathe and very passive about everything he does. I tell him to get his act together or he'll be reassigned.

WEDNESDAY, MAY 8, 1968: This afternoon while I'm in the S-1 office picking up my distribution, a question comes from Milt, the S-1. "Chaplain, have you taken your R&R?"

"Yes, I went to Hawaii in January." I recall the days with Barbara and the kids with a smile. His next question turns that smile into a perplexed frown.

"You want another one?"

I'm sure he's joking, but respond that I thought I was only authorized to have one R&R.

He explains that he gets allocations for the division and some of them go unfilled. "Maybe a soldier gets wounded or sick and can't go. These allocations simply go to waste. I'll get you another one if you can go on short notice. Besides, with all the time you spent in the field, you certainly deserve another one."

"I'd love to. But I don't want to get into trouble," I say.

"There won't be any trouble. They are there for the taking. I'll give you an unused slot, and you won't be taking anything away from anyone. What do you think? Want one, or not?"

I was no longer shy. "Sure. What do I need to do?"

"Just tell me where you want to go."

Something comes to me in a flash. "Australia."

"I'll see what I can do."

I go back to my office feeling like I'm a sweepstakes finalist. It would be wonderful to go to Australia. I've heard nothing but good things about the place from the guys who have been. Suddenly, I stop and think. I hope this isn't another of Milt's practical jokes!

WEDNESDAY, MAY 22, 1968: Today a PFC from Milt's office called to tell me I need to fill out the R&R paperwork for Australia. It looks like it might actually happen! In no time, the paperwork is done and I'll leave on

Tuesday the 3rd of June, the day before our 7th wedding anniversary. Then, when I return from R&R, I'll only have a little over two weeks until my DEROS. I'm thrilled.

MONDAY, JUNE 3, 1968: I am to leave today for Camp Alpha for my flight to Australia. Just before I leave, a soldier comes with a marital problem. He has received almost no mail from his wife and he finally wrote her and said, "If you don't begin writing to me, we'll hang it up." She has written him back and he brings the letter. It reads, "Hang it up, then, you bastard." That's it. No more, just a one sentence letter. Broken love can be so painful. Tomorrow is our wedding anniversary. I am glad Barbara is so faithful.

TUESDAY, JUNE 4, 1968: Our big bird leaves for Australia. While airborne, my thoughts are of June 4th, 1961 when Barbara and I were married. That was, and still is, the most wonderful day in my life. Everyone should have a spouse as loving and committed as my wife.

WEDNESDAY, JUNE 5 THROUGH MONDAY, JUNE 10, 1968: We land in Sydney, process in and I get to my R&R hotel at midmorning. The first thing I do is call Barbara. For the next five days I enjoy the hospitality of the wonderful Australian people. I do the usual sight-seeing, even attend a bush barbecue but the best part of my trip is my discovery of the Australian-American Hospitality Club. It is a group of families who host American GIs here on R&R. For several days I am the guest of The Moses family in their home. It is a three hour drive from Willow Tree, which is five hours by train from Sydney. I have a tremendous time with this gracious family.

The worst thing about my trip is seeing over the hotel lobby television that Bobby Kennedy has been shot. It is such a shock. I think about John Kennedy, Martin Luther King, and now, Bobby? I am sorry for them all, but I know thousands and thousands of families are going through what the King and the Kennedy families are, dealing with death. The senseless loss is staggering, whether you are shot in a hotel kitchen in Los Angeles or a rice paddy in Vietnam, whether you are a famous religious or political figure, or a dirt farmer from Kentucky.

WEDNESDAY, JUNE 12, 1968: When I returned yesterday from "down under," it was my hope that my port call orders would be here on my arrival at Bear Cat. I was told the orders will be here in a day or two.

But, today's the day! As I pick up my distribution, the orders are in my box. What a wonderful surprise. My port call is Tuesday June 24. This is two days before my DEROS. Hurrah! Two days early. That's less than thirteen days from now. I'm practically home. I want the yell, "I'm short!"

TUESDAY, JUNE 18, 1968: Today is an awards ceremony in which I receive another valor medal for the Tet operations. It has been downgraded from a recommended higher award, supposedly because "he's a chaplain, not an infantryman", but who cares? What really matters is that I lived, and next week I'm going home!

WEDNESDAY, JUNE 19, 1968: My replacement is here! He's a major I knew at Ft. Knox whose office was just across the street from me there.

SUNDAY JUNE 23, 1968: I take my replacement around with me to the services. I let him preach and I do the preliminary parts of the services. These are my last ones in Vietnam. Tomorrow, I go to Long Binh to process out for my flight on Tuesday. After my last service, I take a deep breath and think to myself, "I'm through".

CHAPTER NINE

June 26, 1968–March 1, 1996

TUESDAY, JUNE 25, 1968: Perhaps it was due to nervousness, excitement, anxiety, or who knows what, but I literally did not sleep at all last night at the 90th Replacement Battalion at Long Binh. Processing for my flight home at Bien Hoa Air Base was heavenly.

After more processing at Travis Air Force Base, I leave by army bus to the San Francisco airport where I fly directly to El Paso, Texas, arriving there just before dark. My plans have been to stop in El Paso, sign in, get my name on the post housing list, sign out immediately on leave and go home to North Carolina. Then, when my leave is over and I report back for duty at Ft Bliss, maybe housing for my family will be available.

My sponsor meets me at the airport. I can't sign up for housing until tomorrow morning when the office reopens. I call Barbara. It's hard to believe that tomorrow, I'll be home!

WEDNESDAY, JUNE 26, 1968: I go to the housing office, do the brief paperwork, sign out and return to the airport to catch my flight to North Carolina.

The closer I get to Charlotte, the more excited I get. This year has created a new universe for me. I've experienced far more of life in these 365 days than I did in the first twenty-six years of my life put together. My entire concept of the world and life in general has changed drastically—forever. I'm coming home whole—at least physically.

At Charlotte, we touch down and taxi to the gate. I hurry off the plane and spot Barbara. We come together like a magnet and metal. We embrace and cry. Someone grabs my leg. It's like Hawaii all over again. I pick Kellie up, and Grey too. I'm home!

It is a one hour drive to Albemarle. I know Daddy is working second shift in the mill, so we stop to see him. It's almost dark by now and I meet him at the main gate. It's been a year since I last saw him at the Charlotte airport when I left. Many of the other workers come to the gate to see what's going on. Daddy has told everyone that I'm coming home today, but he didn't know I'd stop to see him. Everyone claps when we embrace.

We drive the two miles to see Mother. More hugs, kisses, tears and prayers of thanksgiving. And some good food, nothing out of a can!

Then, it's the quarter mile to our house. The kids are tired, but not too tired for me to tell them some bedtime stories. I linger with them for a while, and then it's just Barbara and me, in our own bed, in our own home. Thank God, I'm home!

I have thirty days leave plus travel time to El Paso. We decide to take only two weeks leave and save some for the future. I visit family, some friends and generally just take it easy for the first three or four days.

Soon, it begins to happen. People ask me to tell them about Vietnam. I don't know what to say. Do I say, "Ninety six of my buddies were slaughtered and over 900 were wounded?" I do respond to some regarding my feelings, but it seems no one wants to hear. Conversations go like this: "I had a terrible experience. We had a lot of killed and wounded. I'm very lucky to have gotten out myself."

Then, at the first pause, "What about all those Buddhists monks who torch themselves? Did you ever see any of that?" Or, "Why is the political climate so volatile?"

I gradually realize that everyone wants to know about Vietnam, but no one wants to know about me. This becomes a pattern, and it's painful. I know it isn't intended, but it feels like Vietnam is more important than I am. As a result, I begin to tuck away thoughts and feelings. Who's to listen? Who's to care? My parents do. Barbara does. But, no one else seems to. Or maybe they can't.

Everyone is glad to see me. They tell me so and I believe them. They hug me. Some cry. All this is genuine. But, no one is here to soothe my soul. My emotional scar tissue has not yet formed. Barbara and the kids are wonderful. But, the wounds remain.

Some veterans report being spat upon or being attacked by antiwar protesters when they return. I do not experience any of that. But, there's no one who really wants to hear my story.

Before we are to leave for Texas, I decide to call the young widow of one of our KIAs. I just want to reach out to her. It's now been several months since her husband died. Nervously, I pick up the phone and place the call.

"Hello. This is Jim Johnson. I was your husband's chaplain. He was a very good friend of mine and I was with him the day he died."

"Oh." Nothing more.

"I just wanted to see how you're doing."

"I'm fine." No questions, no comments.

"How are your children?" I ask.

"Fine."

"Well, I just wanted to call," I say after another uncomfortable pause. "Your husband was a very good man and a very good friend. Is there anything I can do for you?"

"No, thank you."

She has asked no questions and made no observations, and the call is over. I certainly don't feel like I thought I would. In fact, I feel awful.

I'm puzzled. I really wanted to reach out to her, and I haven't. Perhaps I didn't know how.

We have a wonderful time traveling to El Paso. Driving across country, we visit friends, stop in Houston and then San Antonio, where the Hemisfair '68 is going full blast. Grey rides some kiddy rides by himself for the first time ever. Barbara says his feelings of security are the result of my being home. It's wonderful knowing I will not have to say goodbye again.

We head for El Paso and somewhere in west Texas, I reach into the rear seat to get something one of the kids has dropped. I yell out in pain so loudly that I frighten Barbara and the kids who have no idea what's happening. It is my shoulder. It has dislocated again! I quickly brake to a stop and pull over to the side of the road. I feel like I'm back in Vietnam in that canal the day Frank Pina was killed. That was when my shoulder dislocated the first time, and as then, I am able to force it back in place.

I assure Barbara that I'm okay but she isn't convinced. I promise her I'll have the shoulder checked when we get to Ft. Bliss.

We arrive in El Paso and post housing is available the day we sign in. I had been told the waiting time would be one to two months and we were anticipating an even longer wait. I sign for housing the first day and process into post.

Vietnam is now further away as we begin a new life.

I'm shocked when I get to Ft. Bliss and learn that my assignment will be at the post stockade. What a contrast having served with many heroes and now ministering to soldiers who are AWOL, facing petty crimes and a few who're in serious trouble for crimes such as armed robbery and rape. However, I quickly adjust. I find I do have the skills to minister to those wounded by morals, poor choices, mood and personality disorders. Even though physically secure, my office is the only one located actually "behind the wire." I'm proud of this. Again, I'm where the soldiers are.

Ft. Bliss is an air defense post, which means that while many here have been in Vietnam, few have been a vital part of ground combat operations. They know nothing about what it's like to face snipers, ambushes and booby traps on a daily basis. This enhances the sense of isolation I soon begin to have. I think it would've been healing to have had a network of others who had experienced daily combat. I make many friends but I find no one I can truly relate to as far as my recent trauma is concerned. I only have myself, my memories, and my unsettled feelings.

As I process into post, it is noted that I have several combat valor medals, which the Public Affairs Office finds of significant interest with me being a Chaplain. This leads to several interviews by reporters and stories about me are published. I'm quite uncomfortable with the notoriety because I'm still a shy country boy at heart. I'm not sure what to make of all this hoopla. All in all, though, I feel I'm making my adjustment from Vietnam to my new duties quite well. I grow to love El Paso, perhaps because the dry desert is so drastically different from the wet Mekong Delta.

I'm not sure how or when my post traumatic stress begins. There are some dreams, vivid dreams, of specific battles. Sounds in these dreams are in very real. The dreams themselves are frightening. Sometimes I wake up crying. I'm dreaming we're about to be overrun. Always I'm terrified. I had always assumed that although I never carried a weapon, except on two operations, that if I ever needed to defend myself, there'd always be plenty of weapons available. In my head, I knew this was true. However, in my subconscious, my fear and insecurity must have been ever-present. These feelings come out in these terrible dreams.

Other symptoms begin to surface. What is called startle responses, for example. And, like so many veterans, I can't stand the sound of a helicopter. At times, I have difficulty concentrating. Fortunately, the symptoms do not become overwhelming.

A friend who knows about some of my combat experiences suggests I write a book about them. I immediately discount his suggestion. I am not certain why, but soon, I do begin writing. I had kept very detailed diaries and journals in Vietnam and now I begin a process of what I later will refer to as a therapeutic journal. And when feelings surface due to dreams, or in my waking moments, I record these feelings. I simply record what I'm experiencing.

During the next year, I fill many legal pads. My pen becomes my therapist. Eventually, the vividness of my dreams begins to diminish. My feelings aren't gone, but I do begin to heal. The longer I am away from Vietnam, the less preoccupied I am with the trauma that I experienced there.

Soon after my arrival at Ft. Bliss, I had decided I must reach out to the parents of Ron Wood, the lieutenant killed at Can Tho. I had written that I would contact them when I arrived in El Paso, so, I place a call.

Mrs. Wood seems eager to meet and invites Barbara and I to their house for dinner. I'm not completely comfortable about the pending visit. I recall that my efforts to reach the young widow while in North Carolina didn't go well. Perhaps I'm anticipating the same here.

Upon arrival at the Wood's, we're invited into the living room and exchange pleasantries. It's obvious that we must get to the business at hand, and that's Ron. I bring up the subject. His mother cries. His father looks like he'll burst, but doesn't cry. They've lost their only son, their dreams for him, hopes of grandchildren and much of their future. I would be bitter. We discuss the details of how Ron died, and I describe him as the hero that he was. They show me his medals and certificates. Overall, the evening goes well. Even though it has been six months since Ron's death, the pain is still very real. In spite of this, his parents are gracious and caring. As I leave, I think, what a waste, this war that I hated so. But, I am sincerely glad to have made the visit.

In late September, I'm playing in an intramural flag football game and I catch a long pass. As I reach the end zone for a touchdown, I trip, fall and again dislocate my shoulder. This finally prompts me to see the orthopedic surgeon, who informs me that reconstructive surgery is required. The original injury back in the canal in March of 1968 did extensive damage.

I enter William Beaumont Army Hospital and have the surgery, which involves reattaching tendons and muscle with screws. I'm hospitalized for a week and on convalescent leave for another two weeks. A waist to neck body cast is my constant companion for six weeks after that and then there is painful physical therapy.

I am told that for the rest of my life, I'll have significant limited range of motion, which forces me to modify physical activity. For example, I have limited overhead lifting ability, which keeps me from going to airborne school. This bruises my ego, but doesn't impede my career. I'm limited in basketball and my golf swing is affected. "My shot went into the lake, woods, or clubhouse window because of those blasted VC," can always serve as my excuse.

But most importantly, having limited arm movement will always remind me of the awfulness of war.

When Barbara asks, I keep telling her that when I finish, she can read my therapeutic writing. In the meantime, I just stuff my feelings down if they surface. This is not easy at times, especially when it's my turn to accompany the duty officer to tell a next of kin their son/husband has been killed. One notification is especially difficult. An Hispanic couple's only son is killed. The mother's soft, continual sobs bother me greatly for several days.

I conduct a military funeral in Odessa, Texas. After the funeral, some World War II vets in the VFW treat us to dinner in a private club and look at us as if we're all conquering heroes. I appreciate their generosity but I still hate these funerals. Two nights later, one of the enlisted men who served on the funeral detail commits suicide by jumping off a third floor overhang. I know this is another indirect casualty of war.

I become ambivalent about wearing my ribbons. It's almost like my not wearing them is a silent, passive resistance to the pain from my trauma. Yet, boycotting has little effect on my feelings.

Big Bob Wood, the Catholic priest who was the last division chaplain for me in the 9th Division, arrives at Ft. Bliss as the post chaplain. I become one of his "projects." He encourages me, sends me to schools and temporary duty training and becomes my true mentor. He is rough and gruff, but he has a true big brother's heart and I grow to love him dearly. He has become a true mentor.

But, only Barbara ever knows the depth of my feelings, and she really knows very little. I talk about Vietnam, but no one sees the gapes I feel I have in my soul.

My obligation to the army is three years. I'll automatically separate then unless I request and am granted voluntary indefinite status, which means I can stay as long as the army wants me.

Barbara and I have long discussions about staying in or not. I have a definite feeling that being an army chaplain is one of my special divine callings. Yet, chaplains who are captains are returning to Vietnam for second tours, between eighteen and twenty months, after their first tour. This does not sound very appealing.

Finally, we decide that if this is my calling and we like the army life, which we both do, I'll request indefinite status. In January 1969, two and one-half years after I entered active duty, I request and am granted indefinite status. We decide if I must return to Vietnam then it'll somehow be okay. A part of my resolution is that I'll request a job in a support unit, though, not a combat unit.

Once this decision is made, I begin to get more and more inner peace. My career path has now begun. Life is good during the first fifteen months at Ft. Bliss. Barbara is pregnant. Twins, Eric and Stuart, are born in May 1969. Kellie and Grey are growing. We are a family. Barbara and I are very much in love and we enjoy each other as we share family responsibilities. She proves once again how wonderful she is, and I'm glad we've decided to stay in the army.

JANUARY 3, 1969: Christmas day was exactly eighteen months since I left Vietnam. As I said, chaplains who are captains are being sent back for second tours, between eighteen and twenty months after their first tour. "What a Christmas present that'll be," I thought. The closer it got to Christmas, the more Barbara and I prepared mentally for my alert.

I'm at the gym playing handball at lunch, as is my normal routine, since my shoulder surgery. I'm as good or better hitting the ball left-handed as I am right-handed! A gym worker calls out my name from the court doorway, telling me I have a phone call. I know it is unusual to receive a call here unless something hot is up. I wonder if there is something is wrong at home or if there is a riot at the stockade.

I answer and discover it is the deputy post chaplain, Dick Combs. He asks me if I want to go to Germany.

I'm immediately angry. I'm due for orders to Vietnam and this clown calls me at the gym to yank my chain about going to Germany. I don't know of any of my chaplain peers who are captains who have gone to Germany instead of Vietnam. This isn't funny. I pause and say nothing.

"Jim, are you there?"

"Yes sir, I'm here." It takes real effort to remain calm.

"Well, do you want to go to Germany or not?"

"Well," I simply do not know what to say. Could this be on the level? "I don't understand."

"Look, Jim, I have two units training to deploy to Germany this summer and they need two chaplains. You and John Reed are the next two on the list and I've got to get the names of the chaplains to be assigned to them by close of business today. I need to know if you want to go." Dick sounds more than a little rushed.

"Yes sir, I want to go. Let me clean up and come to your office in a few minutes. Will that be okay?"

"Sure. But I've got to have an answer this afternoon. In an hour if possible."

Stunned, I hang up the phone. He's serious. I can't even think straight. For months, I've geared my thinking to a return to Vietnam. Germany has never been in the picture. Yet, that's what Dick said. Germany.

I quickly make excuses to my handball buddies, shower and rush home since the house is on my way.

"I might get to go to Germany," I blurt out to Barbara as I dash inside. She's changing one of the twins' diapers and says nothing, just stands with a bewildered look on her face.

"Where's Germany, daddy?" asks Kellie, who's playing on the floor.

I ignore her as Barbara asks, "What do you mean, Germany?"

"I don't know, but Dick Combs says we might go to Germany. Will that be okay?

She doesn't answer. She's probably convinced that I've gone out of my mind.

I rush out, yelling that I will call her later.

When I walk in the door of the post chaplain's office, I note that Ben, the administrative chaplain, does not even look my way. I walk straight to Dick's office.

"Sit down Jim. Sorry to have called you at the gym. But, Bob is in Washington and I have to make a decision today." He goes on to explain that two air defense Chaparral/Vulcan battalions have been organized and are training for deployment to Germany. Their modified table of organization and equipment has just been approved to include a battalion chaplain and surgeon.

"Since you and John Reed have been here the longest, I'm going to recommend you two fill those slots if you want to go." He pauses. "Well, do you?"

"Do I want to go? Sure! What do I have to do?"

"Nothing now. I'll take it from here. I have a call in to Bob. But I know he'll okay this. Then, we'll have to get the Chief's okay but that should be no problem either. Then, we'll cut orders, move you to the new unit and you'll be all theirs."

"Great. Thank you, Sir. Thank you very much."

"One other thing. Ben is super angry about this. He thinks he should go. He says he left Vietnam before either you or John Reed did and he should go."

This might explain why Ben didn't greet me when I arrived. "Actually, he did leave before me." I hate being this honest because I fear this might sabotage my new present of going to Germany.

"Doesn't matter. The clock begins to tick when a person signs in here, not when he leaves his previous assignment. I've double checked the army regulation on that. You signed in here June 25, 1968. John was next and Ben was after him. Therefore, Ben is standby should either of you not be able to be assigned to the new units."

I see it now. When I stopped by Ft. Bliss on my way to North Carolina, I signed in to get my name on the post housing list, hoping my wait would be short for housing. Little did I know then that I would receive this much larger bonus now. A life altering moment!

I walk out and Ben still doesn't acknowledge me, but I understand. I feel like I've just won the lottery.

I soon transfer to the 7/61st Air Defense Artillery battalion, train in the desert with them and prepare for overseas deployment. In the months prior to deployment, all the officers families become very close. This is a wonderful experience. Barbara and I fit into the unit very well and are immediately accepted.

I gain some significant credibility among the officers because a major's promotion list comes out in January from Department of the Army and I'm on it. I'll be promoted to major!

In June 1970, we pack up and the entire battalion heads to Germany— a long way from Vietnam and the trauma of two and one-half years ago.

1970–1973

The tour in Germany is wonderful. My three years are spent as a circuit-riding chaplain, not unlike preachers in the US of the 1800s. Each day I visit two or three units of the eleven I'm responsible for. I love what I do. Little stimulates my trauma of Vietnam, but it's never far below the surface. A few situations and events take me back. I'm in an air defense unit and we live and work at Spangdahlem Air Force Base. During these three years, five aircraft crash with some loss of life. Each time this occurs, some of my raw feelings attempt to surface, but I diligently keep them in their place.

We take an eleven-day trip to the Middle East in 1972, where I see many remnants of recent wars including bunkers, burned out military vehicles, and sandbagged buildings. Again, I'm careful to keep my inner feelings hidden as I see the trappings of war.

Barbara's parents come for two weeks during June of 1971. While we're traveling, I receive an emergency message that my father has had a heart attack. I hurry to Frankfurt, catch a flight to the states and as I disembark at Dover Air Force Base in Delaware, I call to Albemarle, North Carolina for an update on his condition.

Gerald, my brother, tells me Pop didn't make it. Gerald begins to cry as he relates that our dad died the previous night. I can't believe it. I lean against the brick wall and sob, the first time I've cried like this since that dark night on the *Colleton* in February 1968 when I stumbled onto the body bags of the dead soldiers. I continue to cry unashamedly. Pop's loss is very hurtful to me. But, I make it through.

Two months before I rotate back to the states, I'm finally promoted to major after having been on the promotion list for almost three and one-half years. I guess this makes me "brass" in the eyes of the soldiers, but in the coming years, I work hard not to get caught up in the brass trap. I'm also granted a Regular Army commission, which is all but unheard of for a Southern Baptist chaplain these days.

Throughout the three years in Germany, the pain of Vietnam remains, for the most part, dormant. Little reminds me of 1967 and 1968 and when it does, I just push my feelings down until they goes away.

1973–1974

I'm selected to attend the Chaplain Advanced Course at Ft. Hamilton, which is in Brooklyn, New York. This also gives me the opportunity to work on a second masters degree in Counseling at nearby Long Island University.

Most of my classmates have been to Vietnam, but with the drawdown of the war, few have been there during the past two or three years. Little happens at the chaplain school or at Long Island University to remind me of Vietnam.

It's a wonderful year until June of 1974. As we're making preparations to be re-assigned to Fort Bragg, North Carolina, Barbara's father has open-heart surgery in Charlotte. He dies a week later. He's been like a father to me and now in the space of three years, I've lost two significant males in my life. I begin to reflect upon my own mortality due to these deaths.

1974–1977

I spend the first of my three years at Fort Bragg with an engineer brigade. It's during this assignment that I come to grips with the fact that I won't be able to go to airborne school due to the physical limitations and restrictions resulting from the reconstructive surgery on my shoulder in 1968.

Two events reconnect me temporarily with Vietnam. First, a reservist by the name of Henry Roland comes to Bragg for two weeks. Henry was in the 3/60th, learns I'm at Bragg, and looks me up. Henry's visit reactivates some long lost Vietnam memories. Again, I push them down.

The second is a horrible automobile accident involving two sons of my beloved commanding officer, Colonel Swede Nelson. This wreck occurs on Christmas evening of 1975, kills one son and horribly mangles the other, and both of their dates. For several weeks, I walk with Swede and his family through this terrible experience. This involves a trip to northern Virginia with Swede to clean out his deceased son's house and personal belongings. Being with Swede and his wife Charlotte during this time causes me to recall a little of the pain associated with Vietnam and the families of the slain heroes.

Mostly, however, Vietnam is a long ago war. Reports occasionally surface in the media about Vietnam vets who have become dysfunctional. They have lost jobs or families, they are sleeping under bridges and some are killing themselves. I remain in denial about their pain by simply thinking, "They must be weak, or something." The "something" is what I don't understand nor am I ready to try.

I'm becoming aware that I have special ministry skills with persons in crisis. I'm not intimidated at all when a situation is chaotic. I recognize that oftentimes people rely on me and the calming effect I seem to have when things are coming apart for them. Because of this emerging ministry gift, I decide I want additional training to hone these skills. I request and am granted another year of school. Orders are issued for me to go to Brooke Army Medical Center in San Antonio, Texas for a year of Clinical Pastoral Education (CPE). CPE is a very intense year of specialized training and is usually conducted in a trauma center.

One afternoon just before leaving for Texas, the phone rings. A vaguely familiar voice asks for Jim Johnson. The caller identifies himself as Monk Doty. It has been ten years since I saw him leave Dong Tam as the departing battalion commander. I'm shocked but pleased to hear from him. I've known he's lived in Raleigh and periodically I intended to call him. Yet, for reasons I don't understand, I never have.

We exchange small talk and I learn he has a son in Fayetteville. He wonders if the next time he is down, can he stop by. I tell him that it would be great, but explain that I am moving to San Antonio the day after tomorrow. Eager to visit, he decides to come the very next day.

Monk arrives just as the movers do. It's great to see him and I appreciate his efforts to see me. We talk old times, for he has many questions about things that happened in the 3/60th after he left. Then, he's gone.

1977–1981

Brooke Army Medical Center (BAMC) is a huge army medical center in San Antonio, Texas that is best known as a pioneer in treating burn victims. However, this 700-bed facility also does significant open-heart surgery, treats hundreds of persons with life threatening illnesses such as cancer, renal failure, and lung disease.

My year here is a wonderful learning experience. I discover a great deal about both my strengths and weaknesses. I reaffirm that I'm especially effective interacting with persons who've been traumatized and/or those who are facing death. My Vietnam experiences are helping me significantly, especially since our hospital averages two deaths every twenty-four hours.

This year will be the fifth year since returning from Germany and I fully expect alert orders back overseas. Instead, I'm asked to stay on the staff at BAMC, which will be an additional three years here. This is wonderful!

My work during these next three years is primarily with patients having terminal illnesses, open heart surgeries and those in our five ICUs. As stressful as it is being a staff chaplain in a huge medical center, it's also gratifying to do ministry with patients, families and hospital staff in such critical areas. During these years, the trauma of Vietnam remains relatively tucked away. The war is long since over but occasionally the pain surfaces.

One afternoon while on call, I respond to the emergency room when a civilian postal supervisor is brought in. He has been shot several times by a disgruntled and intoxicated postal letter carrier. He dies soon after entering the ER. His family arrives and I accompany them into the small treatment room to see the bullet riddled and blood covered body of their beloved family member. As I view his wounds and smell the odors of blood and death, I'm transported back in time, to another place where blood and death were common place.

Later, at the request of the Chief of Chaplains Office, Emory Cowan, the CPE supervisor, and I develop a two-week course for reserve and National Guard chaplains that we call "Trauma and Survival." The idea is to prepare civilian pastors who are part-time chaplains for the possibility of being confronted with the horrors of war should they be activated and thrown into combat. We utilize the ER, some surgery cases and autopsies to enhance their learning.

During our development of this course, Emory and I discover that since our return from Vietnam, neither of us have had anyone to really hear our stories from the past. As a result of this insight, I vow to dig out my numerous old journals, diaries and notes that I wrote during my Vietnam tour and then at Ft. Bliss when I returned. But I never quite get around to it.

In 1979, I'm sent to a special school in Richmond, Virginia. When I leave Richmond on one of my three trips there, I'm on an Eastern Airlines flight that has an in-flight emergency while approaching Atlanta. We're told that the left landing gear won't lock in place, which may cause the plane to cartwheel down the runway on touchdown. That won't be fun. We burn off fuel for well over an hour. As we prepare for a possible crash landing, the flight crew collects all loose items. Pillows are passed out and instructions are given on tightening seat belts, bracing for impact and exit instructions. This all sounds strangely familiar, like a pre-combat operations briefing.

Oftentimes, when we've just had a close encounter with death like an auto accident, we're left shaken as we reflect back on what almost happened. However, it's seldom that we're in a situation where we have an hour or so to anticipate what may happen. As I sit in that plane with a hundred or so other strangers, I wonder if I'm going to die in a little while.

I have the strange realization that we in the infantry experienced this same thing prior to each combat operation. Fortunately, we land safely.

In late 1979, my mother becomes ill in North Carolina. She has a non-malignant tumor in her spinal cord at neck level. Two attempts at surgery relieve some of her symptoms temporarily. With the tumor inside her spinal cord, intrusive surgery is impossible. Her life is slowly fading. In early spring 1980, I declare her as my legal dependent and have an Air Force hospital plane fly her from the hospital in North Carolina to Brooke in San Antonio. She's admitted to one of the wards where I work.

Her body slowly shuts down but her mind remains sharp up to the day of her death six weeks after her arrival at Brooke. I'm grateful that I'm selected for promotion to lieutenant colonel just prior to her death. Even though very sick, she's able to celebrate with me. She dies five days later.

I turn forty years old and am painfully aware that, with both my parents now deceased; I'm the next generation to face mortality. Life is moving on.

It's the middle of my fourth year at Brooke and I'm facing reassignment. It has been eight years since I returned from Germany and I know I'm long overdue for another overseas assignment. I volunteer for Korea, orders are cut, I get my assignment and my family prepares for next year's separation. Then, another strange but wonderful series of events happens. The Department of the Army has made some mistakes by programming too many lieutenant colonels to go to Korea. I'm reluctantly offered the opportunity of returning to Ft. Bragg for my next assignment. When the final phone call confirming my assignment back to Ft. Bragg instead of Korea is concluded, I close my office door and let out a war hoop that would make a fog horn sound like a whimper.

I go home and announce that we'll be going back to Bragg in three months and why. Everyone but Kellie is ecstatic. She's counted on graduating from Cole High School and now she'll have to attend a strange school for her senior year. She's already been selected as a cheerleader here, but she'll have to forgo that. Despite my happiness of not having to spend next year separated from my loved ones, I feel badly for her. She's hurt. God bless her.

Still, I'm amazed at my career luck.

1981–1986

The next three years I spend at Womack Army Community Hospital. I essentially do the same work as I did at Brooke. I'm in my eighteenth year in the army. I must now decide whether to retire or stay in beyond twenty years. Being a Regular Army officer, I can stay until my twenty-sixth year even without another promotion. To stay in means I'll get orders for overseas next year, orders that should have come years ago.

After weeks and weeks of agonizing discussion with Barbara about our future, we decide that I'll retire if I can squeeze out another two years at Bragg after this year, which will put me at the twenty-year mark.

I check with personnel to see what's the earliest date I can retire. Another marvelous surprise! Personnel tells me I not only can back up my retirement date a day for each day of leave I sell back, but I have some active duty credit for the two years of Army Reserves I spent prior to entering active duty. I can actually leave service the end of January 1986! This is almost six months earlier than I had originally thought possible.

Now, I tell myself, the trick is to get the Chief of Chaplains Office to let me stay here at Bragg until I'm eligible to retire. I call the chief of chaplains personnel officer. I tell him that I want to retire as soon as possible but I need his help to keep me here for the next eighteen months, which is when I'll be eligible to retire.

We reach an agreement. I'm going to retire after twenty years. With almost twenty months to go. I will spend my last eighteen months as the staff chaplain of the 18th Airborne Corps Support Command where I supervise eleven chaplains and four chapel programs.

A few nights before my retirement, I'm honored with a formal retirement dinner. Several hundred officers and their wives are present, with the officers decked out in dress blue uniforms and spouses in cocktail dresses. Formal affairs like this are fairly frequent in the army. The question of dress has always mockingly been, "Dress blues and tennis shoes?" when inquiring about proper attire for a particular formal event. I decide to take this literally tonight. I don my dress blues and arrive for the party at the Ft. Bragg officers club. Then, after everyone has arrived and during the normal pre-dinner cocktail hour of standing around making small talk, I sneak into the nearby men's room with a brown paper bag. I roll my blues trousers up to almost knee high in order to expose fully my tennis shoes— high top, canvas, Chuck Taylor types from the 1960s, really dorky-looking shoes. I pair these with calf length white socks.

I casually stroll back out into the crowded room. The first few to see me dressed in dress blues and tennis shoes begin laughing. It's contagious and the crescendo rises as more and more people see what I'm wearing. The entire room is rocking with laughter. Even the brass who are present are laughing too. After all, what can they do, kick me out of the army?

I believe this is the way to go out, with a laugh.

Twenty years in the army and now, it's time for a different life. I'm forty-five years old and I have much living to do, I hope.

For those exposed to significant trauma, perhaps the effects are never over. Post traumatic stress can occur at any point. For years, I've managed my feelings associated with the trauma of combat operations in 1967–68. However, as I enter into the late 1970s, demons began to raise their heads. I had to deal with the postal supervisor's murder, my parents death, the Trauma and Survival course we designed and taught, and the airline in-flight emergency mentioned earlier. In the 1980s more situations arise and by the early 1990s, a number of additional things are happening that are troubling my peaceful soul.

In the fall of 1984, the marine barracks in Lebanon is blown up the same week as the insertion of US troops into Grenada. My feelings concerning the barracks tragedy are of anger and sadness, much like I felt in Vietnam. Surprisingly, my feelings are somewhat different for Grenada. The brass treat it like it's a huge war. "It's good to have won one for a change," one general says. In ways I don't quite understand, I find myself resenting this attitude.

While assigned as staff chaplain at Ft. Bragg's Womack Army Community Hospital, a young soldier contracts an infectious disease. His body swells grotesquely and his face and extremities become contorted before the illness quickly takes his life. His father and cousin arrive at Ft. Bragg that evening. The father apparently hadn't understood the severity of his son's illness, so he isn't prepared for the news of his son's death. When the grieving father meets with the company commander, he decides he wants to see his son's body. I'm called to accompany then to the hospital morgue. As the dead soldier's face is uncovered, the father becomes angry. "That's not my son," he says several times. "There's some mistake here. What are you people trying to do to me? Where's my son?" His voice rises with each utterance of his disbelief, and his body is quivering.

At first, the company commander doesn't know how to respond. Then, we both attempt to assure him that, yes, this is his son. The father hears none of this. It's the next day before he is finally be convinced that this is actually his son.

This experience takes me back to the parents of soldiers killed in combat and those who did not want to believe their son had actually been killed.

On another occasion, two cars, with four soldiers each, collide head on. Four are killed and four are seriously injured. The Emergency Room is hectic and for a short while, I'm reminded of arriving dustoffs coming into the 3rd Surg at Dong Tam.

The movie *Platoon* is released in the mid 1980s. Even though I find portions of the movie are somewhat unrealistic, some of the scenes are reminiscent of the feelings of fear from my past. This is the only Vietnam era movie I have allowed myself to see. I will not be seeing any more. It doesn't seem reasonable for me to risk the resurrection of my feelings.

When I learn that "Bad Luck Tony" Normand now lives in Fayette-ville, we meet and review old times over lunch. He gives me "the rest of the story" that unfolded after he was evacuated from Saigon in November of 1967, almost three decades ago. When airplanes take off from Vietnam, instead of climbing in a normal pattern, they ascend sharply to reduce the chance of being shot down. The hospital plane transporting Tony to Japan pitched abruptly upward as it left the runway. As it did, Tony's stretcher shifted, and many of his stitches opened. He was sewn up in Japan, but a severe infection set in and for days, Tony was in and out of consciousness. He was moved to what he later learned was the "death ward", his belly became grotesquely swollen and all hope was gone for his survival. As a last ditch effort, a seventy year old army civilian contract physician appeared one day and told Tony to hold tight to the bed rails. He stabbed Tony's side. From this puncture, nearly two gallons of infection erupted.

During the next thirty days, Tony slowly improved. He remained semi-conscious for most of his recovery, but he told me he recalled yet another amazing memory. An elderly Japanese woman would visit him each day, rub his forehead, mutter comforting words in Japanese. He thought she was a dream at first, until he learned she had been coming to the hospital daily for years, long before the Vietnam War began. She had lost five sons in World War II and as a way of honoring their memory she came to give what she could, her compassion and hope. She was there for Tony when those he loved were on the other side of the world. I thank her for her love, kindness and dedication to my friend. May God bless her eternally.

Eventually, Tony was sent for further recovery and treatment at Eisen-hower Medical Center at Fort Gordon, Georgia. He was chosen "Young Man of the Year" from Alabama the year after he was wounded, and although he was on the verge of being medically retired, Tony fought to stay in the army and to be sent back to Vietnam. With only one kidney, the VC having claim to the other, he was never allowed to return to Vietnam, but he stayed in the army for a total of twenty-nine years. As a special operations commander during the Panama uprising, Tony and some of his staff were standing near the Legislative Building when a lone Pana-manian sniper a block away fired two rounds in their direction. One bullet ricocheted and struck Tony in the upper arm. Shot again! Fortunately, it was a flesh wound and did no real damage. Tony became a battalion com-mander, group commander, and eventually the Chief of Staff of the Special Operations Command at Ft. Bragg before retiring. Good luck or bad luck, Tony is a hero's hero!

In early 1987 I learn that a group of my former Vietnam buddies are trying to locate me for a reunion in Colorado Springs. It is primarily for those of us who were in the 3/60th in 1967–68. I'm almost overwhelmed at the feelings that immediately emerge. I suddenly feel anxious. The sentimental part of me wants to go to the reunion and see my old buddies. But, I'm not sure I can handle the other feelings, those that I can't exactly identify. Barbara and I discuss whether I should go, and she encourages me to do so, and agrees to go with me.

At the reunion hotel, I walk hesitantly into the hospitality room. The first person I see is Will Davis. He has changed little. Soon John Iannucci introduces himself and begins to talk about the battle at Vinh Long, and his memory of the Vietnamese couple who had their family members massacred and then burned. Then, Tim Doty introduces himself and recalls the firefight on October 5, 1967 when we had been hit from the rear and we both were hunkered down in a canal and I gave him the "holy smokes". I see Jim Bledsoe, Monk Doty, Peder Lund, Floyd Buch, Dick Botello, Ed Blackledge, and many others I haven't seen in twenty years. It suddenly feels very good to be with these guys. Some I don't know and others I don't remember, but that's okay. We became brothers back then and now, we discover we're still brothers. A total of about 135 former soldiers and spouses are in attendance.

The next morning, I conduct a memorial service. The place is packed with a standing room only crowd of former 3/60th guys, spouses and even some hotel employees. The service becomes quite emotional for some, and this service is very cleansing for us.

We have a banquet, which is a lot of fun. Tim Doty calls me up on stage where he tells the story of that frightful day in the canal when I gave him the "holy smoke." He then presents me with a pack of Camels, and embraces me.

Several attending the reunion have visible reminders of the war; no legs, only one arm, facial scars; one has lost an eye.

Afterward, I'm exhausted for several days. I realize it's the emotional drain of reconnecting to these heroes that I love dearly, but have been disconnected from for so many years. Going to the reunion was almost like going home.

Back home, Barbara and I take a day off work to attend the annual fire power demonstration that the 82nd Airborne Division puts on each summer. Always very impressive, it includes mass parachute jumps, heavy equipment parachuting, firing of weapons from M-16 to huge artillery, airplanes dropping bombs, even helicopters firing rockets. Five thousand persons are bussed out to the drop zone where the first part of the demonstration is to be conducted. Barbara and I sit at the far end of the bleachers, several hundred yards long that have been erected for spectators.

The show is very impressive as usual. The last segment of this, the first of a two-part demonstration, involves a spectacular air-land presentation.

Today's showing is what is called a LAPES, a low altitude parachute extraction system. A C-130 transport plane, a four-engine Air Force plane for troops and equipment, is to fly about four feet off the ground right in front of the bleachers with the rear ramp open. At the precise time, a parachute will be released at the rear of the plane while the aircraft is flying just above ground level. An armored vehicle packed in honeycomb shock absorbing material will be released from the rear of the plane during flight. When the vehicle hits the ground and slides to a stop, the C-130 should gain altitude and fly away while ground troops positioned nearby quickly unpack the vehicle and drive it away. The entire episode will take only a few moments and is an impressive series of maneuvers.

The first of two C-130s comes in from our left and the second is to follow by two minutes. As the C-130 drops in altitude, I see immediately that the plane's last minute descent angle is too steep. The C-130 pancakes on the ground, blowing all tires. It scoots and bounces along the ground immediately in front of the bleachers with dust flying. As it passes in front of me, it is no more than fifty yards away, traveling from my left to right. I can see the cockpit personnel struggling to get the aircraft airborne again.

The C-130 strikes an army vehicle just to my right and then hits a small ditch, causing the huge plane to buckle. A huge fireball erupts right in front of our eyes as the plane blows apart. The heat, sound and sight of this is like a scene from a movie, only this is very real.

Four persons on board the plane are killed and a soldier in the army vehicle struck by the plane is also killed. All of this occurs seventy-five yards from me.

This scene invades my hidden stash of suppressed memories, and I am mentally tossed back twenty years to the midst of combat.

Each of these situations help to resurrect feelings from my past. However, after each occurrence, I'm able to tuck the feelings back into the place they've occupied for many years, deep in my soul. The emotional antibiotics that I've used, however, work less frequently the older I get. What I begin to experience I can only describe as Gods way of telling me I can still be healed of those old wounds, but I first must acknowledge them in order for cleansing to occur.

For years, I've minimized veteran activities such as Veterans Day. It's not that I wasn't interested, I just felt I needed to keep my mental distance.

While at Walter Reed Army Medical Center for a check-up following a cardiac angioplasty procedure in 1990, Barbara and I plan to take an extra day for some District of Columbia sightseeing. We want to see some of the museums and memorials. After parking, we are walking on the mall and I realize we're near the Vietnam memorial wall. I've never been there, although I've been to Washington several times since it's construction. Barbara asks if I want to go by the wall. I tell her we probably won't have time, but she points out it is close by and I say okay. This surprises me. I think I can just walk by, but I discover I can not.

By the time I'm halfway down the slight decline with the wall on my left, I'm absorbed with the entire environment. It's like the wall has tentacles that reach out and pull me in. I slowly focus on some names, no name in particular, just several names. I understand that each name represents a life that is no longer; a life wasted.

I meander for awhile. Barbara graciously allows me time and space, no idle chitchat. I'm oblivious to other visitors. It's like all the years come together for me at this very spot. It's time to leave, and I'm surprised to discover that I'm crying.

I'm shocked at the emotional impact just walking by this black granite wall has on me. I'm not necessarily overwhelmed, just profoundly sad. I don't sob like I did that night on the USS *Colleton*, but I do cry. I'm not ashamed of my tears, but I'm mystified at how quickly my feelings have surfaced.

The tears stop. Barbara and I don't talk about my reaction.

"Let's go to the Museum of Natural History," I suggest, and we tour several museums. But I'm not there. I'm caught between a wall in Washington D. C. and the Mekong Delta.

Late in 1990, our community is hard hit with the mass exodus of many units going to the Persian Gulf for Desert Storm. Fayetteville, North Carolina, is adjacent to Ft. Bragg and Pope Air Force Base, and our church, Snyder Memorial, is a large one. We have almost fifty families who have a family member deployed.

As the Minister of Counseling on the staff of our church, I develop an "Adopt a Family" program of family support within our congregation. As the deployment continues, it becomes more and more apparent that our nation is gearing up to fight.

It's mid-December 1990, and I've been at Duke Medical Center the past six days for my second angioplasty in fifteen months. It's Friday night and I'm recuperating from complications after the procedure. A letter with a Department of the Army return address is waiting for me when I return home. I open the official looking envelope. "Due to your extensive combat and hospital experience, you and seven other retired chaplains will be recalled to active duty should we go to war and take extensive casualties. You will be assigned to Martin Army Hospital at Ft. Benning Georgia."

I'm shocked! Ft. Benning, of all places! I am certainly willing to be recalled if needed. But why not Ft. Bragg? My first thought is that I have to get that changed. But, I know I can't do a blasted thing about it until Monday.

During this long weekend, I experience such intense feelings. It's almost as if God is giving me time to think and feel, really feel. Being temporarily incapacitated, I can't physically do anything that would help me insulate my thoughts from the past. This weekend, I'm forced to be in touch with these feelings.

Monday finally comes and I do get my alert recall changed to Ft. Bragg. The alert never changes into orders because the "war" is over after 100 hours.

In a few months our community is back to normal. My feelings are not. Three hundred plus Americans were killed in the Gulf region. I genuinely feel for these families. But, strangely, I begin to feel some resentment, which I don't voice to anyone. But I begin to believe that the resentment centers on the fact that more soldiers were killed and wounded in the 3/60th in the few years it was in Vietnam than all American forces and units combined in all of the Gulf War. None of this resentment makes sense to me, and I feel guilty about it. Much positive attention is given to the returning troops and for that, I'm glad. But two decades ago, our returning soldiers were ignored, or worse, chastised and criticized.

While in Philadelphia working on my doctorate in Marriage and Family, one of the requirements was a paper on personal history. I included a few of my Vietnam experiences. Even though I gave some graphic detail about my combat role, I didn't go into a descriptive, blow by blow account. Yet, many of my classmates are astounded at my role in combat and of the awfulness of war. It's as if they knew it existed, but had never known someone who was actually in combat. Several are inquisitive about my experiences, which gives me the opportunity to tell my story informally. Over the past years, few have heard even fragments of my story. The telling feels different, but good.

For six months, I became embroiled in a situation involving a prominent and influential person whose covert activities were fast becoming a threat to himself, his family and potentially to hundreds of innocent persons. This wasn't a physical threat, but a threat to relationships involving trust, confidence and gross disappointment. Character and behavior flaws were swirling within this, and when I learned the sordid details, he was on the verge of emotionally exploding. I knew his blast would injure countless others.

One other person and I had the dubious task of intervening to stop an emotional explosion. This person is hurt; however, not to have acted would have resulted in hundreds of innocent persons being hurt because of his status and influence.

Due to the confidentially of the above scenario, few details can be given. However, during this horrible period of six months where we make our interventions, I find myself experiencing a significant amount of grief. I cry easily, I am hurt, and am angry that I am even involved. A few months after this near tragedy is successfully subverted, I reflect on why my emotions during this time were so prominent. Even though there wasn't a physical threat as in Vietnam, the fact that so many persons stood to be hurt had the same emotional impact on me as if it were a physical threat. My feelings of fear and anger had surfaced once again.

One evening Barbara suggests we go see *Forrest Gump*. After the movie, I say nothing as we get into the car, nothing as we leave the parking lot, nothing as we drive toward the street.

"Something about that movie bothered you, didn't it?" Barbara says.

My scream is immediate. "I HATE THAT SHIT!!!" I'm shocked at my outburst. I begin to cry, can barely see through my tears enough to pull to the side of the street. I mumble more about hating "that stuff", and make little sense to Barbara.

As I begin to calm down, Barbara asks, "What about the movie do you hate?" I'm sure she already knows, but this is her way of allowing me to vent.

"That war shit. That ambush scene was just the way it was." I'm aware that I'm tightly gripping the steering wheel.

The movie was enjoyable until it came to the ambush scene. As the solders depicted in the movie wearing 9th Infantry Division patches are fired upon and are returning the fire, it's as if I'm actually there. The scene could have been any one of a score of firefights twenty-five years before, and the sounds and sights depicted in that scene brought out feelings that crawled all over me like worms in a dead, rotting animal.

Sometime later a news program featured a group of veterans and others gathered on the Washington mall to be addressed by President

Clinton. It was a patriotic ceremony, and just as the President stands to speak, the vets rise. In an act of defiance, their leader orders, "About Face" prompting all the standing vets to turn in the opposite direction from the President.

As I see this on the evening news, I'm somewhat amused but basically ambivalent about whatever is going on between the President and the vets. "I have no dog in this fight," I think. Then, in what appears to me a rather arrogant and condescending manner, the President says, "I listened to you, now you listen to me!"

I suddenly become livid. I feel like spitting at the TV screen. "Who has heard their story?" I yell. "You don't have a clue what their stories are. How can you be so patronizing as to say that?" I'm amazed at how rapidly these feelings surface. I obviously do have a dog in this fight.

The next morning, I'm having breakfast with my best friend, Bill Shipp, at a local cafeteria as we have each Thursday for the past fifteen years. Politically, he's quite liberal and a strong supporter of President Clinton. But even though our politics are different, he's still a dear friend and we would do anything for each other.

Bill says, "Did you see what those vets did to President Clinton on TV last night?"

"Yes, I did." I suddenly feel the back of my neck getting hot with anger. I'm hoping he'll drop it. He doesn't.

"What right do they have being disrespectful to the President?" Bill wonders.

That does it. It's like a B-52 has just released a cargo of bombs on me. "What right does any person have to criticize combat vets and say 'I listened to you,' when no one has heard their story. Bill Clinton and most of America don't have a clue what some of those vets went through. Don't talk to me about disrespect unless you know what it's like to have a buddy die in your arms, or be shot at or live in constant fear of dying." I'm aware that other patrons at nearby tables in the cafeteria are looking our way. But, I continue. "I don't give a rats ass about respect if it's not a two-way street. Vietnam combat vets have had little or no respect or understanding of the distress they went through. They didn't ask to go into combat. They didn't want to get shot or see their buddies shot. They were forced to go by politicians who couldn't have cared less about whether they lived or died."

I'm aware I should probably stop, but I don't. "Unless you've walked where an infantryman has walked in combat, what right does anyone have to judge his actions, especially hot aired politicians? As far as I'm concerned, it's impossible for anyone to understand unless he's there in the rice paddies or gone into a hot landing zone. All those politicians can just kiss my ass." Tears are running down my cheeks. They are tears of anger.

Bill just looks at me. I know he doesn't understand what has just happened. Neither do I.

In September 1993, my task at the annual staff retreat of ministers and spouses from our church is to lead the last day session on "Ministering in a Stressful Environment". I decide to include some of my Vietnam experiences of ministry.

As I'm preparing for my presentation, I become aware that I've never done this before, present my experiences before a group. I've alluded to it before, and I've talked informally to a few friends. But, that's it.

I begin my presentation for discussion. I reflect on my role as a chaplain in combat operations all those years ago. There's no onrush of feelings like there was after the *Forrest Gump* movie, or the scene with Bill at breakfast. But, the feelings do come. I try to fight them, my eyes fill and I'm initially a little embarrassed.

No one in our group of thirteen has ever been in situations like I describe. As I periodically pause to gain control, I'm aware that the group is captivated by the descriptions of some of my combat experiences. A few times I want to stop. Several times, I apologize for my tears. But, this kind and compassionate group encourages me.

Afterward, I tell them they are the first group to ever hear the details of my story, and I thank them.

Each Thanksgiving Day, I think of that awful Thanksgiving in 1967 when a young woman lost both her brother and her fiance. I wonder what has happened to her and I wonder about Pastor Ha and his family.

One afternoon brings another call. I don't recognize the voice, but after a few questions, I realize I am speaking with Quent Holder in Arizona. He was a battery commander in the 3/34th artillery. I recall him with sudden clarity. "Right! Your guns were a huge help to us on many combat operations." It was one of his guns that almost killed me in My Tho in the Tet offensive, but I don't mention this.

Then he asks me if I ever knew Frank Pina. Flashing lights go off in my head. Frank Pina! How could I ever forget him? I tell Quent that Frank was a good friend of mine.

He informs me that Frank's daughter, Teresa, wants to talk to me. I'd forgotten her name over the years, but I make a quick calculation in my head. If she is Frank's oldest daughter, she must be about twenty-eight years old now.

Quent asks if I would be willing to talk to her.

"Absolutely. Tell me more," I say.

He explains Frank was a good friend of his, too, and Teresa has contacted him looking to meet with people who served with her dad.

I tell Holder that two of my children are about the ages of Frank's daughters and that Frank and I used to talk about them. I learn that Teresa lives in Houston and she wanted to be sure it'd be okay for her to contact me.

I'm so excited, after all these years, and call right away, but to my disappointment, I get a recording. After finally making connections, plans are made for us to meet soon in Fayetteville.

On the designated afternoon, Barbara and I have just returned from conducting a three-day couples marriage enrichment retreat at the beach. A thousand thoughts are running through my head. I hear someone coming down the hall, and I stand and greet two smiling faces. One is Teresa and the other is Jennifer, Frank's younger daughter. Teresa looks exactly like her father.

For the next two hours, we talk, and talk and talk. I discover Teresa is on a pilgrimage to learn about her father. She beams as I relate what a responsible position Frank had as a combat company commander and of my respect and admiration for him.

Teresa tells me that she was about two and a half when Frank was killed, and that she remembers absolutely nothing about him. Even pictures of Frank that would surface over the years weren't enough to generate much curiosity, until recently.

Our visit goes extremely well. I immediately like both these young women. When it is time to end the evening, I feel a little sad, but warm and relieved. We exchange addresses and agree to stay in touch.

On Easter weekend, April 1995, I'm in the hospital recovering from complications from open-heart surgery. A nurse says there's someone outside who wants to see me. Her name is Teresa Pina. I am surprised that Teresa is back in North Carolina. I learn she has called home and Barbara told her I was in the hospital.

We talk for a while, and my daughter, Kellie, who now lives in New Orleans, arrives for a visit. The two meet, and neither Kellie nor Teresa realize how twenty-seven years ago, they were very important to two young fathers who happened to be on the other side of the world trying to survive.

The surfacing of Teresa, perhaps more than anything else, proves to be a catharsis for me in connecting my present to my past. Her coming into my life during a time when I'm dealing with the increasingly emerging feelings from Vietnam is, like so many situations in my life, a part of the healing providence of God.

During my recovery period from the heart surgery in the spring of 1995, I have much time to think. I make my decision. I will return to Vietnam and complete my own pilgrimage.

CHAPTER TEN

March 2, 1996–Present

In December of 1995 I put a note in my annual Christmas letter telling my friends that Barbara and I were going back to Vietnam. I receive a call from John Iannucci, who tells me he can't believe I'm going back. I tell him I certainly am, and ask if he would be interested in going along.

"I'm not sure. If I went back with you, do you think we could find that battle site in Vinh Long?" John is referring to the terrible battle where the Vietnamese civilians were executed and burned on February 4, 1968. I'm excited that John is thinking about going back with me.

"We could try. The itinerary says we're to stop overnight in Vinh Long. Are you serious about going?"

He admits he has been thinking about it off and on for about six months. After we talk, John decides the trip is worth taking. He and his wife, also Barbara, will accompany us.

I still marvel at how the trip became a reality. On the way to Louisville, Kentucky for a Mobile Riverine Force reunion in June 1995, Barbara and I had decided we'd return to Vietnam. We knew a representative from Vietnam Tours would be at the reunion and we could talk to him about cost, a major factor.

My prayer to God was that, somehow, the details could be worked out. I talked to the travel representative, who's a former member of the 3/60th. After signing up at the reunion for information, we attended the banquet and I won a door prize donated by another former member of 3/60th, Peder Lund. This was God's answer to my prayer. The prize? Round trip airfare from the United States to Vietnam.

FRIDAY, MARCH 1, 1996: "Closure" is a popular word in emotional and relational healing. However, I'm not sure there is ever adequate closure to the kind of experiences I had on combat operations. A more suitable word is "cleansing." As I prepared for my return trip to Vietnam, it was my fervent hope that I'll be cleansed of the re-surfaced pain of the past few years. On the way to the airport I realized that today was the twenty-eighth anniversary of Frank Pina's death. It seems almost like yesterday.

Our flight doesn't leave for Vietnam until Monday, March 4, so we spend a long weekend in the Los Angeles area sightseeing and relaxing. John Iannucci and his wife, Barbara, are spending the weekend in San Diego and will meet us at our hotel on Sunday evening, where we're all to have dinner together.

It's 5:30 P.M. on Sunday when we return to our hotel room from sightseeing. I call to see if John has checked into his room and find out he and his wife have just arrived. We agree to meet in twenty minutes in the lobby and go to dinner. My Barbara decides to call our children, since we'll be out of the country for a couple of weeks.

I flip on the TV hoping to catch a few moments of a sporting event. As the program comes into focus, I can't believe it! A movie is on and it's *Forrest Gump*. More astonishing is that the movie is within seconds of the patrol and ambush scene that had triggered such intense feelings when I originally saw it. My first impulse is to quickly change channels, but, surprising myself, I decide to watch the scene. As the scene is replayed, I'm immediately overcome with a calmness and peace that is very sobering. It's like God is telling me, "It's okay. This is only a movie. Your combat trauma is long ago." As the ambush and battle scene plays out and then ends, the serenity I am experiencing is incredible! It's like God has given me the perfect antidote for my historical hurt.

I've always had what I call a theology of timing. I believe that "All things work together for good to them that love the lord." Rom.8:28. Timing is a vital part of that working together. I believe very strongly that in the greater scheme of God's intervention in life, there's a divine sense of timing that is far beyond my ability to comprehend. I also believe that what I experience in these few moments with this movie is far more than coincidence or random chance.

It's as if God said, "Let Jim's cleansing begin".

MONDAY, MARCH 4, 1996: As we visited with Barbara and John last night, we shared many of our thoughts and feelings about our upcoming trip. Mine is excitement mixed with anxiety. John's is anxiety mixed with excitement. Perhaps that's reflective of the difference in a former combat chaplain and a combat infantryman.

At the airline terminal, eighteen former GIs gather for our return. Also included are four wives, a former American Red Cross donut dolly and a Bolivian national whose brother was shot in the Delta and died at the 3rd Surgical Hospital at Dong Tam. He wants to visit the actual site where his beloved brother died twenty-eight years ago. One of the GIs is a Medal of Honor winner who is now a coal-miner in Kentucky. He pulled several buddies to safety with the 2/39th Infantry during a ferocious firefight.

Over the Pacific Ocean, I chat for a while with a farmer from South Dakota. He tells me, "The war won't be over for me until I go back. My friends never understood because they felt I shouldn't have been there anyway, as if I could help it. When I came back home, I buried my feelings by working day and night."

Another pilgrim is blind. The last thing he ever saw was some foliage where a rocket propelled grenade was fired and then detonated at chest level, with fragments immediately blinding him in both eyes. He needs to go back to, "smell and hear Vietnam." I'm reminded of the blinded hero that night on the *Colleton*.

The nearer we get to Ho Chi Minh City, the more my anxiety increases. Just saying that name angers some of us. To us it is Saigon, always will be. It's near midnight when we make our final approach to Tan Son Nhut International. This, too, sounds funny because it was once Tan Son Nhut Air Force Base. It is adjacent to Saigon. It's from here that both of my R&R flights arrived and departed. I look out into the black night and notice that electric lights from the countryside have now replaced the ever-present flares of twenty-eight years ago. I see no tracer bullets in the distance. I see no uniformed military police or runway bunkers with firing ports.

As we off load and enter the terminal to process, the immigration and customs people never show a smile or have any kind of pleasant expression. I learn that these, like most Vietnamese government workers, have come down from the former North Vietnam to work and are somewhat favored by the Communist government hierarchy.

Our visa and immigration papers are in order and we're allowed to officially enter Vietnam. However, one of our group is detained because his paperwork is not in order. He's forced to stay at the terminal and take the next flight out. He has traveled from Iceland to New York to Los Angeles to Seoul to Saigon only to be denied entrance. Communist rules apparently aren't flexible.

We're transported by our host to the small guesthouse that will be our headquarters over the next two weeks. Exhausted from the long trip, we finally get to bed at 1:30 A.M.

WEDNESDAY, MARCH 6, 1996: After only three hours of sleep, we're wide-awake. A twelve-hour time zone difference does that. We're on a side street in the middle of Saigon. The sights, sounds and smells are exactly like they were twenty-eight years ago.

Our pilgrims have been divided into two groups and I'll see little of the other group during our stay because they have a different hotel, itinerary, guide and bus. Our group consists of Barbara and I, the Iannuccis, Denny

and Michelle Scoville, and Vic and Mimi Gray. Denny is a former helicopter pilot in the Delta. He wasn't with the Mobile Riverine Force, but
he's a true hero who was shot down several times in the Delta and severely
wounded, spending much time in the hospitals back in the United States.
He's a prominent lawyer in San Diego now and was the lead attorney for
the female navy pilot of the infamous "Tailhook Debacle." Vic is a former
navy advisor who served southeast of Can Tho. He also wasn't in the Mobile
Riverine Force, but spent considerable time in the Delta and later Vung
Tau. Vic is now an executive with the State Department in California. The
ninth member is Rick Corrick from Haw River, N.C., who was a Navy "river
rat" boat crewman. Our itinerary is to see Saigon today. Tomorrow we
embark on a four-day tour of much of the Delta.

Saigon! What an exciting city! We visit the former US Embassy with the
most famous outdoor staircase in the world. Etched on the minds of many
of us are scenes of many Vietnamese scrambling to escape the war by
helicopter in 1975 as the North Vietnamese Army was closing in on Saigon.

Traffic in Saigon is terrible. People are going everywhere in every
direction. Everything from lumber to hogs is transported on the many
forms of two-wheeled transportation. Saigon's intersections are like figure-
eight automobile races.

The Majestic Hotel has a beautiful top floor open-air restaurant and
lounge where we can look out over the river, much of downtown Saigon,
and much of the distant countryside. I have some temporary resentment
from the past as I recall some "Saigon Warriors" would sit up here and,
"Watch the war at a distance," meaning they could see smoke from fire
fights on the distant horizon.

I also recall the "Five o'clock Follies" where the brass would brief the
press on the progress of the war in the preceding twenty-four hours. The
Follies were conducted a few blocks away. Their reports would talk about
VC body counts and operations in a dehumanized way. This sanitized
treatment hurt and angered the American heroes on the receiving end of
AK-47 bullets.

I remind myself that the war was a long time ago and maybe it is indeed
"folly" to still be so affected by feelings from the past. I know I need to
begin releasing some of these decades-old feelings.

THURSDAY, MARCH 7, 1996: Saigon is an interesting city, but it's not
why any of us returned. I want to get back to the Mekong Delta and this
morning we're on the way. Highway #1 South is what was then Highway
#4. The pavement is no longer pockmarked, but it's still just a two-lane
highway congested with much traffic. Included are buses that look a hundred

years old, cars, motorcycles, bicycles, pedestrians and ox carts. Everyone is in a hurry.

Once we're out in the countryside, the rice paddies and tree lines all look as I remember. I have to keep telling myself that no war now exists, no snipers are in the tree line. It'll be several days before I can look at a tree line and not wonder if any VC are lurking there.

Halfway to My Tho, we cross the Ben Luc Bridge. My first fire fight was up this stream in August of 1967. No soldiers are guarding the bridge now like they were then. We travel through Tan An and then to My Tho. We go down a four lane street toward the My Tho River. It won't be until next Sunday that I realize this is the street where such fierce fighting occurred during the Tet Offensive. Now there is no baby at the breast of his dead mother, no dead father with his little children screaming, and no destruction.

We reach the river, turn right and head toward Dong Tam eight kilometers away. The road to Dong Tam looks the same, although it is built up more than I remember. The My Tho River to the left is also the same. I see VC island and have a slight twinge of fear. Then, we're in Dog Patch. The road in 1967 and '68 ended at the canal we called Route 66. Now, there's a modern concrete bridge over the canal connecting Dog Patch with the infamous and once feared West Bank and beyond.

We park on the bridge and look over into Dong Tam. The turning basin is still there, but Dong Tam looks very different. It's now a Vietnamese army installation, but it's so grown up. In twenty-eight years trees have grown and vegetation abounds. Where the airstrip and the 3rd Surgical Hospital once stood now looks like any other tree line. John and I excitedly compare notes as we look over into that area. It really does feel okay.

As the driver turns the coach around, I instinctively glance out into the huge My Tho branch of the Mekong River almost expecting to see the dredges and/or the Mobile Riverine Force flotilla anchored out there.

Back at My Tho, we take a ferry across the river and head to Ben Tre. We stop at the first of several VC cemeteries we'll visit during the next few days. This cemetery has several thousand white markers.

The entrance says, "Resting place of the Vietnam heroes." As we walk through the cemetery, we all have our own somber thoughts. Our interpreter tells us Vietnamese cemeteries are only for North Vietnamese and VC KIA's. After the Communists took over in 1975, families of ARVN KIA's were given the option of digging up the remains of their loved ones and placing them in private graves. Otherwise, they are not even acknowledged.

As I meander through the cemetery, I have no feelings of malice or resentment. These men died many years ago. Some were very young. My prominent feeling is one of regret that war had to take lives at all, regardless of the side the "hero" was on.

In Ben Tre we stop at a visitor's center. Five young Vietnamese women are amazed at my height and all want photos taken with me. We all feel genuinely welcomed.

Then it's to a small stream in downtown Ben Tre, where we board our "cruise" ship, which will be our transportation for the next three days. This boat is about fifty feet long and very old. It has a four-man crew who live aboard.

We're on the way to Vinh Long. It was only a kilometer or two from here where I "celebrated" Christmas of 1967. Our itinerary is to simulate some of what we experienced on the armored troop carriers years ago. The waterways are busy with watercraft of all sorts.

The shorelines are still intimidating, and John and I find we unconsciously scan them, as if B-40 rockets will suddenly come screaming our way. After an hour or so, I find my subconscious vigilance is gradually giving way to observing the natural beauty of the lush vegetation. This is a pleasure I had not allowed myself before, because behind the natural beauty stood the Viet Cong, always ready to try to kill us all.

Mostly the Delta looks the same. The hooches still have thatched roofs and bamboo sides. What's different is that now, electricity is available throughout the Delta. It looks odd to see the centuries old construction of a grass hooch with a 1950 style TV antenna reaching skyward through the thatched roof.

The water is still brown and muddy. Vietnamese are still swimming, washing clothes, fishing, cleaning eating utensils, eliminating body waste from their over water out-houses, and traveling on these waterways.

We dock in Vinh Long in front of our river front hotel. As we off-load, we meet an old Vietnamese man.

FRIDAY, MARCH 8, 1996: John and I had asked the old man we met last night how we might locate the site of the battle of February 4 and 5th, 1968 that was near a country Buddhist pagoda. John has the names of two canals near the Vinh Long airstrip and remembers that we fought somewhere between the canals. The old man told us to meet him this morning and he would try to assist us.

John and I are hopeful but not convinced that we'll be able to find the battle site. We load onto the coach and head out of Vinh Long on highway #4 toward the airstrip. Highway #4 has changed considerably in three decades. We locate the bridges over the two canals, but we don't see a pagoda.

We ride between the canals in both directions and then someone spots a pagoda about 500 meters off the highway down a dirt trail.

I immediately sense that this is "our" pagoda. We all walk toward it. Then, we see the cemetery where the VC ambushed us! Yes! This is it! The pagoda is slightly smaller than I remembered it, but this is it.

This is where we spent that night in hell. John stayed hunkered down in a pigpen. I remember the heroic medevac pilot, the murdered and burned old couple, our wounded, the terror, the many dead VC, Ron's death, and my intense feelings the next morning as I walked through many dead VC bodies.

We walk around the area and many local Vietnamese come out to greet us as their hooches are on both sides of the small trails. John and I decide to walk up some of the "hard ball" trails for old times sake.

As we rejoin the others, a young Vietnamese mother with a child one or two years old is telling the women, "Take my baby to America!"

"What do you mean?" The wives aren't certain if they have understood.

"Better life. You take. Better life."

"No, you will be very sad."

"Here, baby have no good life. You take to America. Better life."

Ironically, a little less than twenty-eight years ago, on this very spot, life was practically worthless. Ron and several other Americans were killed just over the canal. Scores of Viet Cong were killed and sprawled all over this area. The VC had executed and burned the civilians.

John spots the bridge where George Guthy went one on one with a VC that same day. The fact that George was not killed by the VC's RPG was also miraculous. So, we find the battle site, but we also find peace, love and acceptance. Suddenly I'm aware that finding this battle site, with the help of this old man, the renewal of life of these simple but wonderful people, the changing of our feelings of fear and anger to serenity and affection also is miraculous. Days and events of the Tet offensive are now getting further and further away which is still another miracle.

We board our "cruise ship" heading toward Long Xuyen located up near the Cambodia border. On the way we see fish traps, sampans, water buffalo and rice paddies.

Long Xuyen is a dirty, backwoods city heavily influenced by Cambodia, a short distance away. Before dinner, we go to the open-air market and the Vietnamese watch us almost as if we are aliens. All the kids want to touch us. One little girl about ten or twelve is carrying a baby, apparently her little sister of perhaps two. She bashfully follows Barbara all over the market.

Kids try out their English on us. It's taught both in schools and on TV. The people are friendly and eager to greet us. We soon learn that, although individual Americans have visited Long Xuyen before, we supposedly are the first group of Americans to come. I notice that one of the many open front stores is a small appliance repair shop. A store like this would never have been in existence twenty-eight years ago simply because there was no electricity here.

Here, like all the cities world wide, persons with physical difficulties are the street beggars. It's hard to resist wanting to help them, but so many are present it's impossible to help. One of the beggars is a blind Vietnamese man who's over six feet tall. I've never seen a Vietnamese this tall. I wonder if he has an American father somewhere in the United States.

SATURDAY, MARCH 9, 1996: As we leave the city, Denny Scoville asks our interpreter if we can go by the airfield where he once was stationed. It's now a Vietnamese military post. John, Denny and I, along with our interpreter and guide, ask at the gate if we can enter the compound. There is much bowing and politeness. It feels a little odd to be inside a Communist military compound.

Then, it is back down the river now to Can Tho. After checking into the hotel, we tour the city. We stop at a small Buddhist pagoda. The five young monks dressed in their orange/brown wrap around garb insist on giving us tea and a sweet jellylike substance as refreshment. The youngest monk is eighteen and the oldest is thirty-three, only five years old when I left Vietnam. They know nothing of the war that we knew. These devoted young men are easy to like and their friendliness is very genuine.

The waterfront harbor is alive with boats. A silver statue of Ho Chi Minh that is about 100 feet tall dominates the scene. A beautiful park fronts the water. Many Vietnamese families abound. One little girl of about ten giggles and keeps telling Barbara in English, "You my momma, me your baby." Another little girl keeps wanting Barbara to hug her and gets much satisfaction when she does. Other children are selling packages of peanuts in the shell or "ground" nuts as they're called here.

As we're sitting and relaxing in the busy little park, a friendly young man of eighteen asks if he can sit and talk with me. He wants to study medicine and plans to go to Saigon in the fall to study. He asks many questions about medicine in the United States. "My country very poor, your country very rich," he says, not with bitterness, but matter-of-factness. Physicians make very little money in Vietnam. In fact, an evening bartender at the restaurant in Saigon that we patronized several times is a physician by day and a bartender by night. He makes more money as a bartender than he does as a physician. Now this young man tells me he became interested in medicine because his father was a medic in the ARVN. His father is now a rice farmer.

Barbara is especially touched by one family in the park with three children, ages five to ten. All three children have prominent cleft palates and are staying close to their mother as they obviously are very self-conscious about their looks. As a dental hygienist, Barbara realizes that in the United States, surgical correction of a cleft palate is a fairly common procedure, but here in Can Tho, corrective surgery of this nature is practically unheard of. This makes us both sad knowing what these wonderful people lack.

SUNDAY, MARCH 10, 1996: Today, we've left the boat and will travel back to Saigon by van on Highway 1. It'll be an all-day trip. We cross two fingers of the Mekong River by ferry boat and I'm again astounded at the number of physically handicapped who are begging for handouts. One young man in particular grabs my attention. One leg is so misshapen, his foot is literally behind his back. He moves himself about using two wooden blocks to scoot himself across the ground.

We stop north of Vinh Long and spend thirty minutes walking the dikes of a huge series of rice paddies. This feels a little odd because this is a typical rice paddy that we could have made a combat air assault into years ago.

John and I walk down a trail again. The old fear of walking these trails has now mostly dissipated due to our experiences of the past few days. This is feeling better and better.

Back to the van, and we come to Cai Lay, a hot bed of VC activity years ago. As we cross the stream in town, I glance at one of my maps and realize this is the small river where, only five kilometers down stream, we had that horrible experience called "Snoopy's Nose" on September 15, 1967. The Cam Son Secret Zone is nearby and we had many other firefights in this general area. As we leave Cai Lay, I'm grateful that the terrible war is over. But, seeing that stream does bring back some painful memories. But, they are just that now, memories.

When we traveled through My Tho a few days ago, I told our guide that I wanted to locate the orphanage in My Tho and, if at all possible, Pastor Ha and/or his family. He told me then that we'd try to do that on Sunday when we come back through My Tho. However, he warned me that when I was here before, My Tho was a city of 75,000 residents, but today it has a population of 500,000. He does not offer much hope.

As we near My Tho, I make a hand drawn map of the city as I recall it and where, approximately, I remember the orphanage to be located. The

other members of our group know this is important to me, but don't know
the emotional impact the orphanage and Pastor Ha had on me over the
years. I've wondered a thousand times what happened to him. Did he and
his family survive the Tet offensive? If so, did they survive the war and the
communist take over of 1975? Learning what happened to the family and
the orphanage is high on my list of priorities.

The only "investigative evidence" I have is my memory, my hand drawn
map of where I think the orphanage and Pastor Ha's church are located,
and two photographs. One is of the two buildings of the orphanage compound that had some Vietnamese writing on the top portion of the
building. The other is of Pastor Ha and his wife beside my Jeep with several
Vietnamese kids all around. It was made on Thanksgiving Day 1967.

It's 1:00 P.M. and the four-lane street is filled with bicycles, motor-
bikes, pedestrians and cars. All of us are looking for a church—any church
that could have been Pastor Ha's. We cruise for perhaps ten minutes. Then
we spot a small pink church with a cross! I now realize this is the same
street we traveled on last Thursday morning. This little pink church must
be Pastor Ha's church! The last vision I had was on that dreadful day in
February of 1968 when it was pock marked with hundreds of bullet holes.

In one of the many little shops next to the church, we locate a Vietnamese man who is as thin as a pencil and has lost a leg in the war. He
and our interpreter have an animated conversation. Our guide tells me
this man thinks he knows where the orphanage used to be located and is
willing to go with us in the coach to try and find it. He says the man thinks
it's about 100 meters off the main street a few blocks away.

My heart beats faster. We travel a few blocks back down the street. The
last time I was here, it was littered with bodies, blood, and rubble from that
very fierce battle. Now I spot a familiar looking alley. The man points to the
alley and tells our interpreter that he thinks the orphanage used to be down
that alley.

Excitement mounts as we walk to the alleyway! There is a gate, which,
thank God, is unlocked. But thirty feet further down the alley there's a second
gate. It's locked with a padlock! The fence is too high to even see over. My
heart drops. Could this be the alley where the medic and I extracted the
unconscious Lieutenant Dennis McDougall who was shot twenty-eight years
ago? Does the orphanage compound lie beyond this alley gate?

Then the thin man suggests that perhaps we can walk around a few
blocks and approach the compound from the rear or side. Everyone agrees
it's worth a try. We walk in a large semicircle on several dirt side paths, past
many small, thatched roof hooches surrounded by banana trees and nipa
palms.

After we have walked fifteen minutes, I've seen nothing that looks familiar. I'm getting discouraged. I've given the interpreter the photo of the orphanage buildings. I have the other photo of pastor Ha and his wife in my hand.

I'm about ready to give up. I don't want to monopolize the afternoon time of my friends, plus we must still drive the sixty kilometers to Saigon before dark. We stop and try to decide whether to give up the search for the orphanage.

Then, as we're standing in the little dirt street talking, about thirty feet away, beside one of the countless hooches and inside a small wire fence, I notice a young woman who appears to be in her early thirties. She's just standing there in her postage stamp sized yard, and I imagine she's wondering what these Americans are doing on this back street. I suggest to our interpreter that he show her the picture of the orphanage and maybe by chance she might know where it is.

He does and she points and motions up the street, "It used to be just around the corner," the interpreter says. My heart leaps. "However, it's no longer an orphanage. It's a school operated by the government, but it's locked up since school is not in session on Sunday. But this woman says we can see it through the fence."

"How far?" I ask.

"Fifty meters."

"We're here!" I think. Excitement mounts again.

I thank the young woman. Then, as we're about to walk away, I decide to show her the picture of Pastor Ha. "Ask her if she recognizes anyone in this picture," I say to our interpreter as I hand my picture to her. As she glances at the photo, her mouth drops open. Her eyes dart back and forth from the picture to me and to each of our little group. In an astounding gasp and with broken but understandable English, she stammers, "That's my father!"

Time stands still for me. Twenty-eight years, twelve time zones and 12,000 miles are all here at this one dusty little street, melting the past into the present. We have found the needle in the haystack!

She asks the interpreter who we are. I tell her that I was an army chaplain—a pastor—and that her father was a good friend of mine. She begins to cry and then tells me her father died of cancer in 1988. I'm sorry that he has died, but very grateful to know that he made it through the war. She invites us all inside her house.

By now we're all in tears and keenly aware that a miracle is occurring. Of 500,000 people in this city, we ask one isolated young woman for directions on a no name back street that's no more than a path, and she, of all people, is Pastor Ha's daughter?

Inside her modest home, she sheepishly looks at the picture again and half smiling through her tears says, "That's me," as she points to a four-year-old little girl being held in her father's arms. We all openly weep.

For the next forty-five minutes she fills me in on the past. Yes, they made it through the Tet offensive and the war, although she doesn't remember much of the war, she was so young. When the communists took over in 1975, Pastor Ha's ministry was restricted to the church building itself. He couldn't visit his parishioners or do any kind of ministry outside the church building.

"It was very hard on my father," she says. "But, at least they didn't kill him," After a few years, the government did loosen up and allow him to do ministry in the community.

The government allowed the family to keep this house she's living in, and it still belongs to her mother, who moved to Saigon after Pastor Ha died. She tells us that her mother is coming from Saigon to visit in about two hours and asks if we can stay. Of course, I want badly to do so, but our group must return to Saigon for the night and travel on Monday and Tuesday.

I get Mrs. Ha's phone number and give her the guesthouse address and number in Saigon where we're staying. I assure her that I'll call her mother when we return on Tuesday. I also leave the pictures as a gift for Mrs. Ha and bid a tearful farewell.

As we're walking back to the van, Vic says, "We may not have been in church today, but we have certainly been in the presence of the Lord."

Yes, we have. The past hour has made this entire return trip to Vietnam worth it. God has directly intervened in my life again today.

Life is good. I have just been part of a miracle. The road to Saigon is busy. We stop at Ben Luc at my request. Some abandoned reinforced concrete bunkers are still in place where our maintenance unit once was located. Here was my first taste of monsoon mud. I look out over the small river flowing under the Ben Luc Bridge. As I meander on the riverbank, my soul is somewhat at ease knowing that I don't have to go into battle up this river like I once did. This is the place where, once, people tried to kill me.

Now, its back to Saigon. The past few days have been marvelous. I'm feeling more and more at peace and less and less at war.

MONDAY, MARCH 11, 1996: This morning, we're off to Vung Tau on a Russian made pressured air cushioned vehicle, a passenger craft built to hold 200 persons. The boat moves rapidly down the Saigon River. Soon, we're in the countryside heading toward the South China Sea. Then, we travel through the Rung Sat Special Zone. Thank God, we no longer will beach to slither like a blasted snake through that thicket sown by the devil himself. It's good to see the Rung Sat, but from the comfort of this Russian speed boat in the open water and not from the undergrowth of the triple canopy foliage. I can still feel the squishing of mud as we used to move on hands and knees through this swamp.

Then, we're to the South China Sea. I see the very familiar horizon of Vung Tau with its distinctive mountain range jutting out into the sea. Vung Tau is fast becoming a resort area. Numerous foreigners are here on business, but I doubt that the average Vietnamese will ever enjoy this resort. How can they as they only make fifty to seventy-five dollars per month?

TUESDAY, MARCH 12, 1996: On the way out of Vung Tau, we pass the airfield that I flew in and out of several times when the flotilla was docked here. A Soviet made helicopter is warming up on a nearby runway now.

We travel on what once was Highway 15 from Vung Tau to Long Binh. We pass several rubber plantations. We make the once familiar turn at Long Thanh toward Bear Cat. We pass some Vietnamese basic trainees who are on a road march. They're dressed in half military and half civilian cloths very similar to Vietnamese soldiers of thirty years ago.

We arrive and as I stand in the midst of what was once the Bear Cat compound, I don't even know it. Nothing is here except civilian hooches, banana trees and nipa palms. Nothing is left that would allow me to recognize Bear Cat as I remember it. A little later, Long Binh is the same. Nothing is recognizable of what Americans had built. If I didn't already know that this was Long Binh, nothing would have hinted otherwise. Nearby Bien Hoa Air Base is now used by the Vietnamese Air Force.

Traveling back southwest toward Saigon on Highway 1, I recall having made this trip countless times visiting our wounded in the hospitals. Then I see the sign—a billboard advertising a nearby golf course. I wonder how many Vietnamese nationals even know what golf is.

Then it's back "home" to our guest house. We only have two more days in Vietnam before our flight out on Thursday night.

As I arrive in the lobby of our guest house, the proprietor tells me, "Someone wants to visit you tonight. Here's the phone number to call."

A male voice answers and states, "My mother wants to visit you at your hotel, will that be OK?" It is Mrs. Ha's son, Minh. We agree to meet at 6:00 P.M., which is in an hour.

Word is passed to our group and we all meet in the lobby, which is the size of the living room of a small house. Right on time, Mrs. Ha and Minh arrive on her small motorcycle. Thirty years makes a difference in looks, but she's still an attractive woman at age sixty-three. We have a wonderful visit with them. Mrs. Ha has brought me several pictures of Pastor Ha, their church, his funeral and all her children and grandchildren. She also has the pictures I gave to her daughter on Sunday.

Minh takes the picture I took at the Thanksgiving party in 1967 and announces, "And this little eight-year-old boy here in this picture is me." He tells me that he has always remembered that day because, "An eight-year-old boy will always remember his first and only helicopter ride and that day you sent a helicopter to fly my family and me to Dong Tam for the party." I remembered the orphans being transported in a two and one-half ton Army truck. But until Minh reminds me, I had totally forgotten that, as a special recognition and honor to Pastor Ha and his five kids, I had arranged for them to fly the eight kilometers in one of our helicopters.

Minh goes on to tell us that in 1975, when the communist overthrow was eminent, he left Vietnam and traveled to Holland, where he's lived ever since. Minh is now a successful businessman in Holland and this is his first visit back to Vietnam in several years. I don't believe his being in Vietnam at this time is chance. It is God's wonderful scheme of timing that is absolutely miraculous.

WEDNESDAY, MARCH 13, 1996: Today and Thursday are free days for us. Our group decides to travel northwest to Tay Ninh City, attend the noonday Cao Dai service and then visit the Cu Chi tunnels on our return trip. Tay Ninh was the 25th Division area and this part of Vietnam is new to me.

On the way, we make several stops to experience the Vietnamese economy at work. We visit a rice noodle "factory," which is nothing more than an open air extended hooch with open fire steam cookers where rice is transformed into noodles. We then stop at a peanut farm. These Vietnamese have obviously learned crop rotation—these fields are rice paddies in the rainy season and peanut fields in the dry season. Across the highway, a Vietnamese farmer in his typical conical hat is plowing, using a docile ox as his tractor.

The Cao Dai complex in Tay Ninh is not the Vatican, but the grounds of this religious headquarters include hundreds of acres of landscaped gardens and beautifully colored buildings. The main temple is huge, with many ornate religious symbols. We tour the temple barefooted and are allowed to watch the service from the balcony that encircles the huge floor area. The chants, music and proceedings are foreign, but touching and sincere. The Cao Dai priests are dressed in religious garb of various and distinctive colors. This religious experience is much more sophisticated than my one and only previous Cao Dai experience in 1967, near Dong Tam, while on our MEDCAP.

Heading back south, we stop at a chopsticks factory. Later we see a molasses factory, where sugar cane is harvested and stripped. The stalks are cooked, molasses poured into molds, and then cooled into brown sugar like cubes.

The Vietnamese economy is alive and struggling. Life may not be good, but this is certainly better than war.

Between Tay Ninh and Cu Chi is Nui Ba Den, or the "Black Lady Mountain," as the Vietnamese refer to it. The mountain simply juts out of the earth from relatively flat terrain. This mountain is one of the highest points in Vietnam. A friend of mine, who was a gun ship pilot in the war, told me that they used to fire unused ordinance on the sides of the mountain as a free fire zone, since the VC were known to hole up there. The top of the mountain was controlled by Americans. As I look at the mountain, I'm just thrilled that it's no longer "them" and "us."

We stop at another VC cemetery. This one is much larger than the one we visited at Ben Tre a few days ago. It has rows and rows of grave markers that go almost as far as I can see. My feelings today are not of anger, but of sadness that people must die in war.

We arrive at the Cu Chi tunnels where we're grouped and given a "propaganda" briefing by several young communist soldiers. John and I are somewhat resentful of the tainted way in which the briefing is conducted. The complex once had over 250 kilometers of interconnecting tunnels. The VC here were moles in every sense of the word. I'm impressed at the complexity and engineering ingenuity of the VC, as they even had underground hospitals, dining and other facilities. Even their venting system was an engineering marvel. This complex was literally right under the noses of ARVN and American units and wasn't made public until after the war.

Displays of various weapons, including pungi pits, are interesting. Other war memorabilia includes GI dog tags, C-ration cans, uniforms, papers and shell casings. John and Denny even are allowed to fire live ammunition from both AK 47s and M-16s at a nearby firing range. This time, the firing is for fun, not survival.

Our next stop is at Cu Chi's equivalent to our Vietnam Memorial Wall. A huge memorial to the VC killed in action has been constructed nearby, and it's not yet officially opened. However, they graciously open it for us to tour. It's an inside complex, beautifully and reverently constructed and decorated.

This memorial is just for the VC killed in the Cu Chi area. The wall is thirty-five feet high and 200 feet around and contains over 41,000 names, with birth and death dates of VC soldiers. It's estimated that over two and one-half million VC and North Vietnamese soldiers lost their lives in the war. What a price.

I'm particularly moved at the age I see of one VC soldier. He was only ten years old.

THURSDAY, MARCH 14, 1996: John and I had decided a few days ago that we would use our last day in Vietnam to return to Dong Tam and My Tho. Our flight leaves tonight at around midnight. We rent a van with a driver and head back down Highway 1 by Ben Luc, Tan An and My Tho. We stop at the My Tho river and I see where we made our beach landing during the Tet offensive on February 1, 1968 as we came ashore for that awful twenty hour fight.

Then we head to Dong Tam, go by Dog Patch and cross the new bridge over Route 66 to the once feared west bank. We leave the van and John and I explore the area. The locals, as usual, are curious about us. They're all busy, but wave and grin through betel-nut stained teeth like their predecessors did twenty-five years ago.

We stand on the canal bank and look again over into the turning basin. It's easy to visualize where the 3rd Surgical Hospital was located. I imagine that on this very location, VC spotters probably were once positioned to observe their mortars exploding on us across the canal in Dong Tam. Now, instead of VC, smiling kids are everywhere around us.

I feel a significant amount of reverence as peace now reigns. Today, I, too, am at peace. Thank you, God.

We go back to My Tho, locate the alleyway that leads into the orphanage and walk into the orphanage compound that we didn't get to see on Sunday. All gates are open today. The buildings have all been rebuilt long ago and enlarged. The classroom building has been extended. The pond that was once in front of the building has been filled in and is now a playground. The trail that we maneuvered down on February 2, 1968, while in contact with the VC, is still here. The open area where our dustoff choppers had landed to evacuate Dennis McDougall and the other wounded as a result of the errant artillery round is now filled with several two story buildings. The hooch that was blown up by the artillery round is now the school administrative office.

I pause at the very spot where Dennis McDougall was shot and think how close he came to dying, and maybe how close the medic and I came, as we went to pull him to safety. I say a silent prayer. All of us came close to dying that day. Just past the alleyway is the street of destruction and terror that is now just a normal, busy street. Pastor Ha's church still stands and is progressing. The bullet and rocket damage has long since been repaired.

My memories of destruction, rubble, fear and death are now replaced by beautiful sunshine, children laughing and playing nearby, birds singing and the new image of peace. It's healing and cleansing to stand here in sneakers, baseball cap and shorts instead of combat boots, jungle fatigues and flack jacket.

Perhaps time is also a miracle in My Tho.

As we travel back to Saigon, my mind and soul are full. I've experienced so very much in the last few days. It's now mid-afternoon and late tonight we "di di Mau" (get out of here) on our "freedom bird" home.

I marvel at what I have experienced in this country, both then and now. There's been a marked absence of the trappings of war—no army vehicles, bunkers, flares and outgoing artillery. Helicopters and fighter jets in the sky have been replaced by TV antennas and power poles. Males are present in the hamlets and villages and not hiding or off with the ARVN or Viet Cong.

I'm full of admiration for the Vietnamese people. The average monthly wage is only slightly more than what Barbara and I might spend on a special celebration dinner for just one night. Yet, they are such hard workers. Even the kids work to pay for their schooling. The little middle-aged cook at the guest house was a non-commissioned officer in the Vietnamese Navy during the war. Now, as a cook, he makes less per month than what Barbara and I spend just for gasoline for our automobiles.

The Vietnamese work is mostly manual labor. I've seen some tractors, but most factories are sweat shops with little mechanical or automated help and few pieces of machinery. Living is austere. The countryside has little paint.

The people are friendly. I've experienced no animosity of any kind. Everywhere I've gone, I've seen smiles. The Vietnamese are still trying to survive. Crops are abundant. Not only is there the ever present rice, but they raise corn, peanuts, tobacco, grapes, rubber, fruits, sugar cane, melons and many kinds of vegetables. They also harvest salt and manufacture a number of other commodities for export. The Vietnamese are trying hard. The schools run in two shifts and the literacy rate, I'm told, is now among the highest in the world.

On several occasions, I've been able to spend considerable time with three former Vietnamese officers during my stay here. All three were pilots for the Republic of Vietnam Air Force. One told me that when the overthrow of the country was imminent, the only thing he could do was go home and wait. All three were sent to communist "re-education camps" which were to last for three weeks. But, when they arrived, they learned this was more like a concentration camp than a re-education camp. When asked about the camp, one teared up and said he was isolated there for two years. Another was there one year and the third for three years. One of their brothers-in-law was there for six years. He would escape and each time he did so, he was given more time. Some education!

It has now been over twenty years since the war's end and generally, the Vietnamese attitude is, "The war is over and we must go on." This is true survival. None of these three wonderful men can leave the country, but life has gotten better for them. The government, though, has apparently made no attempt to utilize their skills or abilities in any positive way. One temporarily became a 'cyclo' driver in Saigon after his release from the re-education camp. His average wage during that time was one dollar per day. Going from a jet pilot to cyclo driver could easily cause a self-esteem problem, but, these men now are on the high side of successful by Vietnamese terms.

As we near Saigon, I begin to wonder about the former VC. Why did they fight? They fought for promises. Were these promises delivered? I doubt it. What did the war accomplish for the VC? I see little or no change in the lives of the average Vietnamese as a result of the "Revolution." Plenty of VC, though, have their names on cemetery markers. Just recently, the graves of sixty-eight VC killed and secretly buried at Tan Son Nhut Air Base during the Tet offensive were found after all these years. I take no joy in that.

I wonder if the Vietnamese experience post traumatic stress disorder like many of us have. Who are the victims of this war? Who are the victors? How would this war have been different if LBJ and Ho Chi Minh, their staffs and politicians were forced to walk in the Mekong Delta mud for a five-day combat operation? So many questions, so few answers.

As we arrive at our guest house, I have one answer. This trip has been vastly more than I expected it would be. These people are at peace. I am being cleansed.

FRIDAY, MARCH 15, 1996: It's a few moments after midnight. We've just lifted off from Tan Son Nhut and the night is black. I've been up since 5:00 A.M. yesterday and we still have forty hours of flying and waiting time ahead, but my mind is wide awake.

So much has happened in the past few days. As we reach 10,000 feet, I'm aware of a dramatic difference in my feelings now and the last time I took the Freedom Bird home in 1968. Then, I wanted to leave it all behind and thought I had. Now, I want to carry it with me.

The war is over, thank God. I came to be cleansed and I really have been. This doesn't mean that feelings won't resurface for me in the future. But, I've now completed my tour for real.

I'm a little sad, too. I've developed some significant personal alignments in these few days. The Ha family is alive and they have not only survived, but have excelled. Yesterday, I met a former ARVN soldier near Dong Tam and we talked at length. He shook my hand vigorously and thanked me as "my friend" when he learned I was here with the US Army years ago.

The owner of the guest house and his wife, Hue, were kind and gracious to us. Their children have become almost like nieces and nephews to us in our short visit. They all wanted to ride to the airport with us and did. We all shed tears as we bid our farewells, knowing that we probably will never again see one another, but still feeling an intense bond and love. Hue is in her late thirties and speaks no English, but her expressions, touch and tears as we say our good-byes speaks volumes to us all.

Then, there is our Vietnamese guide and interpreter. This man has gone the extra mile for us and done so with love and understanding. This has been more than a job for him. He was especially moved by my encounter with Pastor Ha's daughter in My Tho. Later, he tells us that late that night, he went home and was telling his wife what had happened and they both cried tears of joy for me.

I reflect on the Vietnamese people and all their needs. As a people, their urge to survive and excel is phenomenal, especially when they have so little. They have limited health and dental care. If they have no money, they get no care. Entitlements, as we Americans know them, are nonexistent.

Our American group has bonded as well. We've lived, traveled, ate, slept, cried, laughed and experienced Vietnam together. I know that when we reach Los Angeles in a few hours, we'll all go our separate ways and probably will never be together again as a group. But, we've all accomplished what we came back to do.

Later, John Iannucci says it best when, as he reflects on our return visit, he says, "For me, Vietnam is no longer a war. It now is a country."

Epilogue

Teresa Pina has traveled again to Fayetteville from her home in Houston, Texas. Barbara and I are taking her out to dinner tonight. It is two days before Christmas, 1996.

During dinner, she mentions her plans to go to Frank's grave. I had always assumed Frank was buried at Arlington or some other national cemetery. During the conversation, she tells me that Frank is buried right here in Fayetteville in a large private cemetery directly across the street from the Veteran's Administration Medical Center. I've driven by this cemetery hundreds of times and have even conducted funerals here. But, until now, I never knew Frank was buried here.

She asks if I'd be able to go to the cemetery with her. I'm honored and delighted.

On Christmas Eve I meet Teresa, we have lunch, stop at a florist to buy some flowers, and drive into the cemetery. It's a gray windy day. We walk the short distance from the street to her father's grave. His plain military headstone states name, rank, date of birth and death. We place the flowers. I'm wondering what Teresa is feeling and apparently, she's wondering the same about me.

"Jim, how do you feel?" she says.

I'm the one who usually asks that question of others, either in counseling sessions or of people with whom I'm attempting to minister.

"I'm okay."

"Are you sure?"

"I'm sure. Thank you for asking."

Here's the little girl I had wondered about and even worried over during the years since Frank's death. Now, as a grown up woman, she simply attempts to minister to me, and does.

I'm very grateful for her question. I'm all right. I really am. And we leave the cemetery.

The summer of 1997 thirteen hundred former soldiers and sailors who served or were associated with the Mobile Riverine Force gather near Cincinnati at Ft. Mitchell, Kentucky for a reunion. Even though none of us know but a select few others, we're all bonded by our history and our memories of events that occurred so many years ago. Pictures and memorabilia bring us all together quickly.

Reconnecting is part of continuing life. Will Davis, who was the company commander of our Bravo Company, is here. He's long since retired and recently has gotten a new lease on life, having received a kidney transplant after being on dialysis for four years.

Terry Gander and Kenny Lancaster were squad buddies. They have reunited for the first time in almost thirty years. Both were wounded at Snoopy's Nose. Kenny still has three pieces of fragments next to his spine from the day he was hit on October 10, 1967. As Terry would later tell me in a letter when referring to Kenny, "What a great guy. If the Lord ever meant for me to have a blood brother, it would have been him. We hadn't seen each other since discharge from active duty and had no trouble taking up our friendship where we left off. The reunion did surely bring us back together." We're able to cross reference many other buddies in a, "What happened to such and such," and, "do you remember such and such battle."

Dennis McDougall is here. He's the young lieutenant who was shot in the chest in My Tho on that horrible morning in the alley in front of the orphanage during the Tet offensive. We spend considerable time reconstructing when he was shot, what happened and what he remembered. He thought he was dying and was indeed very close. Being semiconscious, he didn't even know about the artillery round that had come in on top of us until I tell him today.

"You mean I almost got killed twice in the same morning?" he says when I tell him about that. We laugh.

The most fascinating revelation is about the blood, mucous and fibrous tissue like material that he was throwing up as the medic and I were attempting to keep his airways clear and keep him calm, stabilized and alive.

"I thought I was throwing up pieces of liver or lung. I knew I was shot and hurt badly and it felt and tasted like body tissue I was bringing up. But, it wasn't."

"That's what we thought too. So what was it?" I ask.

"You won't believe this. Before we moved out that morning, instead of C-rations for breakfast, I ate a small watermelon that was in one of the Vietnamese hooches and then drank a bottle of strawberry soda."

His story made us laugh, and made both of us feel so good to be alive.

On Saturday, June 28, 1997, twelve former GIs and eight wives are gathered for dinner at Mike Fink's floating restaurant directly across the Ohio River from River Front Stadium in Cincinnati. Most of us have been in the area since Thursday for the bi-annual reunion.

This is the last night of this year's reunion and we twelve all served in the 3/60th from 1967–68. As somewhat of a farewell, we decide to get away from the convention hotel and have dinner here. The restaurant is packed. We're sitting at a long table in the middle of the huge dinning room with at least 150 other patrons within eye shot of us.

We're not here as former officers and enlisted men, although our table is about half of each. Rather, we're all brothers, having been through hell together years ago.

Between salad and the main course, Dennis McDougall comes over to my seat.

"Jim, just look at our table. We're a table of heroes!"

It's sobering to look around our table. There's Charlie Taylor who served with C/5/60th. This is his first reunion and if there were ever a heroic young lieutenant, he's one. At Snoopy's nose on September 15, 1967, he called artillery to within twenty-five meters of his position risking injury and death to himself and his men in order to avoid being overrun by the fast approaching VC. Tony Haug, his squad leader, is also here. Tony eventually went to officer candidate school and became a career army officer.

John Christy was in constant battles. He now works with low income housing in St. Louis. Greyson Raulston was an infantry lieutenant who later returned to Vietnam as a helicopter pilot. He stayed twenty years in the army. Chuck Howe, a much beloved platoon leader, is now a farmer in South Dakota. John Iannucci, David Graves and Charles Fleming were all buddies in the same squad. They're the heroes who were drafted, walked point, were wounded, left and went on with their lives. They only were reunited last year, somewhat like a lost family.

Then, there's Dennis, who returned to the paddies and jungles after being shot in My Tho. He didn't have to return.

At the head of the table, because his wheelchair won't fit elsewhere, is Barry Barron who lost both legs to a mine. He became an accountant, plays wheelchair basketball and recently killed two deer bucks within fifteen minutes with a bow and arrow.

Dennis goes on. "Imagine the number of Purple Hearts, Bronze Stars, Silver Stars and Air Medals that those of us at this table were awarded, not to mention those who should've been but weren't even put in for awards."

A table of heroes. Even though I've never considered myself a hero, and probably most of us feel the same way, this is truly a table of heroes. I'm honored to even be sitting here with them. They are all my heroes.

It is the Fourth of July, 1999 and the temperature is to be near 100 degrees. The town of Fort Mitchell, Kentucky is having a parade. Our semi-annual Mobile Riverine Force reunion is being held at the Draw-bridge Estates Convention Center nearby and the city officials have invited any veterans who wish to march in the parade.

"Jim, I've never had my parade," Charlie Taylor says. "Have you had yours?"

"I don't guess I have."

"Then let's march. It was hotter than this in the delta."

John Iannucci says it'll be an honor for him to march with me. Henry Roland is here from Tennessee for his first reunion. He wants to march with us and includes his ten year old grandson, Joseph.

The hotel has made a red, white and blue float with Mobile Riverine Force banners. Our veteran group of about forty are to walk behind the float. We are wearing 9th Infantry Division and Mobile Riverine Forces tee shirts. Ahead of us and behind are fire trucks, marching bands, politicians in convertibles, clowns, etc.

As we begin the one and one-half mile stroll, people are lined up on the sidewalks, sometimes four and five deep. When we approach, they stand, clap, yell and salute us. At first, I tend to look around to see what their applause is for. Then, I realize it's for us! I'm surrounded by my heroes. And people are clapping. It doesn't matter that it's been thirty years. Tears come to my eyes in the bright sunshine.

This parade is for me. Thank you.

Index